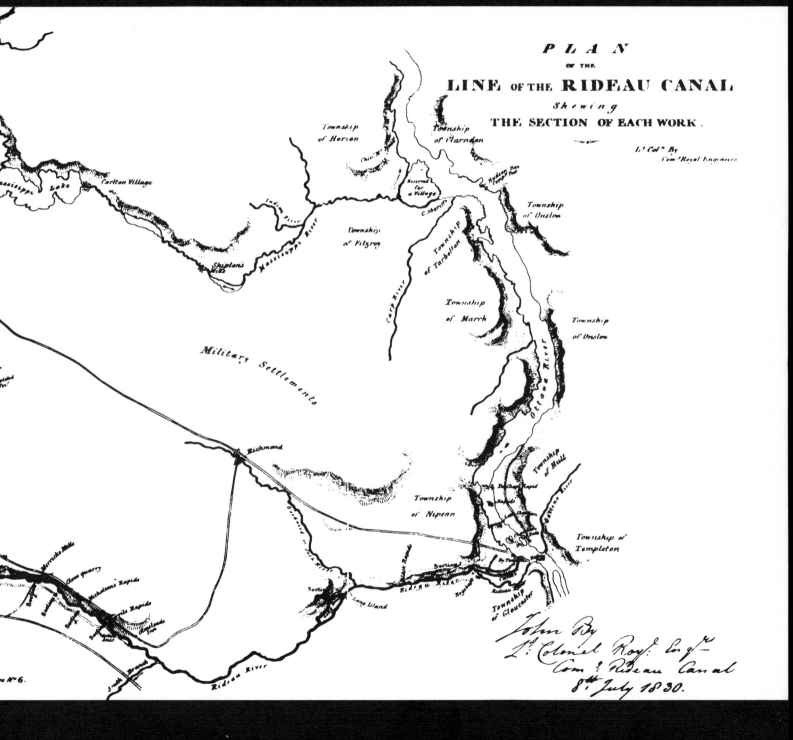

PLAN
OF THE
LINE OF THE RIDEAU CANAL
Shewing
THE SECTION OF EACH WORK.

Lt. Coln. By
Com.g Royal Engineers

John By
Lt. Colonel Royl. Engr.
Com.g Rideau Canal
8th July 1830.

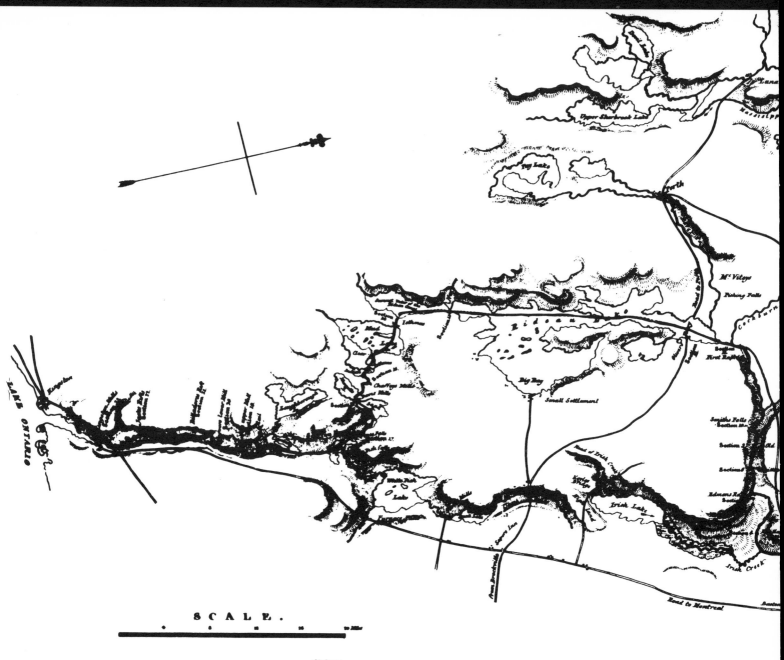

SCALE.

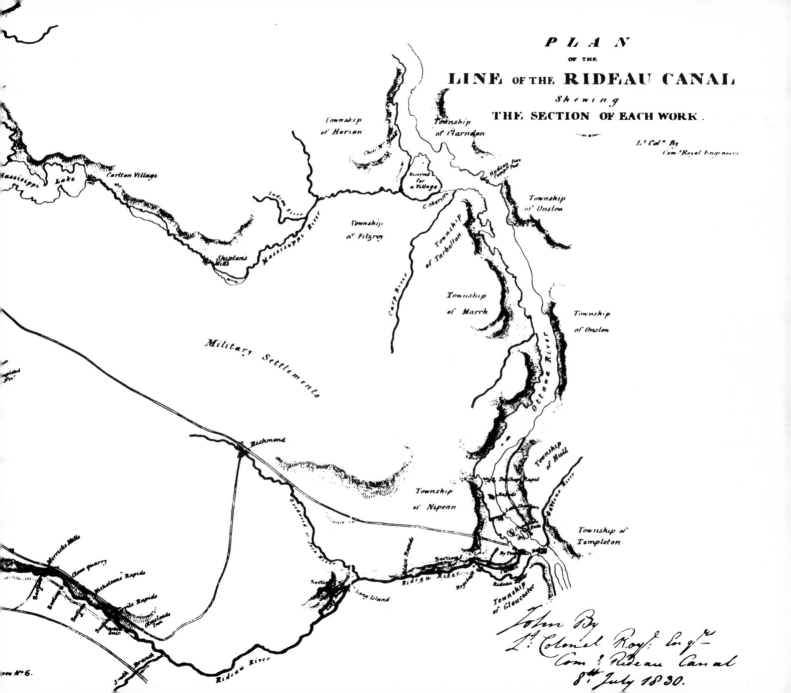

PLAN
OF THE
LINE OF THE RIDEAU CANAL
Shewing
THE SECTION OF EACH WORK.

Lt Coll By
Comr Royal Engineers

John By
Lt Colonel Royl Engr
Comr Rideau Canal
8th July 1830.

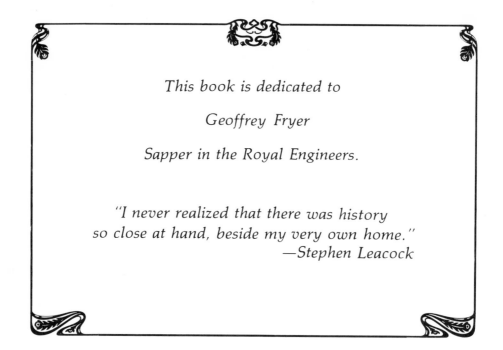

This book is dedicated to

Geoffrey Fryer

Sapper in the Royal Engineers.

"I never realized that there was history
so close at hand, beside my very own home."
—Stephen Leacock

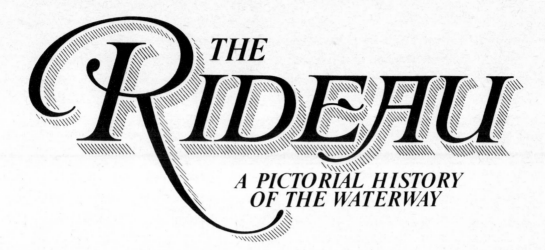

THE RIDEAU
A PICTORIAL HISTORY OF THE WATERWAY

Editor:	Adrian G. Ten Cate
Text by:	Mary Beacock Fryer
Reproduction Photography:	Bruce Wallace
	Peggie Wallace
	Dennis Wallace
Cartography and line drawings:	John C. Lamontagne

ISBN 0-920032-04-4

Published by

BESANCOURT PUBLISHERS, BOX 848, BROCKVILLE, ONTARIO K6V 5W1
CANADA

PRINTED AND BOUND IN CANADA BY BROWN & MARTIN LIMITED, KINGSTON, ONTARIO

Editor's Foreword

Our decision to produce this pictorial history originated with the discovery that a wealth of material existed and that very little of it had ever been published. It reposes in public and private collections, but has never been brought together in one volume. For us, pictorial history has become something of a tradition; one that began with a similar work on Brockville in 1973, and continued with a book on the Thousand Islands of the St. Lawrence River in 1977. With the approach of the sesquicentennial of the completion of the canal works along the Rideau and Cataraqui Rivers and the intervening lakes, we felt that the time was right for us to bring out this book.

Like the Thousand Islands, the Rideau Waterway, rich in history, visually delightful, is visited by thousands of Canadians and Americans every year.

While this is by no means a complete record, the volume serves to provide a good example of the material available.

In some instances outstanding material had to be deleted, because of limited space.

In certain sections, material is included because it relates to the region, or to events affecting the area, in the hope that a more complete record would be preserved.

The book describes the area from the days prior to the Rideau Canal construction, the construction period itself, the subsequent industrial and navigational development, the beginning of the tourist trade, pleasure boating and park development.

An attempt has been made to correlate illustrations with the chronology of the text, and many original maps and drawings of the canal construction have been included in a special section.

The first colour section shows original colour illustrations of historical interest while the second colour section shows more recent views along the waterway.

Often it was found that an aerial view was more descriptive of a particular area along the waterway than any other angle of observation and for this reason the reader may note that we have made use of this method on several occasions.

This is a private publication produced by a dedicated group of individuals without any government assistance or the help of a large publishing company.

Over a five year period we consulted many experts, and talked with scores of local people who know and love their history, yet, we freely confess that we may have overlooked some facets along the way. Any suggestions for corrections and for improving either text or illustrations are most welcome. Any material submitted to us will be duly acknowledged and credited to the individual or organization in our next edition.

We sincerely hope that our readers find the results of our efforts in presenting part of our heritage fascinating and that this book will often be referred to and enjoyed.

To gather the material and to edit this book, together with my co-workers, has been a genuine pleasure.

THE EDITOR

Acknowledgements

During the years it took to gather and research the material contained in this book there were often times that it appeared to be an impossible task. Peggie Wallace frequently provided the added stimulus for us to persist in our endeavours. We deeply regret her passing prior to going to press. This book is a tribute to her and all she did to make it a fine effort.

The text of this book was written by Mary Beacock Fryer who is an expert on the history of the region as seen in her previous books such as *Loyalist Spy, Escape* and the *Pictorial History of the Thousand Islands.*

We are greatly indebted to Madeleine and John Lamontagne for their assistance with detailed cartography, line drawings, photographs, proofreading and the assemblage of the endpaper aerial photographs. Throughout the project they were always available to provide us with excellent suggestions to improve the book.

Special recognition goes to Bruce, Dennis and Nancy Wallace of Brockville Photographic Specialties for their untiring efforts in reproduction of frequently aged and faded photographs, and obtaining specific illustrations to fit strict space requirements.

The collection of material and its verification would have been impossible without the friendly cooperation of the staff of Parks Canada. Without the help of John Bonzer, Mary Switzer, Keith Dewar, Brian Tychie, Bill Wylie, Robert Haig and Robert Passfield this book would never have been possible.

The staff of the Public Archives of Canada and of the National Map Collection went out of their way to locate maps, prints and historical photographs. Mr. Nagy and Mrs. Gobeil and Uno deserve special mention.

The staff of the Ontario Archives, Queen's University Archives, Ontario Department of Industry and Tourism, the National Capital Commission and the Rideau Valley Conservation Authority were of great help in directing us to original source material and illustrations.

The library personnel of the Kingston, Smiths Falls, Metropolitan Library of Toronto, Ottawa and Brockville often guided us in our research.

The curators of the Redpath Museum, the Kingston Marine Museum of the Great Lakes, Fort Henry, Fort Frederick, Royal Military College, the Westport Museum, the National War Museum and the Bytown Museum provided access to their materials and archives.

The executive of the Ottawa, Kingston, Smiths Falls and Rideau and District Historical Societies were of assistance in providing special data or illustrations.

Many private individuals gave us material to use or added information to the text. We are especially grateful to the Manotick Classic Boat Club members and Howard Pain, Joseph T. Kenney, Margaret, Horace and David Roberts, Robert Clark, Ray Mucklestone and Martin Kaldeway.

Marjorie Reynolds for help in typing and correspondence over the years.

A special thank you goes to Keith Watson and his son Thomas for flying numerous aerial photographic missions to obtain the needed views for the book.

William A. Martin of Brown and Martin Printers provided remarkable patience as well as tremendous enthusiasm combined with sound technical advice to make this volume a technical success.

My sincere compliments to my wife Doris for her patience and encouragement to make this book a reality.

Contents

COVER PHOTOGRAPHS (Courtesy of Parks Canada)
FRONT COVER:
    centre—Clowes Lock
    lower left—Ottawa Locks
    lower right—Upper & Lower Nicholsons Locks
BACK COVER:
    top left—Davis Lockstation
    top right—At Davis Lock
    centre—Edmonds Lock
    lower left—Upper Brewers Lock
    lower right—Long Island Dam

I

To Build a Canal

The name Rideau Canal—that most often used—hardly describes the route linking two important cities. Kingston, one of the earliest settlements in Ontario, stands at one end of the waterway; Ottawa, a relative newcomer on the urban scene, at the other. In between lie many lakes that lead into the Cataraqui River, which in turn empties into Lake Ontario. Only 12 miles is actually canal; the rest of the 124 mile system follows lakes and streams. Today the waters flow through a predominantly recreational area, cottage country, and a setting for pleasure boating. The region has much more—quiet, pretty towns and villages with a distinctive architecture, and defence sites, the last a reminder that we must be grateful to the British taxpayer and the Duke of Wellington—the Iron Duke—for the creation of the water link which today gratifies the senses of so many who come seeking an unusual holiday, the opportunity to travel the way people did a century ago, at a leisurely pace.

Historically the Rideau Waterway is part of a larger system that joined Montreal to Upper Canada at a time when no one dreamed of the day when Canada's capital city would stand near the midpoint. We have Queen Victoria to thank for the choice of the remote lumbertown, on the grounds that it was at a safe distance from the United States. Americans had captured Montreal during their revolution, and burned Toronto in the spring of 1813. Fear of American invasion was responsible for the building of the peaceful waterway, which, with its stone locks and canal walls, dams and restored blockhouses, now stands as a quaint anach-

ronism, the symbol of a bygone era.

In the 1820s and 30s, British North America was still a cluster of colonies. Canada at the time meant only two provinces, although the governor-in-chief of the lower one was the commander-in-chief of Upper Canada and the Maritime Provinces, ultimately responsible for their defence. All the other provinces had lieutenant-governors, and the governor-in-chief ruled only Lower Canada directly. On certain occasions this job was divided. For example, in 1836, Archibald Acheson, 2nd Earl of Gosford, was the administrator, while Sir John Colborne, who had just retired as lieutenant-governor of Upper Canada, was sent to Lower Canada to take command of the troops. An emergency was on the horizon and Colborne had more military experience.

The era of canal building—called canal fever—was also a time when the security of Canada rested with the garrisons of British regulars stationed along the border and in each important population centre. Thus Quebec City, Montreal, Kingston and York—in 1834 Toronto—each played host to redcoats, and officers' uniforms were an integral part of any social function. At each place, too, as well as at the forts guarding the border, were representatives of the Commissariat and Ordnance Departments, responsible for dispensing provisions and equipment to the soldiers. Both departments were deeply involved in building the link canals that joined together, in one waterway, two rivers and intervening lakes.

The drainage pattern was rather untidy—a jumble of lakes and streams that wound tortuously towards Lake Ontario, the St. Lawrence and Ottawa Rivers. The landscape was created during the last great ice age to cover the northern part of North America. As the glacier built up, the land was depressed under hundreds of feet of ice before which animals fled or perished, and all plant life was obliterated. The ice scraped at the rocks beneath it, and when it began to melt, most of the soil had been removed, leaving a bare, gouged, chaotic scene wherein streams slowly began to drain away the surplus water. Thousands of years are needed to allow erosion to cut streams to the point where they empty swamps, time which had not passed before man became interested in the country.

1. Orientation

Each summer, hundreds of small craft ply the Rideau Waterway, its many lakes, streams and portions of man-made canal. A canoe tripper finds a bargain. His is the only craft that passes through without paying a fee.

Commencing in the heart of Ottawa, a boat will be lifted from 131 feet above mean sea level at the entrance to the canal up 227 feet to Upper Rideau Lake. There the descent begins, and between this lake and Kingston, the boat is carried down 162 feet to Lake Ontario, 246 feet above mean sea level. The voyage is 123.53 miles—206 kilometres. Some of the locks are electrified, but at most the lock master and his assistants hand-operate them by what they call "crabs", much as their predecessors did when the canal first opened. Each crab is an iron gear wheel, a winch to draw in or slacken the chains that open and close the square-timbered, iron-bound lock gates. The name may derive from the appearance of the rounded, sprawling winches.

A short distance up the Ottawa River from the Rideau Falls is the entrance to the canal. The Rideau itself is blocked by Green Island, on either side of which are steep limestone cliffs. In two steep waterfalls, the Rideau plunges down the cliffs flanking the island. The waterfalls are so much like curtains that early French Voyageurs gave the river its name—Rideau. From the turning basin in the Ottawa River, the *Ottawa Locks* have a combined lift of 79 feet and look like a flight of giant steps. The canal flows through the city, passing under ten bridges.

The next set of locks is *Hartwells*. Then come the *Hogs Back Locks*. Here stands the 48 foot high, arc-shaped Hogs Back Dam, which gave its builders no end of trouble, and a spectacular sight, of huge blocks of cut stone, artfully fitted together. At mile 7.43, the channel enters the Rideau River itself.

Next comes the *Black Rapids Lock* and the first electrified one. Five miles on along the Rideau are the *Long Island Locks*. Beyond swing bridges at Manotick and Kars, lies a side channel to Kemptville and two miles inland is the town wharf. The channel has been allowed to silt up, and passes under a very low bridge, giving access only to small craft.

Rideau Falls and Green Island with Ottawa's City Hall.

6

Ottawa River with the Rideau Canal and locks, the Parliament Buildings are on the left.

Hartwells Locks and Carleton University today.

Hogs Back locks and dam at Mooney's Bay.

Aerial view of the village of Burritts Rapids and the locks.

Houseboat entering Clowes Lock with the dam on the left.

Old Slys Locks.
(Parks Canada).

The Smiths Falls combined locks with the electrified replacement lock to the right of the bridge.

Pleasure craft in the Narrows Lock.

Westport on Upper Rideau Lake.

Blockhouse and lock at Newboro Lake.

Chaffeys Lock with the mill on the left and the Opinicon Resort on the right.

Aerial view of Davis Lock and the defensible lockmaster's house.

The locks at Jones Falls with Hotel Kenney on the left and the defensible lockmaster's house on the right.

Kingston Mills with Colonel By Lake in the foreground.

Farther up the Rideau, past a high level bridge at Becketts Landing is the *Burritts Rapids Lock*. Next come the *Nicholsons Locks*. Following is the flight of *Merrickville Locks*. Beyond Merrickville the Rideau widens, and where it narrows is the *Kilmarnock Lock*. Upstream the Rideau widens again, and narrows at *Edmunds Lock*.

Old Slys Locks are at the boundary of Smiths Falls, and towards the centre of the town are the old *Smiths Falls Combined Locks* but these are no longer in operation. The three steps have been replaced by one large, electrically operated lock called 29A. Next comes the *Single Smiths Falls Lock* and three miles on along the Rideau is the *Poonamalie Lock*. Two thirds of a mile beyond is the entrance to Lower Rideau Lake. Here the scenery changes. Hitherto the path was between undulating farmlands; now the lake sprawls among hills of pink and gray granite denoting the Canadian Shield.

At mile 65 is the entrance to the Tay River that leads north from Port Elmsley to Perth. The *Beveridge Locks* lie a mile up the Tay from Lower Rideau Lake. Between Drummond and Gore Streets is the Perth turning basin and wharf.

Back in the main channel, ahead lies Big Rideau Lake, where a high level bridge at Rideau Ferry carries the side road to Perth from Highway 15 between Kingston and Ottawa. Five and one half miles beyond is the exit channel for Portland, on the south shore, and the village wharf is seven miles away. From this exit the main channel leads to *Narrows Lock*. Beyond is Upper Rideau Lake, the highest point on the waterway—408 feet above mean sea level. A side channel leads to Westport, five miles away at the northwest corner of the lake. The main channel leads to Newboro, at the southwest outlet into Newboro Lake, passing under the Highway 29 high level bridge that joins Smiths Falls to the St. Lawrence River at Brockville.

Newboro Lock is the third electrified lock, and for the first time the boats are descending. A side channel leads to the ghost town of Bedford Mills. The main channel flows down Newboro Lake through Indian Lake to *Chaffeys Lock*. Beyond is Opinicon Lake and very picturesque *Davis Lock* connects Opinicon with Sand Lake. Another four miles brings a boat to the first of the *Jones Falls Locks* between Sand and Whitefish Lakes.

Beyond is a turning basin above the steepest flight of locks on the waterway. Here is the tallest dam on the canal, 60 feet, and for the time it was built, a marvel of engineering. Huge blocks of stone were hewn and hauled through the wilds by oxen or carried on scows and set in this concave dam to eliminate a fall of water that made possible the construction of the locks.

On Whitefish Lake is a side channel to Morton. The wharf is one mile up Morton River. In the main channel, entering Little Cranberry Lake is a side channel to Seeleys Bay, less than a mile away. Past the Brass Point swing bridge the channel traverses Cranberry Lake. Towards its lower reaches a narrow channel leads to Battersea and into long Loughborough Lake. Back on Cranberry Lake the channel enters the Cataraqui River.

The descent continues at the *Upper Brewers Mills Locks* and down the Cataraqui is *Lower Brewers Mills Lock*, also called *Washburn Lock*. Downstream again is the first of the *Kingston Mills Locks*. Below is a turning basin at the top of the last flight of locks and the last landmark is the Kingston-Lasalle Causeway, with a lift bridge and beyond lies Kingston Harbour.

Between Ottawa and Kingston lie two centuries of Canadian history, from the days when Indians paddled their canoes among the byways and lakes that have since been joined together, through a period of busy commercial activity. At the present, the waterway is for the most part a tourist attraction. Today it is maintained as a national park, a paradise for vacationers, cottagers and boatmen of many countries.

2. The Native People

Following the melting of the last glacier, plants and animals began to re-establish themselves on the bare stretches of clay, slowly but surely, building up a complex ecosystem of inter-dependent species of flora and fauna. Characteristic of all recently glaciated landscapes, the drainage pattern was erratic, particularly towards the western portion where the waterway passes through the Canadian Shield. At the site of Kingston the stream the French named the Cataraqui empties into Lake Ontario, but upstream the waters twirl about, dropping over many waterfalls from a maze of ice scooped lakes, spreading themselves wherever they could penetrate among the granite hummocks.

Another stream, the Gananoque River, drains the same group of lakes, but the eastern portion, although strewn with waterfalls, shows a different character. One larger river, the Rideau, flows across the more amenable landscape towards the east. Scattered among the streams and lakes were vast stretches of swamp, needing the downcutting of water erosion to create drainage channels for them to the major rivers. When the weight of ice had been lifted, this land rose, and with its rising were created the twin waterfalls that grace the mouth of the Rideau and are responsible for its name.

The Indians who first saw this land came to hunt. No village site has been identified, although several spots are known to have been campsites. It was Algonkin land, a tribe of the eastern woodlands, skilled workers in birch bark who did not cultivate

Rim sherd St. Lawrence-Iroquois pottery, this type found at Lower Beverley Lake. These Indians hunted and fished along the Rideau corridor as late as the year 1550.
(John F. Fielding).

domestic plants. The forests of mixed coniferous and deciduous trees provided a habitat for a wealth of deer, moose and fur bearing animals, large and small, the more open lakes a variety of fish. Many of the swamps were choked with floating vegetation, islands of cranberry and cattails, with shifting channels which a canoeman had to learn. Even for the native inhabitants, this cross route was little used. There were more pleasant places to camp, along the shore of Lake Ontario, and the better waterways, the St. Lawrence and Ottawa Rivers, upon which to travel inland.

When the French began to explore beyond the lower St. Lawrence, they used the Ottawa River to paddle to the west. The upper St. Lawrence they shunned on the advice of their Huron friends, because of the presence of a hostile group of Iroquois who had a village at a place called Toniata, among the Thousand Islands. In 1615, Samuel de Champlain journeyed to the Hurons' country by way of the Ottawa River, passing the mouth of the Rideau. After the governor of New France, Louis de Baude, le Comte de Frontenac, established his fort on the site of Kingston in 1673, Indians paddled down the Cataraqui River to trade their furs. They had all they could do to concentrate their interest on the St. Lawrence and Ottawa Rivers. The Seven Years' War, which made Canada a British province in 1763, did not awaken much interest in the Rideau country. Not until the closing months of the American Revolution did white men evince a real curiosity about the chain of streams and lakes that might link Cataraqui with the Ottawa River.

Indian trade beads widely used by the French traders from 1543-1759.

Indian pottery fragments found in the Rideau region. These fragments date from the years 500 to 1300. (Brockville & District Historical Society).

3. The First Settlers

In April, 1783, General Frederick Haldimand, the governor-in-chief of Canada, received the preliminary articles of peace that spelled the end of Britain's attempt to subdue her thirteen rebelling colonies along the Atlantic seaboard. When the independent United States were being born, Haldimand had within his province five regiments of provincial troops—2,600 men—refugees from the Thirteen Colonies or residents of Canada. Most of the latter were serving in the Royal Highland Emigrants, raised to the British establishment as the 84th Regiment of Foot. The other corps—the King's Royal Regiment of New York, led by Brigadier-General Sir John Johnson, Butler's Rangers under Lieutenant-Colonel John Butler, the Loyal Rangers under Major Edward Jessup, three companies of King's Rangers under Major James Rogers—were American loyalists. The men had fled to Canada and enlisted, serving as part of the garrison or raiding into the northern colonies. Now they could not return to their homes and had to be resettled. Also present along the lower St. Lawrence were nearly 6,000 wives and children and other American loyalists who had become displaced persons. In the spring of 1783, Haldimand sent his Surveyor-General, Major Samuel Holland, to the neighbourhood of Cataraqui to explore for land upon which many of the loyalist refugees and soon to be disbanded provincial troops could be located. By the autumn, several parties of surveyors were in the field, exploring and preparing reports to submit to His Excellency on the quality of the lands in this remote wilderness. Two of these parties were to penetrate the unknown country by way of the Ottawa River, and each was led by an officer from Major Jessup's Loyal Rangers.

One was commanded by Lieutenant David Jones, whose home had been near Fort Edward, New York, before the rebels drove him away. He served during General John Burgoyne's abortive attempt to invade New York State in the summer and autumn of 1777, and is best remembered as the fiancé of Jane McRae, whose murder became a powerful weapon of propaganda in the hands of the American rebels. When Burgoyne's army of regulars and loyal provincials reached Fort Edward on their southward march, Jane was attempting to gain their encampment and her lover. Some of Burgoyne's Indian allies captured her, and after killing the poor girl carried her scalp of flowing blond tresses to the British camp. The horror and grief young Jones suffered over Jane's hideous demise saddened him for the rest of his life. This was the man Major Holland sent to explore the Ottawa River as far as the Chaudière Falls, above the present site of Ottawa. In the report he wrote, dated October 31st, 1783, Jones observed:

> we now Proceed Down the South Side and Discover as follows from the Shudiar (sic) Falls found the Land very Rough and Mountainous until we arrived at the River Redo (sic) here it appear'd more level But not fit for cultivation.

> The Timber is chiefly Pine, Seader (sic) and Hemlock and Remains such Down to the aforesaid Madam Parraus about seven Leagues, from thence found the land Good Down to the Little Nation, this good Land lys back and Extends In Length about four Leagues the Land is bad Full of Pine & Seader Swamps and Continues much the same for about Five Leagues or even to the Rapids.

> David Jones
> Lieut.

The other officer, Lieutenant Gershom French, may have been the first white man to travel most of the Rideau Waterway. French was from Manchester, Vermont, probably a former Green Mountain Boy who had served with Ethan Allen in the land war against New York. He was a rough, occasionally rowdy frontiersman, court martialed in 1781, for selling to civilians supplies drawn from government stores for the use of his regiment. At that time he was stationed at Fort St. Johns, on the lower Richelieu River, but he was an experienced farmer and surveyor who knew good land when he saw it. The record he left of his journey redeems him.

Like Jones, French got his first glimpse of the Rideau River in October, but he had set out earlier with a party he described as "seven men of the Provincials, Two Canadians and an Indian Guide with two Bark Canoes". He reached the mouth of the Rideau on October 2nd, and "by a Carrying Place of a Mile entered our Canoes into the River." He did not mention that this portage was around the waterfalls at the entrance to the Rideau. He continued:

> 3rd.—A party sent South East from the Carrying place, Reported they had been a League and found the Soil every where good and deep, Tim-

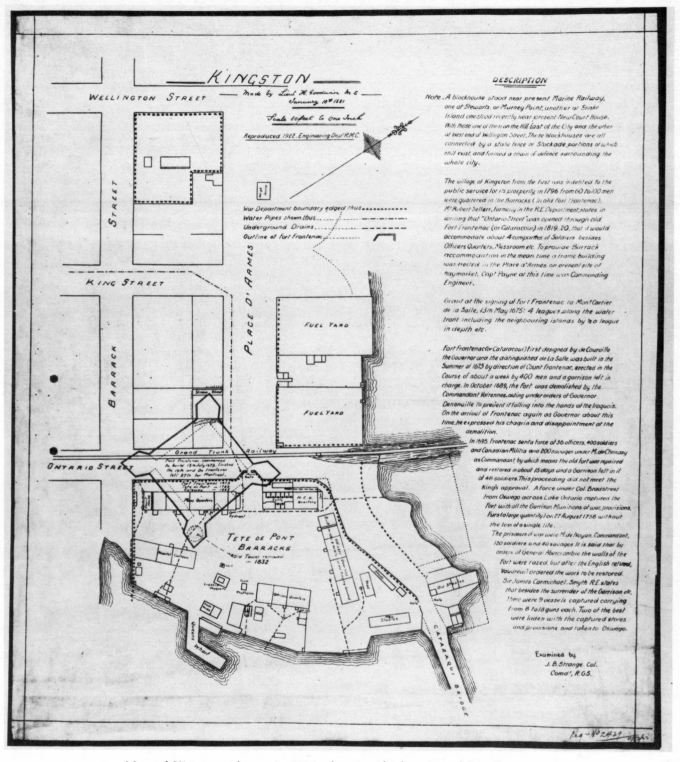

Map of Kingston, drawn in 1881, showing the location of Fort Frontenac.
(National Map Collection, Public Archives of Canada).

Frontenac at Cataraqui, 1673 by A. Sherriff Scott.
(Agnes Etherington Art Centre, Queen's University).

The Cataraqui Land Forces Command and Staff College at Kingston is on the site
where Frontenac established a fort in 1673.

bered with Maple, Elm and Butternutt, but did not discover any Springs or Water in their Route.

From the Carrying Place we steered up the Rideau South 15 Degrees West, five miles in deep still Water, and thence for about 7 miles further in a Rapid Current. In this days Journey the Canoes were navigated by two men each, a party Travelled on each side of the River, myself always being in one, changing sides occasionally, and frequently leaving the Shore a half a mile distance.

The Banks of the River in general raise about twelve feet above the High Water from thence the Land continues very Level, it is a Dark Soil 7 to 10 inches Deep, with a Sandy Loam below, clear of Rocks and Stones, Timbered with Maple, Beech, Birch, Elm, Butternutt, &c., with an Edging of Cedar and Pine always covering the Banks of the River, and wherever the Water is Rapid, the Shores are Lined with Lime Stone, in the Route there was two Excursions made on each side of the River to the distance of a League in which myself and party's found the Lands Everywhere good, we Encamped at the entrance of a small Rapid river from the North West forming a convenient Mill Place.

The latter set of rapids is the falls now called Hogs Back. On the 4th, the canoes found deep water, the land similar to what French had seen on the 3rd. The following day, paddling on, French noted:

A Considerable River Enters here from the East which leads to a Branch of the River de la Petite Nation, from whence the Indians have a Communication to Oswegatchie

Indians travelled along the Nation River until they were at the closest point to the St. Lawrence, crossing it and paddling on to Fort Oswegatchie, then a British post on the south shore at the site of the city of Ogdensburg, New York.

Lieutenant French continued, finding several more waterfalls and good stretches of land, although in places he found it too rocky. On October 7th, he reported that his canoes "entered in a Lake." This was above the waterfall where Merrickville would one day be established. Here he found more good land, and again some rock, and on the 9th, he wrote:

We proceeded South 30 Degrees West 5 miles to the S.E. Point of the Lake, from whence by a Carrying Place of a Mile and a Quarter, we entered our Canoes into the River Gananoncoui.

French had travelled 101 miles of the present canal route, exiting at the site of Seeleys Bay, across the short portage to South Lake which drains into Gananoque Lake, the source of the stream of that name. He found some good land but once he started down the river and all the way to the St. Lawrence, his party found rock, swamp and poor quality timber. While he declared the land unfit for cultivation, his party found numerous waterfalls that would make fine millsites:

discovering a few small Tracts of good Land near the River, but scarcely sufficient in a place for a Farm, to a Fall of 10 Feet, where the Gananoncoui Discharges itself into the St. Lawerence about five Leagues N.E. from Cataraqui, where we arrived on the morning of the 14th.

Summing up, French concluded:

From the Mouth of the Rideau to its Head, a distance of at least Eighty Miles, the Lands are good on both sides the River and may be all cultivated, except for a few Swamps and Stony ridges, which in the whole, will not amount to more then five Miles on a side. However there is not many Streams of Water to be found, back from the River, and the Lands fit for Meadows hardly bear proportion to the Plow Land, which latter is of the best Soil, and will produce Winter as well as all other sorts of Grain, and to the greatest perfection with proper Tillage.

The Timber is neither too heavy nor too light and in general is very Tall and Straight without any Underbrush, and I should suppose that a Man will be able to clear, in the American Method an Acre fit for seeding in eight days.

Because of logging, the woods French described consist today of smaller trees, and considerable undergrowth, and are more difficult to penetrate than they were for these first explorers, who had trouble only with the stretches of swamp. French finished his journal thus:

From our entrance in the River Gananoncoui to its fall into St. Lawrence, I did not discover as much good land Conveniently situated as would serve one Farmer.

Quebec 29th October, 1783.   G. French
                                 Lt. and Asst. Engineer.

The Gananoque River is not part of the Rideau Waterway, but French's description is relevant. That line was mooted when plans to canalize the route from Montreal to Kingston were being made. More important, French proved that it was possible to travel nearly all the way to Cataraqui without using the St. Lawrence.

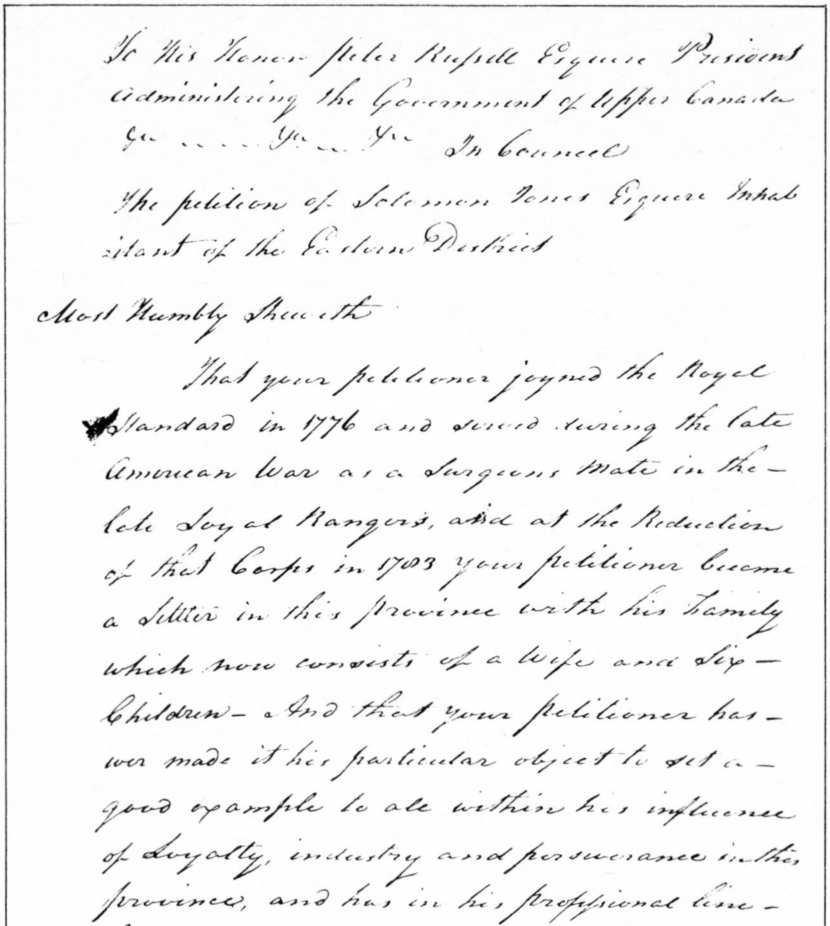

*To His Honor Peter Russell Esquire President
administering the Government of Upper Canada
&c ___ &c ___ &c ___ In Council*

*The petition of Solomon Jones Esquire Inhab
itant of the Eastern District*

Most Humbly Sheweth

That your petitioner joined the Royal
Standard in 1776 and served during the late
American War as a Surgeons Mate in the
late Loyal Rangers, and at the Reduction
of that Corps in 1783 your petitioner became
a Settler in this Province with his Family
which now consists of a Wife and Six
Children — And that your petitioner has
ever made it his particular object to set a
good example to all within his influence
of Loyalty, industry and perseverance in this
Province, and has in his professional line
been a sufferer in administering to the poor
and needy settlers in the Infant State of this
Country — Therefore your petitioner humbly
prays that your Honor will grant Mr Jones
and his Family such further quantity of unap
=propriated Lands in the Eastern District
as may appear proper or consistent
with
with your Honors powers and goodness

And your petitioner as in duty bound
will ever pray —

York June 10th 1797

Solomon Jones

*Example of land petition of Solomon Jones, 1797.
(Public Archives of Canada—Upper Canada Land Petitions—J3-33).*

For the moment, Governor Haldimand did not act on Gershom French's findings, although he did pay attention to David Jones's description of the Ottawa Valley. Grants of land along the shores of the Ottawa River were made to officers of the Royal Highland Emigrants. The governor chose instead to send the American refugees to the more accessible lands along the upper St. Lawrence and the Bay of Quinte, with the exception of Butler's Rangers, most of whom would settle near Fort Niagara, the base from which they had operated and where their dependents had gathered. All the provincial troops stationed along the lower St. Lawrence, and Lake Champlain, were to be disbanded in December, 1783, but word reached Haldimand too late to be implemented for the troops serving at his upper posts. Therefore the Royal Highland Emigrants and the second battalion, King's Royal Regiment of New York, that were at Carleton Island, near Cataraqui, and Butler's Rangers, were not disbanded until June, 1784.

By that date the migration of the first battalion, King's Royal Regiment of New York, the Loyal Rangers and King's Rangers was under way. Haldimand left the province in the autumn of 1784, never to return, and Lieutenant Gershom French's journal lay dormant, the portion of the Rideau Waterway he had visited left largely unexplored for a generation. Nevertheless, the land through which the Rideau Canal would be built had been purchased from the Mississauga Indians on October 9th, 1783, by Captain William Redford Crawford, of the second battalion, King's Royal Regiment of New York. He had acted on behalf of his superior, Sir John Johnson, who was the Superintendent of Indian Affairs as well as Crawford's regimental commander.

Today Gershom French's wilderness and the water route to Kingston which he did not follow, have received a complex form of local and regional government. The waterway crosses or borders on five counties—Frontenac, Leeds, Grenville, Lanark and Carleton. For a time the Township of Gloucester, to the south side of the Rideau at the junction with the Ottawa, was part of Russell County, until placed within Carleton. The Rideau countryside is further subdivided into twenty-one townships. The first local government established by Haldimand's successor, Sir Guy Carleton, the 1st Baron Dor-

chester, in 1788, was by districts, each with its own court, presided over by magistrates appointed by the governor-in-chief. Each had a land board to grant holdings to new settlers, and to older ones entitled to receive more than their original tracts. The area from the last French seigneury on the west side of the Ottawa River to a point a few miles east of Kingston was the District of Luneburg—comprising all but the far western portion of the waterway. Kingston and the land beyond the end of the Bay of Quinte lay in the District of Mecklenburg, German names chosen by Lord Dorchester to please King George III.

Originally His Majesty, who had learned nothing from the American Revolution, decided to make no fundamental changes in the form of government permitted Canada under the Quebec Act of 1774. His loyal American refugees would be made to fit within the seigneurial system, and all new townships established for them would remain Crown land. The king would be the seigneur, each loyalist his tenant, expected to pay a quit rent of one halfpenny per acre per annum once he had been settled on his land grant for ten years. Apart from the loyalists themselves, one man who heartily disapproved of this measure was Lord Dorchester, who in 1783, had argued vehemently that grants to loyalists should be free of all seigneurial obligations. Many loyalist leaders sent urgent petitions begging to be allowed their traditional rights as British subjects after they discovered the King's intentions.

By the time Canada was divided to accommodate the aspirations of the loyalists to be free of seigneurial duties and French civil law, those in the older townships were becoming interested in the Rideau country. The Province of Upper Canada was established in 1791, with English civil law and freehold tenure—a vast relief to the residents, who despised the laws and customs of the French Canadian majority in Lower Canada. When John Graves Simcoe, the first lieutenant-governor of the new province, reached his new subjects in the spring of 1792, the shores of the Rideau were attracting considerable attention. Loyalists' sons and daughters were each entitled to 200 acres upon reaching age twenty-one, or in the case of a daughter, earlier if she married, and the reduced provincial officers were entitled to much larger grants than disbanded privates. Thus many people had the right to petition the district land boards for their acreages.

The most thriving place Governor Simcoe found was Kingston, where the mouth of the Cataraqui River provided a harbour, not entirely satisfactory, however, since the prevailing wind blew steadily into it, a drawback in the age of sail. The township bearing the same name was the first to be surveyed along Lake Ontario, and the work was supervised by Captain Justus Sherwood, Loyal Rangers. His and other parties of surveyors were at work in the autumn of 1783, while Lieutenant Gershom French was making his way there from the Ottawa River.

The first group of settlers to arrive at Cataraqui was led by Captain Michael Grass, who had been a prisoner at Fort Frontenac during the Seven Years' War. He sought shelter at the time of the revolution at New York City, which was occupied by a large British garrison, and many other loyalists gathered there for protection. In the spring of 1783, with Governor Haldimand's permission, Grass escorted to Canada 200 families who wanted to settle near the old French fort at the foot of Lake Ontario, rather than in Nova Scotia.

Captain Grass has been called the founder of Kingston, but a British regular officer, John Ross, has a better claim to the honour. Ross was a captain in the 34th Regiment of Foot, who, with the rank of major of provincials, commanded the second battalion, King's Royal Regiment of New York. As the revolution was ending, Ross's battalion, which had been on duty at Oswego and Carleton Island, moved to the site of Kingston. Knowing that the bases might be within the territory awarded to the United States in the peace treaty, Governor Haldimand ordered Ross to leave small garrisons at the two posts and establish a new British base on the site of Fort Frontenac. There the men of Ross's battalion, and detachments of regulars, built barracks and a new naval establishment.

It was Major Ross who received the first waves of loyalists in the spring of 1784, and distributed certificates for farm lots, together with tools and provisions before each settler and his family proceeded on to erect a cabin on their land grant. Ross was also one of the first magistrates appointed to keep the peace in Kingston Township. He returned to Britain in 1785, and because of the presence of

Richard Cartwright, a man of initiative, the village laid out at the mouth of the Cataraqui River was soon flourishing as a commercial centre, as well as fortress and naval base. For a time Colonel John Butler's secretary at Niagara, and later a merchant there, Cartwright decided that Major Ross's settlement afforded greater opportunities. Cartwright opened a store and had his own fleet of bateaux to carry goods up and down the St. Lawrence River. Governor Simcoe looked over the site of Kingston, and after holding a meeting of his Executive Council, continued with his family and escort on to Niagara, to the village known as Butlersbury, after Colonel John's lost home in the Mohawk Valley. This community Simcoe chose as his temporary capital, rechristening it Newark in 1792.

There, in the autumn, after elections were held, the first Parliament of Upper Canada met. Beforehand, Simcoe divided the populated portions of the province into 19 counties for electoral purposes only. The four districts, whose names he changed to Eastern, Midland, Home and Western, respectively, remained the units of local government. Leeds, Grenville and Frontenac were among the original counties established by Simcoe, and they sent two members to the Parliament at Newark. John White represented Frontenac and Leeds, while Ephriam Jones was Grenville's choice. At the first session, the members introduced a bill legalizing town meetings, the form of local government with which the New Englanders were familiar. In the face of Simcoe's stern disapproval—the bill smacked too much of Yankee democracy—the legislation passed the following spring. The magistrates in each township had the right to call a meeting twice a year so that people could choose officers to look after minor matters, such as statute labour to build roads, and the appointment of fence viewers for animal control. In 1798, the old districts were subdivided to form four new ones. From the Eastern the Johnstown District was created, basically Leeds and Grenville Counties. At the same time the number of counties was increased to 24 and one of the new ones was Carleton.

The lands along the Cataraqui River were not among the first townships surveyed for loyalist settlers. Several of Haldimand's explorers had branded them rocky, and recommended against establishing settlements. As the waterfront lots were gradually taken

Near Nicholsons Rapids, 1830 by James P. Cockburn.
(Public Archives of Canada—C12513).

up, the shore to the east of the Cataraqui River became more appealing, and by 1792, the boundaries of Pittsburgh and Loughborough were demarkated. The lot lines of individual farms were not run until 1807, when one of the few qualified surveyors, Reubin Sherwood, began working with a party of men. Sherwood was a character, and a cousin of Captain Justus, also a surveyor. Born near Fort Edward, New York in 1769, Reubin was brought to Fort St. Johns when he was ten years old, and his brother Adiel, who also figures in this narrative, was an infant at their mother's breast. At age fourteen Reubin was serving in the ranks of the Loyal Rangers, in which his father, Thomas, was an ensign.

Originally Pittsburgh was rectangular, extending along both sides of the Cataraqui River. In 1850, the Township of Storrington was created by taking land from Kingston, Pittsburgh and Loughborough Townships—31 lots from the first, 289 from the second, and 62 from the third. Today the Cataraqui River divides Pittsburgh from Storrington. The village of Kingston dominated its surroundings, although ten miles up the Cataraqui River stood Kingston Mills, where the government—in keeping with its then seigneurial role—had built the first saw and grist mills, so that the settlers could have flour ground and boards cut for their homes.

The land farther up the Cataraqui was generally rocky, with only pockets of good soil, but reports of the lands along the Rideau River were more promising. Since roads to reach inland concessions were nearly non-existent, the rights of loyalists' sons and daughters and the half pay officers could best be served along the Rideau. Accordingly, in 1791, Lord Dorchester ordered that the Townships of Oxford and Marlborough be laid out on either side of the river towards the eastern end of what soon became Grenville County. Over the next twenty years, all the townships bordering the Rideau River and the lakes had been marked out, but few settlers went there until after the War of 1812.

The first person known to have taken

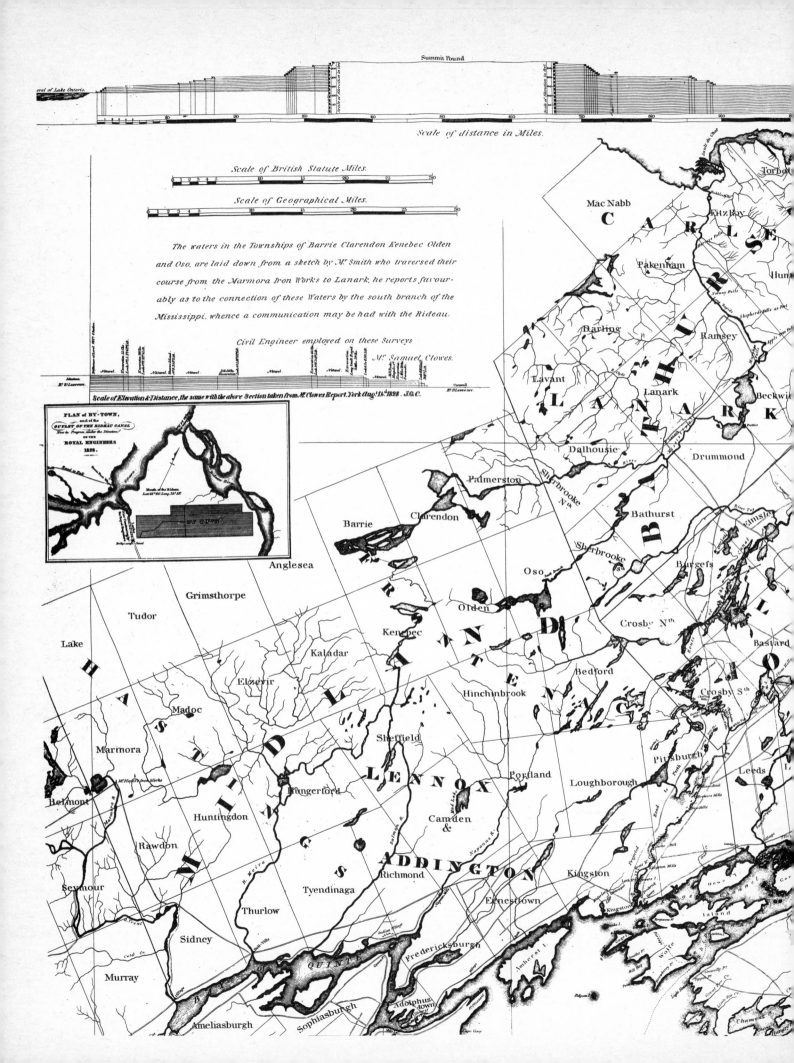

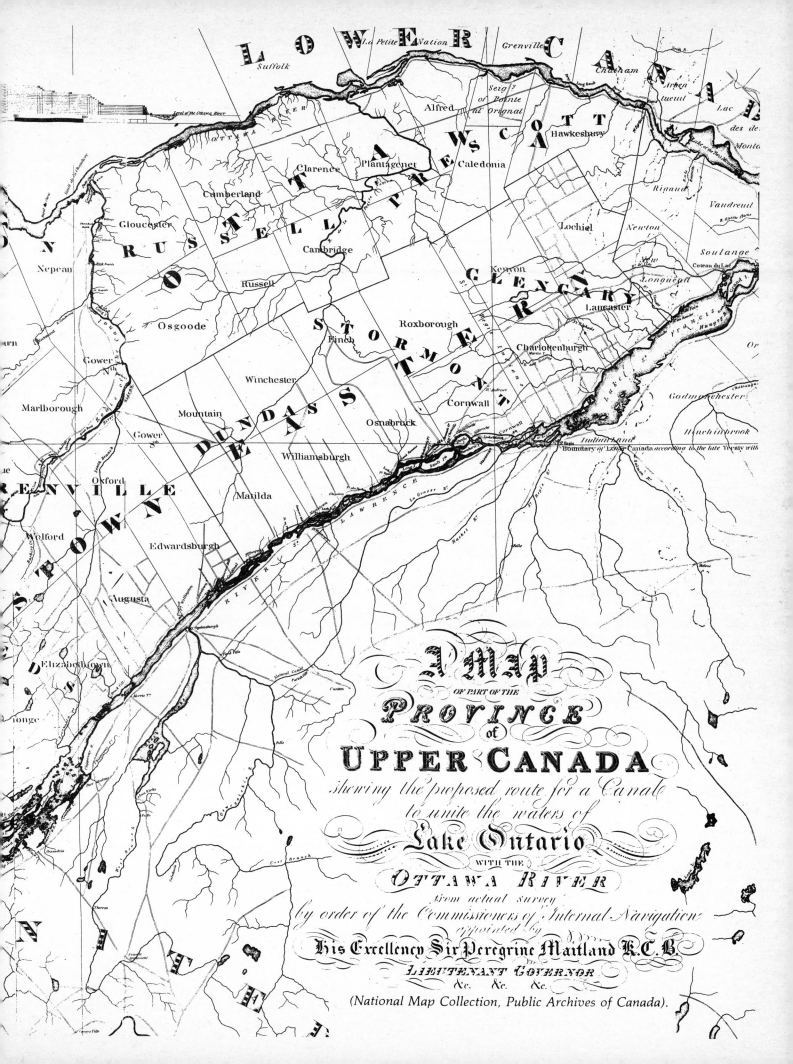

A Map
OF PART OF THE
Province
of
UPPER CANADA
shewing the proposed route for a Canal
to unite the waters of
Lake Ontario
WITH THE
OTTAWA RIVER
from actual survey
by order of the Commissioners of Internal Navigation
appointed by
His Excellency Sir Peregrine Maitland K.C.B.
LIEUTENANT GOVERNOR
&c. &c. &c.
(National Map Collection, Public Archives of Canada).

Smiths Falls "My Canoe Portage" by James P. Cockburn.
(Public Archives of Canada—C12603).

up land beside the Rideau was Roger Stevens, an ensign in the King's Rangers, but not from the part of the corps that had served in Canada. A resident of Vermont, he received his commission from Major James Roger's younger brother Robert, of Seven Years' War fame. By 1776, Robert was a drunk and dissembler, who three years later sent his brother James to Canada to raise a battalion of loyalists. Afterward Robert flitted about from Halifax to London and New York City, sending men whom he had promised commissions—and stacks of unpaid bills—to James, who admitted to Governor Haldimand, "the Conduct of my Brother of late has almost unmann'd me."

Like all the officers from the King's Rangers, Roger Stevens was a character. Captured by the rebels and imprisoned at Lichfield, Connecticut, he escaped and served with Burgoyne until captured again. This time he escaped from the rebels with the help of his brother Abel, later a settler in Leeds County. Roger succeeded in reaching Canada, and he worked for Captain Justus

Sherwood of the Loyal Rangers, who was head of Governor Haldimand's secret service.

Roger brought in some useful information, but Sherwood, and his deputy, Dr. George Smyth, who was also the Loyal Rangers' surgeon, complained that his expense accounts were padded. Furthermore the intelligence provided by Roger's brother Abel, still in Vermont, was hardly worth the trouble. Roger was also chatty. When he was on a visit to Quebec City with dispatches, the governor's secretary warned Sherwood that news of Stevens's presence, and the content of his packet, was widely known before he even reported at headquarters.

Roger lived in Montreal until 1788, when he arrived in the District of Luneburg where Justus Sherwood was then the chairman of the land board. The former head of the secret service awarded Stevens 200 acres in Bastard Township—lot 2, concession 9—but he soon struck out to look for land that suited him better. By 1790, Roger was homesteading, with no certificate to the land he occupied, above the modern village of

Merrickville, by J.P. Cockburn, 1830.
(Public Archives of Canada—C10656).

Burritts Rapids. Like many other settlers, he was determined to have a millsite rather than depend on farming for his existence. Stevens claimed that his ensign's rank entitled him to 2,000 acres, although there is no evidence that he ever recruited the prescribed number of privates to qualify for a signed commission.

In 1793, he petitioned for more land, stating that he had "erected a good Saw-Mill on the great Falls on the River Rideau and have made the necessary preparations to build a Grist-Mill next fall", reminding the Executive Council of Upper Canada that he had "commenced the Settlement on the Rideau." Two years later he drowned at the mouth of the creek that now bears his name.

Roger Stevens was soon followed by Stephen Burritt, another King's Ranger, one whose name does appear in Major James Rogers's records. On a muster roll dated January 10th, 1782, is "Stephen Buret, a private." According to family tradition, Stephen and his brother Adaniram, were among the loyalists who fought at the Battle

of Bennington in 1777 and afterward spent some time as prisoners of the rebels. Escaping, Stephen made for Canada, and was joined after the war by his father, Daniel, and four brothers. As a loyalist Stephen received lot 29, concession 1, in Augusta Township, and there Daniel resided for the rest of his life. Soon after 1790, Stephen made his way to the Rideau with his brothers, Daniel Junior and Edmund. Building a raft they floated down to what is now Burritts Rapids and founded the settlement that straddles the Townships of Oxford and Marlborough. There Stephen's son Edmund was born on December 8th, 1793, the first white child on the Rideau.

Stephen Burritt was the first permanent settler at the rapids which still bear his name, but Terence Smyth of Elizabethtown had a sawmill operating there. The elder son of Dr. George Smyth, the deputy head of the secret service, Terence had been a dispatch carrier. He never received a commission because the rebels captured him and he spent months in Albany Gaol, which interfered

Home of Col. William Merrick and later Mr. William Pearson, Merrickville, Ontario.
This photograph was taken in the early 1900's.
(Public Archives of Canada—C54494).

with recruiting. The younger Smyth was rarely on the Rideau, and the Burritts' closest neighbour was Roger Stevens, who was squatting a mile to the west.

The next arrival of note was William Merrick, who hailed from Massachusetts. A millwright by trade, Merrick stayed a while in Elizabethtown, on the St. Lawrence, and hearing that there were many good power-sites on the Rideau, he pushed inland with his wife Sylvia and chose a waterfall six miles above Burritts Rapids. His log cabin and the mills that followed were the foundations of the village soon called Merrickville. While the township names usually commemorated some British dignitary—the children of George III or some crony of Governor Simcoe's—and so did some of the first loyalist towns that were originally called after their founders, some towns along the Rideau managed to retain the names local people chose. Merrickville spread across the river into the Townships of Montague and Wolford, and the founding father soon built a stone house. It had an extension with bunk

beds for the use of Indians hunting in the vicinity. Not long after they reached the banks of the Rideau, William and Sylvia fell ill with fever and ague. Some Indians lingered and nursed them back to health using local herbs. Later, when William built the fine stone house that is still a landmark, the native hunters were always made welcome by the Merricks and their children.

Samuel Dow and Joseph Easton soon followed William Merrick. Samuel was the first blacksmith in the neighbourhood, while Joseph founded the village of Easton's Corners, and opened the first tannery. Others who joined Merrick were Joseph Haskins, Richard Olmstead, and Caleb Edmunds, and all opened mills. On the whole, the development of the Rideau townships was rather slow, and two in particular were impeded by absentee owners. In Oxford many lots were granted to reduced provincial officers, who already had farms and comfortable homes along the St. Lawrence, while Wolford suffered through the generosity of Governor Simcoe. In his zeal to have the province populated he informed the British government that many people in the United States were loyal at heart, and would welcome encouragement to move to Upper Canada. In response to advertising, Americans came into the province. Some were genuinely loyal, but many were speculators who took their grants and held them in order to sell them when land values had risen.

The Township of South Gower, surveyed in 1799, was a narrow wedge at the east end of Grenville County. Its concessions numbered from the Rideau, while those in Oxford and Wolford numbered from south to north. An early settler was Peter McAlpine Grant, a Scot who had served in the American Revolution. He went to the third concession, and during the War of 1812, he served as a lieutenant in Captain Reubin Sherwood's militia company. Patrolling in a canoe, Grant and Sherwood kidnapped Major John B. Esselstyne, of the New York Militia and an unidentified captain. Not long afterward, the two American officers were exchanged for two officers of the Leeds Militia, Major Bartholomew Carley and Captain Adiel Sherwood, Reubin's brother. Both men had been captured during an American raid on Brockville in February, 1813.

Another settler in South Gower was David Beach, who brought his family to the Rideau country in a two-wheeled ox cart drawn by a team of horses in 1800. They travelled in the winter, and when one horse died, David purchased an ox, and with this ill matched pair finished his journey. The bottom of the ox cart was the front door of Beach's first cabin.

West of Kitley, which does not touch the waterway, lies Bastard Township, surveyed in 1796, by which time several families were in the neighbourhood. The founder was Roger Steven's brother Abel, who looked over the area in 1793, and returned to Vermont for some of his friends. Stevens was a Baptist elder, and most of the people who joined him were members of his flock. Over a five year period, Elder Stevens brought some 100 families to Bastard and Kitley. The names of both townships commemorate a family in Devonshire, England, Governor Simcoe's home county. John Pollexfen Bastard was a member of the British Parliament, and his family home was known as Kitley.

Of the other Rideau townships in Leeds County—Elmsley, Burgess and North and South Crosby, only the last had many settlers before 1812. Like many others this township was surveyed by Reubin Sherwood, and the first settler was Walter Davis, a loyalist who had lived in Augusta. In 1800, he moved to South Crosby with his family and adopted son, Thomas Ripley. They located on lot 9, concession 2, at the east side of the township, and years later Thomas recalled the night when their fire went out. The nearest neighbour was seven miles away in Bastard Township, and his foster father walked the fourteen miles through the bush to procure live coals. Davis was soon joined by Ashel Beach, Ebenezer Halliday and his sons.

At the eastern end of the waterway, in what later became Carleton County, the surveys of Marlborough and the four townships that touch the Rideau, began in 1793. This work was supervised by Deputy-Surveyor John Stegmann, and the new townships were named North Gower, Osgoode, Gloucester and Nepean. The following year Stegmann drowned in Dow's Great Swamp, which, during canal building was converted into the lake that is such an asset to downtown Ottawa. Below the falls of the Rideau, along both sides of the Ottawa River, the land was flat, of rich alluvial sand and clay left when the Champlain Sea receded. This spot, where the Ottawa, Rideau and Gatineau Rivers converge, and where there were many good powersites, soon attracted the attention of the land-hungry from soil-poor, overcrowded New England. It was closer than the lands along the Ohio River where some Yankees were moving in quest of good land.

The man who led the way up the Ottawa Valley was Philomen Wright, a prosperous farmer and businessman from Woburn, Massachusetts. After some years of negotiation, part of the time assuring the authorities in Quebec City that he would defend the King and his Parliament, Wright set out from Woburn with 27 settlers in February, 1800. The time of year seemed unpromising, but winter was an easier season to travel through wilderness than when the weather was mild. On six ox-drawn sleighs they carried farm equipment, mill irons, and supplies to the tune of £2,000. Wright made

Kingston, U.C., 1827—View from Barriefield, showing: 1, H.M.S. "Grampus"; 2, Stone Frigate, now the site of the Royal Military College; 3, Fort Frederick; 4, Commodore Barrie's residence; 5, Marine Cottages; 6, Marine Hospital; 7, St. George's (Anglican) Church; 8, Market House; 9, Dean's schoolhouse; 10, Ordnance Stores; 11, Cataraqui Bridge, connecting Kingston and Barriefield.
(Metropolitan Toronto Library Board).

for Hull Township, on the north shore of the Ottawa River in Lower Canada, facing the Upper Canadian shore above the falls of the Rideau.

In April, the Council of Lower Canada ordered a survey of the boundaries of Hull Township and in 1801, Wright hired a surveyor to lay out farm lots. The village Philomen founded on the shore of the Ottawa River was known as Wright's Landing until the name was changed to Hull. The founder built saw and grist mills and entered the timber trade at a crucial time, when France was at war with Britain and her blockade had cut off the Baltic ports. The mother country's normal source of tall masts and spars for the Royal Navy was lost. Wright stepped into the breach, rafting logs down the Ottawa to the St. Lawrence, beginning the lumber trade that was the economic base of the future capital region for more than a century.

Land speculators were active in Nepean Township, but the first real settler was Ira Honeywell, whose father, Rice, was a one-time American rebel who settled in Augusta

Township on the shore of the St. Lawrence, Ira homesteaded three miles above the Chaudière Falls. The first development on the site of downtown Ottawa was a dock and a log store, erected in 1809, by Jehiel Collins, who soon sold his enterprise to his clerk, Caleb Bellows. The spot was known as Bellows Landing until 1816. By the time the War of 1812 broke out, the other three townships—North Gower, Gloucester and Osgoode—were vacant, although in 1809 the founder of Gloucester, Braddish Billings, was employed as a lumber jobber by Philomen Wright. Born in Boston in 1783, Billings was brought to Brockville by his parents when he was nine years old. At age twenty-six, imbued with ambition by his Yankee origins, he was bent on success.

By 1813, Braddish had won the heart of Samuel Dow's daughter, Lamira, who at age seventeen was the schoolmistress at Merrickville. She only taught one summer before her wedding, and her salary was supposed to be $7.00 per month. When she tried to collect in the autumn the farmers had no cash. The Reverend William Brown, a Methodist nick-

Westport, Upper Rideau Lake, by Thomas Burrowes.
(Ontario Archives).

named Priest Brown who had hired Lamira in the first place, suggested the farmers give her promissory notes for the delivery of wheat to a merchant in Brockville, thirty miles away. Undaunted Lamira set out on foot, but to her chagrin the merchants insisted she accepted goods for the notes, not cash.

Lamira walked back to Merrickville and taking a wagon she drove through the settlement collecting what each farmer owed her in wheat. Returning to Brockville, Lamira sold the wheat on the market and used the money for her hope chest. Following the wedding, Lamira and Braddish had a fairly typical honeymoon for the time and place. They spent it canoeing down the Rideau, portaging around the Hog's Back Falls to his land, some 100 yards from where Billings Bridge was built later. Those plunging rapids were the most treacherous on the river. Soon after Braddish and Lamira's daughter Sabra was born—the first white child in Gloucester Township—they were returning by canoe from a visit to the Dows in Merrickville. At the portage they met Philomen Wright, and

the two canoes collided. Wright reached shore, but the Billings family was swept downstream into the white water. Lamira kept her head and Braddish showed his skill, for he brought them through in one piece. They may have been the only people ever to pass down the Hog's Back Falls. Even the Indians portaged when they reached that dangerous place.

Braddish prospered through the timber trade, acting, too, as an agent for the sale of settlers' log rafts, maintaining an office in Montreal. Billings was as hard-nosed a businessman as any other Yankee, but one who got the better of him was the author's ancestor, Caleb Seaman, who owned land at Rockport, on the St. Lawrence. Through Braddish a Montreal man named William Johnson ordered 6,000 staves. Caleb agreed to cut them, and received £120 when they were ready. After the rough journey down the rapids of the St. Lawrence only 3,000 staves reached Montreal, whereupon Johnson sued Billings for the balance. The court ordered Billings to provide the missing 3,000 staves at no additional cost to Johnson. This

31

anecdote showed the need for some kinder form of transport that was a valid argument for building the Rideau Canal.

4. When War was the Catalyst

After the United States declared war on Britain—and therefore Canada—in June, 1812, the Rideau country, a safe distance inland, was not affected directly. Many of the settlers joined the battalions of militia raised in each county, and many who had served in provincial corps during the American Revolution were made officers. In 1813, Stephen and Daniel Burritt were stationed at Fort Wellington, on the shore of the St. Lawrence east of Prescott and opposite Ogdensburg, New York, where Fort Oswegatchie, the former British post, had a garrison of American troops.

Early in the November dawn, as the story goes, a cannon ball dropped into Fort Wellington's officers' mess. Daniel Burritt seized it and returned it to its owners by way of one of the fort's cannons. The ball struck the Ogdensburg Court House, where an artillery officer picked it up and put it away for safe keeping. Like most residents of the border communities he disapproved of making war on friends and relations who just happened to live on the wrong side of the river. Later he presented the ball to the Burritt family, and now it is a prized heirloom in the possession of Stephen's great great grandson.

The war that might have lost Upper Canada to the United States—but for the stupidity of the Americans—ended on December 24th, 1814, with the signing of the Treaty of Ghent. A year later the Napoleonic Wars were concluded, and Britain, somewhat startled, found that she still owned the province. The vast empty spaces should be settled with loyal British stock, and for the security of the territory an alternate water route to Montreal was imperative. Now the lands along the Rideau Waterway and the entire route from Kingston to the Ottawa River below the Chaudière Falls came into the limelight, attracting the attention of the Iron Duke himself.

Soldiers stationed in Canada and most of Wellington's army were about to be disbanded, and would face unemployment during the post-war lull. Those in Canada should be encouraged to remain and settle, while some of the returning troops might be willing to emigrate. Then, too, the poor in the British Isles should receive encouragement to depart, relieving the high unemployment caused by the early stages of the Industrial Revolution. Disbanded soldiers would be given land on the basis of rank—1,200 acres for a lieutenant-colonel, 1,000 for a major, 800 to a captain, 500 to a subaltern, 300 to a quarter master-sergeant or sergeant-major, 200 to a sergeant, and 100 to a private.

For civilians, Lord Bathurst, the Colonial Secretary, advertised that the government would supply food for the voyage and a grant of 100 acres for each family willing to move to Canada, as well as 100 acres to each son on reaching age 21. To ensure that these civilians would take the offer seriously and try to improve their holdings, a deposit of £16 had to be paid for each man over 16 and another £2 for each wife. The money would be refunded once a family had stayed two years on the land. Although many impoverished people had no savings, the immigration of those who could afford the deposit began. Following the war, the stream of Americans seeking land resumed almost at once, and most were from New England, New York and Vermont—states that had voted against what they regarded as President Madison's unpopular war.

Following his success against Napoleon, the Duke of Wellington became the Master General of the Ordnance Department, concerned with defence, and he studied ways to secure Upper Canada against any other depredations by the United States. Had the Americans decided to concentrate their strength along the upper St. Lawrence, instead of dissipating their energies at Niagara and Detroit, the entire province could have been isolated and no doubt annexed. A safe water route between Montreal and Lake Ontario was necessary.

The matter of a canal from the Ottawa River to the upper St. Lawrence or Lake Ontario had been discussed even before the War of 1812-14 had ended. Sir George Prevost, the governor-in-chief, had written to Lieutenant-General Sir Gordon Drummond, the administrator of Upper Canada, proposing a canal system through the Rideau River and the labyrinth of lakes. Moreover, Brigadier Jacob Brown of the New York Militia, captured at the Battle of Crysler's Farm in

Cataraqui (Kingston)—A south-east view, 1783—This is the first picture of Cataraqui, showing what was left of Fort Frontenac in that year. In 1671 the place was known as Cataraqui, and visited by De Courcelles, the Governor of New France. He was succeeded by Count Frontenac, and the fort was built by him, and named in his honour. Water colour by James Peachey, ensign, 60th Regiment.
(Public Archives of Canada—C1511).

Count Frontenac on the way to Cataraqui. Painted by P.H. De Rinzy in 1899.
(Public Archives of Canada—C13325).

Kingston Mills by J.P. Cockburn
(Public Archives of Canada—C12627).

Jones Falls, Upper Canada ca. 1838 by Philip John Bainbrigge.
(Public Archives of Canada—C11835).

Merrickville, Rideau Canal, ca. 1838 by Philip John Bainbrigge.
(Public Archives of Canada—C11849).

Merricks Station No. 9, 1827-1832—46½ miles from Bytown, by W. Clegg.
(Public Archives of Canada—C1209).

Perth, the capital of the District of Dalhousie, from the north-east bank of the Tay River, sketched 20th August, 1828 by Thomas Burrowes.
(Ontario Archives)

Opinicon Lake to the north-west with the steamer "Hunter", November, 1840, by Thomas Burrowes.
(Ontario Archives)

Upper Rideau Lake:—Canoe en route to Bytown;—Westport in the distance, by Thomas Burrowes.
(Ontario Archives)

Hon. Thomas Mackay's Mills, distillery and part of New Edinburgh, Rideau Falls,
sketched in 1845 by Thomas Burrowes.
(Ontario Archives)

Lock and dam at the Davis Mill.
Barges passing from the lock to the steamboat "Bytown", by Thomas Burrowes.
(Ontario Archives)

Lock at the Isthmus, the last ascent to the summit water of the canal from Lake Ontario,
1841 by Thomas Burrowes.
(Ontario Archives)

Hotel Kenney at Jones Falls. This hotel was established in 1877.
Original painting by F.M. Taylor in 1895.
(Mr. T. Joseph Kenney)

Steamer "James Swift" in the Jones Falls Locks, 1896, painted by F.M. Taylor.
(Mr. T. Joseph Kenney)

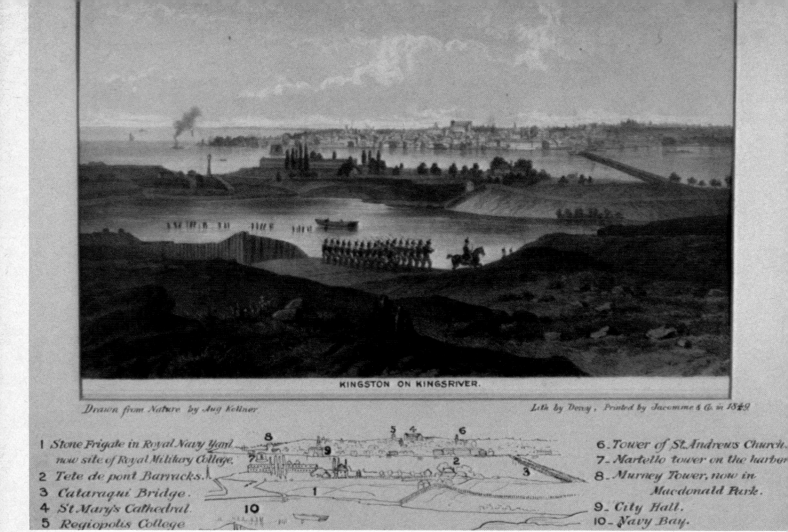

KINGSTON ON KINGSRIVER.

Drawn from Nature by Aug Köllner.   *Lith by Devoy, Printed by Jacomme & Co in 1849.*

1 Stone Frigate in Royal Navy Yard now site of Royal Military College.
2 Tete de pont Barracks.
3 Cataraqui Bridge.
4 St Mary's Cathedral.
5 Regiopolis College

6 Tower of St Andrews Church.
7 Martello tower on the harbor.
8 Murney Tower, now in Macdonald Park.
9 City Hall.
10 Navy Bay.

Kingston in 1849, by Aug Köllner.
(Metropolitan Toronto Library Board)

Ottawa City (lower town), Canada West, from government hill looking down the Ottawa River and showing the locks of the Rideau Canal, 1855. Original painting by Edwin Whitefield in 1855.
(Public Archives of Canada—C600).

November, 1813, admitted that his superiors had realized their mistake and were planning to concentrate on the upper St. Lawrence and Kingston in the near future—intelligence later confirmed when James Munroe became the Secretary of War in September, 1814. Fortunately for Upper Canada, the prospect of coping with the British veterans who had subdued Napoleon brought the Americans to the peace table, and the treaty was signed before Munroe's plan could be tested.

Sir Gordon Drummond's immediate reaction to a canal system linking Montreal to Kingston through the Rideau was caution. The scheme would weigh heavily on the British taxpayer, which, as matters turned out, was prophetic. Prevost was unconvinced, and seeking another opinion he ordered Lieutenant-Colonel George MacDonell—Red George who had successfully raided Ogdensburg in February, 1813—to improve the rapids and roads from Cornwall to Prescott, and to explore the Rideau route.

MacDonell's report, prepared in December, 1814, was favourable, but it did not reassure Prevost, who suspected that the red-pated colonel was making light of some difficulties improving the Rideau would impose. MacDonell's was the first of many reports on the feasibility of developing an alternate route to the St. Lawrence. In view of the difficulties the builders encountered, not one of them was thorough. After reading what MacDonell had to say, Sir Gordon Drummond informed Prevost that he had consulted several regular officers at Kingston, and he still thought that a canal through the Rideau would be too costly. One who gave his support to the scheme was Captain Sir James Yeo, Royal Navy, who commanded the British and provincial ships on Lake Ontario. Should the Americans establish themselves somewhere on the St. Lawrence between Montreal and Kingston, Yeo warned, they would soon render both the navy and army on the lake impotent.

Yeo had only one solution; make Kingston a strong base, and open a waterway to Montreal via the "River du Rideau." (When the time came to build the canal, another naval commander at Kingston, Commodore Robert Barrie, used his clout to persuade the Board of Ordnance in London to make it wide enough for steamboats, ending a lengthy debate on the subject.)

Red George MacDonell estimated that the canals would cost from £20,000 to £25,000, but Yeo felt that even though the improvements might cost three or four times this amount, it was a small price to pay for the security of Upper Canada. One who feared the enormous expense was Lieutenant-Colonel George Nicolls, the Commanding Engineer in Canada, who, after a tour of duty in Nova Scotia would be on hand for the final stage in the construction of the canal. Despite his reservations, by October, 1815, Sir Gordon Drummond had received orders from London to secure estimates on the costs of building canals to bypass the Lachine Rapids in the St. Lawrence, the Carillon and Long Sault in the Ottawa River, and to link that river with Lake Ontario by way of the Rideau River and the lakes. However, the war was over, and the authorities could now debate at leisure.

In April, 1816, Colonel Nicholls sent Lieutenant Joshua Jebb, of the Royal Engineers, to do his latest study on the feasibility of making a navigable waterway along the Rideau. Meanwhile, Sir Gordon Drummond was wondering how best to dispossess the settlers already along the route in order to replace them with disbanded soldiers and their families—people of unquestioned loyalty to the King—an indication that the home government mistrusted people of American origin, even those of loyalist descent. Drummond put the matter before the lieutenant-governor of Upper Canada, then Sir Francis Gore, who discussed the proposal with his Executive Council. Replying to Drummond, Sir Francis hedged:

> I fear that any attempt to engage the Proprietors in the Rideau Townships to exchange for other Lands, will be fruitless;—Every aid, however, in my power, will be afforded, if the agents can induce a willing concurrance; but I should not feel myself justified to make the proposition as an Act of Government.

Drummond's hope of settling disbanded troops facing the Rideau died, but such men could be placed close at hand, to assure a strong militia in the event of more trouble from the south.

Lieutenant Joshua Jebb began his journey of exploration along the Rideau in June, 1816, starting from the Ottawa River. He forwarded preliminary reports to Colonel Nicholls, one on the difficulty of mounting the 30 foot waterfalls at the mouth of the Rideau; another on the intricacies of construction as far as Long Island. Later Jebb wrote that the waterway should be by way of Irish Creek, which branched southwest from the Rideau River five miles above William Merrick's mills. The way was shorter, and the land along the creek more fertile. Although the canal would be primarily for military use, Jebb and the other officers realized the advantages to be gained if it were of some use to the future inhabitants.

By mid July, Jebb had written his report, delimiting the stretches of navigable water, pinpointing the waterfalls and rapids, noting where expensive cutting through solid rock could not be avoided, checking the water depth for the passage of "boats", by which he meant bateaux, whaleboats or Durham boats. Floating islands of bog, Jebb observed, could easily be removed, and there should be a strongly fortified blockhouse at a spot he called Koyle's bridge, where a new road from Brockville crossed the Rideau near the site of Smiths Falls and turned west towards Perth, then a brand new settlement. Jebb also thought some land transport would have to be integrated with the canal. Cutting a channel to the Gananoque River would be very costly, and Jebb offered a novel solu-

tion. A road of five miles could be cut to Rideau Lake, and it should be a railway so that carts could carry stores and all sorts of military supplies. The rails would be of cast iron, no problem for the engineer had found some bog ore only a short way downstream. Should this ore be difficult to smelt, Jebb recommended rails of wood, although these would be less durable.

The canal would wend its way through Cranberry Lake and into the Cataraqui River. For some time after Jebb sent in his report, the Irish Creek route was favoured over the longer route along the Rideau by way of Smiths Falls. Meanwhile, the section of the Ottawa River needing canalization came under scrutiny. From August to November, another Royal Engineer, Lieutenant Richard Baron, explored that stretch of water, and his report as well as Jebb's was submitted to Lieutenant-Colonel Elias Walker Durnford, who had replaced Colonel Nicholls as the Commanding Engineer in Canada. Despite snags that would delay the start of construction along the Rideau for a decade, an advertisement for contract tenders appeared in the Upper Canada Gazette in March, 1817.

Sawmill at Kingston Mills, as it appeared in May, 1828, by Thomas Burrowes. (Ontario Archives).

Old Fort Henry built in the 1820's to protect the naval yard at Point Frederick, Kingston.
(Royal Ontario Museum).

5. Settlement after 1815

In accordance with British policy of filling up the land near the Rideau with loyal disbanded troups and needy civilians from the motherland, a period of rapid land colonization followed the cessation of hostilities with the United States and France. Many of the settlers were Scots seeking to better their lot, and while conditions in Ireland were bad, few families could afford the deposit money. Americans, particularly New Englanders, continued their northward trek. Grants to reduced officers from the American Revolution had left gaps, and the reserves for the clergy and Crown established under the Constitutional Act of 1791, added to the problem of unoccupied farm lots that interfered with contiguous settlement. Still, for the lots that were available, settlers began moving inland, usually from Prescott, Brockville and other St. Lawrence River towns. A rash of new villages sprang up at the powersites in the back townships.

The first wave of disbanded soldier-settlers reached the Rideau townships in 1815. The previous December, the government announced that free land grants of 100 acres would be allowed privates, and 200 for non-commissioned officers, who wished to remain in Canada when their regiments were reduced. They would also receive provisions for one year, varying sizes of axes, spades, hand and crosscut saws and other implements from a depot to be located at a convenient spot on the Rideau. The veterans were to remain on their lands for a minimum of three years, and to make "reasonable improvements." By the end of September, 100 privates and sergeants had settled in the townships of Oxford, Wolford, Montague, Marlborough, Kitley and Bastard.

One community outside the townships bordering the waterway is worthy of inclusion because of its direct links with Rideau Lake. Perth, in the Township of Drummond, north of Elmsley, was established on the Pike River, renamed the Tay by its Scots founders. It was intended as a military settlement, but the first Scots to reach the site were civilians who had sailed from Glasgow and Greenock in the summer of 1815, and arrived at Quebec City in mid September. Since the season was well advanced, 300 of the would-be settlers wintered at Cornwall, sustained by provisions from a military store-

house. Thirty families continued on to Brockville, and were lodged in an old barracks, huts built for them, or billeted on farms in the vicinity. A depot of supplies was set up at Oliver's Ferry (now Rideau Ferry) across Rideau Lake, and surveyors under Reubin Sherwood's direction went up the Tay River to lay out lots. The site of Perth had been chosen because it was at the portage to the Mississippi River, to the north, which flows into the Ottawa River. The surveyors made heavy weather of their work, for they found that the land around the intended community was swampy and nearly impenetrable.

Eager to see their future homes, several of the Scots housed in Brockville set out for the Rideau. After exploring the swamp where Sherwood's men were struggling they returned to Brockville and sent a petition to Sir Francis Gore, the lieutenant-governor, asking for land along the Bay of Quinte. In reply Gore ordered them to proceed to the location north of the Rideau that had been chosen for them as soon as the spring would permit. Settlers were for a specific purpose that would not be fulfilled unless they located close to the Rideau.

In command of the Scots travelling from Brockville were several officers of the Glengarry Light Infantry Fencibles, a detachment of which would also be settling at Perth. Alexander MacDonell, the paymaster, Lieutenant Angus MacDonell, and the regimental surgeon, one Dr. Thom, were responsible for moving supplies to the depot and distributing certificates for farm lots. They found that the survey of the lots was depressingly slow, and Alexander MacDonell complained that Reubin Sherwood was rarely on the spot and his men needed more guidance. Not until March, 1816, was a road completed all the way to the depot, where a government storehouse was to be erected. Nor was the surveyors' work accurate. Chains that broke had been repaired by joining the next sound links, which shortened each by 4 inches per lost link. Others were mended with willow links that stretched. As a consequence, some lots were a few acres short, others overly generous. Sherwood was a capable man, but he had overextended himself. Qualified land surveyors were rare birds, and Reubin had parties working in too many places to keep track of what each was doing.

An impatient Alexander MacDonell went to Kingston to talk with Colonel Francis Cockburn, the Deputy Quartermaster General there, who agreed to investigate the matter. On March 16th, accompanied by Captain Otty, Royal Navy, Cockburn reached Brockville, where MacDonell joined them, with Reubin Sherwood and Joseph Daverne, the latter the clerk of the government warehouse now nearing completion. They drove in sleighs along the best road, which took them to Stone Mills, 26 miles from Brockville at the east end of Upper Beverley Lake, and on 12 miles to the site of Portland. Next they drove down Rideau Lake to Oliver's Ferry, left their sleighs and crossed on snowshoes to a small lake which Colonel Cockburn named Otty in honour of the naval officer travelling with him. From there they selected the townsite for Perth. By

March 26th, Sherwood had blazed a trail from this spot to Rideau Lake at the point where Port Elmsley would later stand and a road would link Perth with Merrickville.

The settlers who had wintered at Brockville set out in wagons along the route used by MacDonell and his party, and went down Rideau Lake in a scow that belonged to a local resident. An ox sled carried their worldly possessions around the waterfall on the Tay, and a second scow took them the rest of the way to Perth. To every four families the government storehouse dispensed a grindstone, crosscut saw and whip saw. As well, an individual family was issued with an adze, hand saw, drawing knife, shell auger, two gimlets, door lock and hinges, scythe, snath, rasping hook, two hoes, hay fork, skillet and camp kettle, while each family member received a blanket.

Rideau—1815. Sketch of the route for boat navigation from the Ottawa River, up the Rideau, also the route from Bastard by the way of Gananoque, and by way of Kingston Mills, by Reubin Sherwood.
(Public Archives of Canada—C85689).

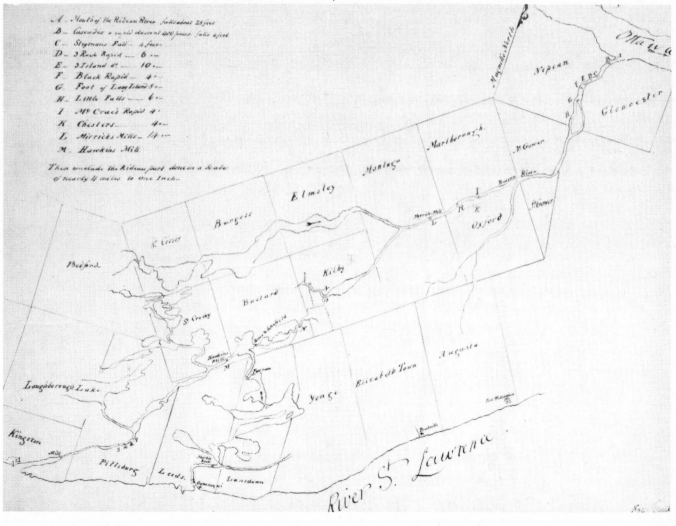

*Richmond,
on the River Jacques,
or Goodwood,
a tributary of
the Rideau River,
September 1830,
by Thomas Burrowes.
(Ontario Archives).*

The surveys lagged behind the arriving settlers, and MacDonell complained that Reubin Sherwood was not supplying him with sufficient accurate information on where the best land was to be found. Equally frustrating, many of the tools the government supplied were unsuitable for the forests of Canada. Most were neither heavy enough nor durable. The base line for a series of new townships to accommodate the civilians and the soon to arrive soldiers was soon called the Scotch Line in honour of the origin of most of the inhabitants.

In June, the first of the disbanded troops arrived with their families. These were Glengarry Light Infantry Fencibles, and part of the Regiment de Watteville. The first had been raised among Highlanders who had settled in Glengarry County and other places, some of whom were lured into the wilds by the offer of free land; the second was a Swiss regiment that had been in Britain's service for many years. Put on the British regular establishment in 1801, the corps had served with distinction during the Peninsular War, and was posted to Canada in April, 1813. The men were from many backgrounds. Some had served under Napoleon, and when taken prisoner they willingly enlisted under Major-General Louis de Watteville. At Perth confusion reigned, and Alexander MacDonell complained again, this time that Reubin Sherwood had spent too much time surveying Drummond Township, where much of the land was swampy, instead of working in Bathurst, to the west, where the land was superior.

After waiting around some of the de Wattevilles became disenchanted and joined Lord Selkirk's settlers making for the Red River Valley. Others vanished into the United States. The Glengarrys, refusing to be discouraged at the lack of organization around them, remained, no doubt persuaded by their officers not to desert the newly arrived Scottish civilians.

Meanwhile, two other groups of disbanded British regular soldiers who had been on duty at Quebec City were making their way up the Ottawa River. Both landed at Caleb Bellows's dock, and one group, from the 99th and 100th Regiments, founded the village named after the then governor-in-chief of Canada, the Duke of Richmond. The landing, thus far called after Bellows, was soon renamed Richmond, as was the road that linked it to the new military settlement. Richmond village was located on the Jock River, a tributary on the north bank of the Rideau River in Nepean Township. The other group went to Pinhey's Point, in the Township of March, to the north of Nepean. The three military settlements were to form a second line of defence, supporting the townships along the St. Lawrence, and the generous grants of land to officers were in keeping with their status as gentlemen. A few of the disbanded soldiers chose lots on the south side of the Rideau, and of the de Wattevilles, 10 chose Burgess, 26 went to Bathurst, while 2 remained in Drummond.

46

Residence of Capt. P. Cole, W.Eng. the officer in charge at Isthmus during construction of the Works from 1830 to 1832 by Thomas Burrowes. (Ontario Archives).

From these beginnings the town of Perth evolved, with its stone buildings one of the most substantial communities in the Rideau country. Another important settlement was Smiths Falls, which developed later, and was named after Thomas Smyth, a lieutenant in the King's Royal Regiment of New York who had settled in Elizabethtown. He was the younger son of Dr. George Smyth, the surgeon in the Loyal Rangers who had been the deputy head of the secret service during the American Revolution. Like his brother Terrence, Thomas had been a dispatch carrier. Early sources refer to him as Major Smyth, the commission he held later in the militia. Part of his grant as a reduced officer was 400 acres on the 4th concession of Elmsley Township, but for many years he did not visit the land and was unaware that he owned a splendid millsite. In 1810, he mortgaged this land to a Boston man for £223, 11s, 3d, but he was never paid and he assumed that the 400 acres still belonged to him.

In 1823, with some associates, Thomas built a rudimentary sawmill at the falls, then in the midst of the wilderness. Before a year had passed, Smyth was ordered to appear in court at York (Toronto), and he lost the title to his land. He must have been aware of what the outcome would be, for he removed the working parts of the mill before he went to court. The land was sold at a sheriff's sale in Brockville and purchased by Charles Jones, a loyalist from New York State. A grasping businessman, Jones sold the Smyth land to Abel Russel Ward for £600, a considerable increase over the amount Thomas hoped to gain through the mortgage. Ward

was the founder of Smiths Falls, which was called Wardsville for a time, then Smyth's Falls until the present spelling was used. Abel rebuilt Smyth's mill and by the summer of 1827 it was in operation when construction on the canal had also begun.

A third town whose foundations were laid following the War of 1812 was Kemptville. Lyman Clothier, from South Gower, came to the South Branch of the Rideau in search of a millsite. The exact date of his arrival is not certain, but thought to be 1813, and shortly afterward he built a dam across the narrow stream, and a sawmill. Later he added a grist mill, and as usually followed, a village began to mushroom. Tradesmen and craftsmen were attracted by the powersite. Wherever farmers had to come to have boards sawn and grain ground was automatically a mecca for other commercial activity. Another prominent settler was William Bottum, whose father Elijah had ended the American Revolution as an ensign in the Loyal Rangers. Bottum was the first clerk of Oxford Township, and the local postmaster.

The village was known as Clothier's Mills, or prosaically, The Branch, once it had a blacksmith's shop, harness shop and general merchant. Then in 1829, when the residents wanted a more impressive name for their community, they honoured Sir James Kempt, then the Administrator of the Government of Canada, who had toured the canal route the year before. Another Upper Canadian town had lost the opportunity of having the founder's name kept alive for the benefit of later residents.

6. Definite Plans to Build the Canal

On February 19th, 1817, the lieutenant-governor's office in York published a notice calling for tenders from persons wishing to contract for all, or any part of, the water communication between:

> La Chine and Kingston, by the course of the River Rideau, navigable for Boats drawing two feet water, and ten feet width, also for Boats drawing three feet water and twelve feet in width.

Each contractor was to specify the number of locks and the places where he proposed to build them, the number of floodgates in each lock, and the time when he expected the work could be completed. The route, in agreement with Lieutenant Joshua Jebb's report, was to be by way of Irish Creek.

At the same time, tenders were invited for the communication by Rideau Lake through to Mud (Newboro) Lake and from thence to Kingston. Even the larger dimensions to be submitted would take only Durham boats, shortsighted when steamboats were already operating on the St. Lawrence between Montreal and Quebec City and on Lake Ontario. Common sense decreed that any canal contemplated should be large enough to accommodate the steamboats, a technological advance that was not likely to disappear.

Few contractors responded, for the mood in Upper Canada had altered with the coming of peace. By 1818, people were discussing improving the St. Lawrence, the better waterway and the one that could attract American commerce to Canadian ports. However, with the approval of the governor-in-chief, the Duke of Richmond, the Royal Engineers continued their investigations of the Rideau, because of its military significance. For this reason the British government gave it priority. The lieutenant-governor, Sir Peregrine Maitland, and his councillors in Muddy York favoured the St. Lawrence, but the cabinet in London felt that as a commercial waterway it was the responsibility of private money, or some form of provincial funding. The situation was delicate, a tug of war between the desires of the Upper Canadian leaders and the British officers concerned with defence, a conflict not unusual between politicians and soldiers.

The lieutenant-governor of Upper Canada led the politicians, the governor-in-chief nursed the desires of the military. Charles Lennox was the 4th Duke of Richmond, and Sir Peregrine Maitland's reluctant father-in-law. When Maitland asked for the hand of Lady Sarah Lennox, one of seven daughters, His Grace refused. Peregrine was a capable soldier who had been one of Wellington's officers, but he had no private fortune. Undeterred the young couple eloped, and through the intervention of the Iron Duke personally, Richmond unbent somewhat towards Lady Sarah. The Maitlands and the other members of the duke's family travelled to Canada aboard the same ship, Sir Peregrine to serve in Upper Canada while His Grace and Excellency remained in Quebec City.

In the summer of 1819, the governor-in-chief embarked on a tour of Upper Canada. With two sons, three daughters and a retinue of attendants, he left Quebec City aboard a steamboat on June 21st, and stopped for a few days at Sorel—a great mistake. During that visit he was bitten by a fox, but stories are at odds on how this happened. According to one version, he was given a tame fox as a pet, while to another he was rescuing his dog Blucher from a wild one. Either way, His Grace was unaware of the pending consequences as he proceeded up the St. Lawrence and across Lake Ontario to inspect the defences at Niagara and view the falls. He visited the Maitlands at York, and by the beginning of August he had reached Kingston and was planning to travel to Hull, looking over the route of the proposed Rideau Canal.

Colonel Francis Cockburn, one of his aides, had been at Perth, preparing for His Excellency's visit there, and he met the vice-regal party at Kingston. Most of the members returned to Quebec City the way they had come, but the duke remained behind, attended by Cockburn, Colonel George Bowles of the Coldstream Guards who was his military secretary, a servant named Baptiste, and the dog Blucher. On horseback the men plunged into the wilds. Brushing away the swarms of mosquitos, the dog in tow, the nobleman and his escort reached Perth on August 21st, and remained three days. His Grace, Colonel Bowles noted, was unusually irritable, and looked far from well. Despite some urging, he refused to curtail his journey, and on the 24th, the men set out for a store fifteen miles distant in Beckwith Township, to the east of Drummond. There they spent the night and planned to proceed towards the military settlement at Richmond in the morning.

The party travelled six miles to a shanty owned by a man named Saunders, and here the duke agreed to rest while his aides made arrangements for an overnight stop at Sergeant Vaughan's cabin, beyond which the going would be so difficult that the party would have to walk. At the cabin Colonel George Thew Burke, the superintendent of the Richmond settlement, met them, and with Colonel Cockburn he returned to Richmond to prepare for the duke's coming. Bowles remained to care for His Grace, who was limping badly when he reached the Vaughan cabin. By August 26th, when he entered Richmond, the governor-in-chief was having difficulty swallowing. Cockburn had arranged for rooms at a tavern in the heart of the settlement kept by Andrew Hill, a former sergeant-major in the 100th Regiment, and his wife Maria.

The Hills put their best foot forward to entertain near-royalty in the backwoods. The 1st Duke of Richmond was an illegitimate son of King Charles II by his mistress Louise de Querouaille, Duchess of Portsmouth. The King bestowed the dukedom on his offspring, declaring the heir the Earl of March during his father's lifetime, a name commemorated in the Township of March, north of Nepean. Following a special dinner, the 4th Duke paced his bedroom floor, and Mrs. Hill overheard him talking with Colonel Bowles and the whimpering of the dog Blucher. In the morning the governor-in-chief declined breakfast, and his aides sent for Surgeon Collis, who was to meet the party with bateaux at Richmond Landing for the journey to Montreal. Because the road was so rough, the duke set out with Colonel Bowles and the servant Baptiste in a canoe, while Colonel Cockburn and Colonel Burke took the horses, planning to meet the canoe at Chapman's, three miles downstream.

Colonel Bowles and Baptiste took the governor into Chapman's log cabin, and there Surgeon Collis, who had hurried inland from Richmond Landing, bled him, which probably worsened his condition. In his dying hours the duke dictated messages to his relatives, one a word of forgiveness to Lady Sarah Maitland for her elopement with Sir Peregrine. His Grace asked to be remember-ed to the Prince of Wales, his kinsman on the right side of the blanket, and to the Duke of York with whom he had once fought a duel. On the evening of August 28th, he succumbed to rabies. The body was taken back to Hill's tavern in Richmond—afterward known as the Duke of Richmond's Arms. Mrs. Maria Hill prepared the corpse for transport to Richmond Landing, and Philomen Wright awaited it with a team and "waggon" at the ford over the Jock River. He conveyed His Grace's remains to the Ottawa River and put them on a boat for Quebec City. The deceased governor-in-chief lay in state until September 4th, and after the funeral service he was interred in the vault at the Anglican Cathedral.

In the Rideau country, a boulder marks the site of the Vaughan cabin where His Grace had rested, a cairn the site of the Chapman cabin where he expired. In 1926, a plaque commemorating the mournful event was erected by the Historic Sites and Monuments Board of Canada, and in October, 1951, a direct descendant, Lady Alexander, visited Richmond to view the plaque. Her husband, Earl Alexander of Tunis, was the last British governor-general to reside at Rideau Hall, a building with strong ties to one of the canal contractors.

The next governor-in-chief of Canada was a Scottish peer, Sir George Ramsay, the 9th Earl of Dalhousie. The knighthood was earned (1813), the earldom inherited (1787), and he was created 1st Baron Dalhousie in 1815, for his services under the Duke of Wellington, which made him a peer of the United Kingdom. From 1816 until the death of the Duke of Richmond, Dalhousie had been the lieutenant-governor of Nova Scotia.

As head of the Ordnance Department, the Duke of Wellington was in charge of canal building in the colonies, and within a decade he would be Prime Minister of Great Britain. When Dalhousie reached Quebec City in 1820, he was well aware of the Iron Duke's keen interest in the construction of a canal along the Rideau. While the British public adored their great war hero, the politicians of the mother country were in the midst of an economy drive and not receptive to the notion of having expensive projects in a remote and worthless province such as Upper Canada weigh too heavily on the shoulders of British taxpayers, not after the cost of the Napoleonic Wars. Furthermore,

Lieut.-Colonel John By, Royal Engineers, founder of Bytown and superintendent during the construction of the Rideau Canal.
(Public Archives of Canada—C28531).

Esther By—Wife of Lieut.-Colonel By, R.E.
(Metropolitan Toronto Library Board).

the assembly of the province was maturing, and its wishes could not be wholly ignored—a fact brought to light vividly in 1837. Nevertheless, the Rideau Canal was a hot issue, and when in 1820, military settlements were suspended to cut costs, the Rideau country was exempted, an indication that by hook or by crook the canal would go ahead.

As usual, American activities sparked a response. They were caught up by canal fever, and working on a link between Lake Champlain and the Hudson River. Since 1817, they had been building the barge canal that would soon tie Lake Erie to the Hudson River at Albany. An improved Canadian route was essential to prevent trade being diverted into New York State. The government of Lower Canada decided to build a canal at Lachine, and to deepen the bateau canal at Coteau du Lac. The ground breaking ceremony took place in July, 1821, to the strains of the band of the 60th Regiment, and the first link in the long route inland had started.

Eager not to be left out, the Upper Canada Legislature passed an act to enable the improvement of navigation within the province, and set up a commission to report on the cost of these alterations. Chaired by the Honourable John Macaulay of Kingston, a member of the Legislative Council, the commission sat for four years studying estimates for bypassing Niagara Falls, the rapids of the St. Lawrence and building the Rideau route.

Macaulay hired a Kingston civil engineer, Samuel Clowes, to make surveys, and in April, 1824, Clowes submitted his findings. He disliked Lieutenant Joshua Jebb's proposal to have the canal cut by way of Irish Creek, where he suspected the water supply might not be adequate, and recommended the longer way through Rideau Lake. He then provided the commissioners with three sets of estimates:

	Depth of Lock	Width at Top of Lock	Width at Bottom of Lock	Cost
I	7'	61'	40'	£230,785
II	5'	48'	28'	£145,802
III	3'	32'	20'	£ 62,258

At best Clowes was optimistic, even for those times, to envisage a canal system with 47 locks and a lift of nearly 300 feet. He was either unaware of the amount of building involved, or eager to sell the scheme to the Macaulay Commission, and therefore to the legislators. The commission's final report, published in April, 1825, stressed the military importance of a canal along the Rideau, but it also pointed out the advantages the loyal inhabitants who had been planted in the vicinity would enjoy. Thus very early in the planning, the canal so often described as a defence measure was intended to have a commercial role as well.

The report was submitted to London through Lord Dalhousie in the summer, and the home government offered a loan of £70,000 to assist in building canals on the Rideau. The Upper Canada Legislature declined, arguing that the St. Lawrence route was more vital to the province's economy. Next, unable to achieve the objective through civilian channels, the British government ordered a military commission sent to Canada to examine the country's defences and to bring back estimates on the cost of the Rideau works, with locks the same size as those on the recently completed Lachine Canal.

This commission was headed by Major-General Sir James Carmichael Smyth, and the members were Colonels Fanshawe and Lewis of the Royal Engineers. The commissioners agreed with Samuel Clowes's recommended route, but proposed locks 20 feet wide, 5 feet deep and 108 feet long, and felt that such would cost £169,000. Also the canal should have tow paths so that troops could be marched along them while their supplies and other military stores were brought on barges, bateaux or Durham boats. Still no thought was given to building a canal large enough for steamboats.

The commissioners travelled the entire route and suggested that the British government undertake the work, because the costs would be more than Upper Canada could afford. To the Duke of Wellington they reported that the settlers were very poor, and incapable of understanding the importance of the Rideau route for defence. For them, better transport for their produce to the markets of Montreal by way of the St. Lawrence took precedence. The home government accepted the Smyth Commission's recommendations, convinced that another attack by the Americans would mean the loss of Upper Canada.

Private G. Allan
Royal Sappers and Miners

Captain Hall
Royal Engineers

Reproduced by permission of H.M. The Queen from the original oil
paintings by A.J. Dubois Drahonet at Windsor Castle.

Sergeant J.J. Johnstone
Royal Sappers and Miners

Britain had no choice because of prior commitments. In 1819, work had been started on the Grenville and Carillon Canals in the Ottawa River by the Royal Staff Corps. If the Rideau Canal were not built, others would benefit mainly Philomen Wright and his lumber village of Hull—and Wright was not a man who needed government assistance. Having decided to proceed, there remained the choice of the superintendent who would plan and build the project, and the task of selecting him fell upon General Gothar Mann of the Ordnance Department. The man he found was one who would dominate the setting, stand straight, chin jutting, ready to overcome every adversity, yet deal humanely with his workmen while battling the bonds of red tape and bureaucratic insensitivity—Lieutenant-Colonel John By, Royal Engineers.

This gentleman's name presents a literary problem, owing to shortness and double meaning, giving rise to a sentence such as: By the time By stood by the Rideau, and so on. Henceforth he will be known as Colonel John, the Superintendent, or Superintending Engineer, as often as Colonel By.

7. John By Takes the Helm

To compare John By's last resting place, the churchyard at Frant, in the green, rolling countryside of Sussex, England, on the border of Kent, with the forest primeval and its stretches of swamp among the granite rock knobs, is to admit that the Superintendent was to say the least, adaptable. His story begins in the London Parish of St. Mary Lambeth, on August 10th, 1779. George By and Mary Brian were his parents, and John was their second son. George By and several members of the family had been in the Customs Service, but young John chose an army career, entering the Royal Military Academy at Woolwich. He received a second lieutenant's commission in the Royal Artillery on August 1st, 1799, before his twentieth birthday, and in December he transferred to the Royal Engineers, his life's work.

Promoted to first lieutenant on April 18th, 1801, he spent the next ten years in Canada. In the interval he became a second captain on March 2nd, 1805, and first captain on June 24th, 1809. He did duty in Quebec City, and helped build the small canal at the Cedars, above Montreal, before he was recalled to serve in the Peninsular War. While in Spain he took part in the siege of Badajos. In January, 1812, he returned to England and was sent to three different gunpowder mills. First he served at the mills in Faversham, then at Purfleet, and later Waltham Abbey. He supervised the construction of a small arms factory at Enfield Lock while he was at Waltham Abbey, and on June 23rd, he was promoted to the rank of brevet major. When the Peace of Paris ended the Napoleonic Wars, the government planned a fireworks display for St. James's Park, London. The Board of Ordnance was in charge of this celebration, and Major John By, who was well acquainted with the properties of gun-powder—the only explosive known at that time—helped with the arrangements. Later he displayed versatility by designing a truss-bridge with a span of 1,000 feet, which qualified him for some of the construction he was to undertake in Canada.

In 1821, the British Army had been reduced after the heavy drain of the long war against France, and Major John By was put on the half pay list temporarily. He was able to perform enough administrative duties to secure promotion to lieutenant-colonel, in the Royal Engineers, the rank he held when appointed to build the Rideau Canal.

Colonel John was of medium height, dark, inclined to portliness, but jovial and vigorous. His personal life had not been entirely happy for his first wife, Elizabeth Baines, died young leaving no children. On March 14th, 1818, he married Esther March, a young woman of some wealth and as adaptable as her spouse. They had two daughters, Esther and Harriet Martha, and with his three ladies the Superintendent landed at Quebec City on May 30th, 1826. They were to remain together throughout Colonel John's sojourn in the rough, inhospitable country. The colonel came full of enthusiasm, eager to leave his mark in the world and gain at least a knighthood for his pains. He left Canada broken by his toils and frustrations, his project completed, but under a cloud of disapproval that forced him to defend his actions against hordes of detractors.

He came with orders to build the canal between the Ottawa River and Kingston, and in the face of discouraging setbacks he did as he had been told. The survey work done by Samuel Clowes and Sir James Carmichael Smyth was superficial, and when Colonel John began his task he was confronted with unforeseen obstacles and challenges. Each advance was an experiment, for a canal had never before been cut through largely uncharted, poorly explored terrain. The waterway he was to improve—mild understatement—would follow the route recommended by Clowes, rather than by Irish Creek, would have a minimum depth throughout of 5 feet whether through canal, lake, river or swamp, and the locks were to be the same as those on the Lachine Canal and under construction on the Ottawa River. Such would be sufficient for the transport of gunboats and supply barges, and Colonel John was to build it for the magical £169,000 which General Sir James Carmichael Smyth had recommended.

Even before he left England, John By admitted to General Mann that the work might well cost four or five times that amount. Smyth had used construction costs for the Lachine Canal as the basis for his estimate, and Colonel John knew he faced a more formidable task. He had seen Lachine, where the excavation had been straightforward, requiring only digging and no blasting through solid rock. On the other hand, the Rideau country was trackless wilderness with scant resident population to provide labour. He would have to carry all his supplies long distances and build barracks to house workers—all of which would add considerably to the costs.

With these reservations in mind Colonel John listened to a final briefing from General Smyth, who warned him to resist pressures from local politicians to build the canal to the Gananoque River, which would bring it to the St. Lawrence eighteen miles east of Kingston. This exit would be vulnerable to attack by enemies lurking among the Thousand Islands. The canal must end at Kingston. In a last letter to General Gothar Mann, Colonel John informed him that the proposed canal route was 131 miles, through country little known, needing 45 locks and 10 weirs to the extent of 4,050 feet. He would require the assistance of one captain and two subalterns of the Royal Engineers, a clerk of works, an overseer of works, and the right to hire more if he thought necessary. During the winter of 1826-27, he hoped to have some timber felled, clear tow-paths, and collect materials for dams. Mann approved the junior officers, and informed Colonel John that he would be independent of the Commanding Engineer in Canada, Colonel Elias Walker Durnford.

The day after Colonel John and his family reached Quebec City, Lord Dalhousie received new orders. Lieutenant-Colonel John By, and Lieutenant-Colonel Wright, in charge of the works on the Ottawa River, would be under Commanding Engineer Durnford after all. For John By, this turned out to be a blessing. Durnford was to defend him when a parliamentary enquiry was investigating the costs of the Rideau Canal.

When the Superintending Engineer received his orders to report to Durnford on any problems he encountered, he was in Montreal with his family. Fired with enthusiasm he was soon writing to General Mann in London. The Rideau Canal should be wide enough to permit steamboat navigation, so that it could divert trade on the Great Lakes away from the Americans. Their Erie Canal was a mere ditch, with flimsey wooden lock gates that could be pushed open manually. A large canal for steamboats could carry British goods that would then find their way to American markets through the lake ports. Furthermore, steamboats would be superior to gunboats and Durham boats for transporting troops in safety. A steamboat such as Colonel John proposed could carry 700 troops at a time, and be armed with four 12 pounder guns. Larger canals would also ensure that Britain controlled the shipping on the lakes, both military and commercial.

Hull, (Lower Canada), on the Ottawa River—at the Chaudière Falls, sketched 1830 by Thomas Burrowes. (Ontario Archives).

Steamboats then being built on the Great Lakes and the St. Lawrence, the colonel went on excitedly, measured up to 130 feet long and 50 feet wide and required a draft of 8 feet. A canal to accommodate them over the Rideau route might cost £400,000, but the revenue from tolls would soon repay both the interest and principle. His letter on its way to General Mann, Colonel John waited anxiously for a reply, and was soon struck down by dysentery, as was his assistant, Captain Daniel Bolton, of the Royal Engineers, who had joined him at Montreal in August. Not until September was the colonel fit to travel up the Ottawa River to the mouth of the Rideau to begin his work as the Superintendent. When he set out he had hired John MacTaggart as his clerk of works, and two overseers, while Lieutenant Henry Pooley, Royal Engineers, had joined his team. He was also relieved by the order to report to Colonel Durnford, who would share the responsibility of decision making.

Meanwhile, Lord Dalhousie received detailed, complicated instructions on how the Superintendent was to dole out funds for labour and supplies—rules he would find impossible to follow when engaging and paying his contractors. The Parliament voted a sum of £25,000 for the first years' construction, of which £15,000 was for the Rideau, the rest for the Grenville Canal. The work was to be done entirely by contract, and tenders would be accepted. Colonel John quickly discovered that few men could arrange for workers and supplies in the wilds without receiving substantial sums in advance of starting to organize their operations. Consequently, the Superintendent regularly drew sums before they were authorized. The difficulties over receiving public funds when his contractors required them were the bane of Colonel John's existence for the next six years, and the subject of anxious enquiry in London, where neither the Board of Ordnance, nor the members of the House of Commons could be made to understand the problem.

In the middle of September, 1826, Colonel John, accompanied by Lieutenant Pooley, set out to look for the best place to dig the entrance to the canal at the Ottawa River end, hoping that if the government did not own the land, and the spot was not on a Crown reserve, Sir Peregrine Maitland, the lieutenant-governor, would help him acquire it. On the 21st, Colonel John set up a headquarters in Hull, the only remotely civilized place, where Philomen Wright was then about 70 years old, and delighted that at last the canal would go ahead.

In 1826, Hull boasted in addition to saw and grist mills and Wright's fine house, the Columbian Hotel with a livery stable, a steamboat service above the rapids of the Ottawa River, a local militia unit of which Wright was the colonel, a supply of cannon, muskets and swords, three churches and schools. The steamboat that operated on the river belonged to Wright. Built in 1819, it was called the *Union of the Ottawa*, or more often the *Union*, and it would be the first vessel to navigate part of the canal.

The view across the river from Hull was less than enticing—rocky cliffs and shady forest mainly beech and hemlock. In the townships of Nepean and Gloucester were six houses and a few log cabins. Ira Honeywell, the first to settle in Nepean, had a clearing at Britannia Bay. Braddish Billings's home was on the Rideau, and not far from him was an eccentric, Captain Andrew Wilson, a retired naval officer who had served with Lord Nelson on the *Victory*. Wilson was building a substantial log mansion which he named Ossian Hall after the ancient Gaelic poet, and was himself writing a history of the Royal Navy as well as poetry.

At Richmond Landing stood Caleb Bellows's dock and store, and a Yorkshireman named Isaac Firth was operating an inn. Firth had come to Canada in pursuit of Miss Dalmahoy, a feminist from Edinburgh, Scotland, who reached the country in 1818 to establish, of all things, a millinery business. She soon won renown for the otter hats she turned out for canal workers. The other local character at the landing was Ralph Smith, who kept a still in the woods, supplying some of the hooch that chased out the winter blues. Then there was Nicholas Sparks, an Irish entrepreneur who owned 200 acres through which the canal would pass. Both Sparks and Braddish Billings were quick to donate parts of their lands that were needed. Altruism was hardly the motive of either landowner. The canal would enhance their lumber operations no end. Billings went a step further by erecting buildings to house workers and setting up a blacksmith's shop.

Uniforms of the Corps of Royal Sappers and Miners, 1823 by T.W.J. Connolly.

The acreage around Richmond Landing belonged to Captain John LeBreton, a half pay officer whom Lord Dalhousie viewed with dark suspicion. While dining with several officers at the Richmond settlement in 1820, His Excellency mentioned that he wanted to purchase the area around the landing for a government storehouse. Not long afterward Captain LeBreton heard that the land in question was to be disposed of at sheriff's sale in Brockville. He hurried there but found he did not have enough money. LeBreton visited Levius Sherwood, a lawyer in town and the son of Captain Justus, who had run the secret service during the American Revolution. Levius agreed to advance the half pay officer cash in return for an equal share in the property. Captain LeBreton got the land for £499; his portion became known as the LeBreton flats, while the other half was Mount Sherwood.

Before long, LeBreton offered his land to the governor-in-chief for £3,000. Lord Dalhousie was convinced, although LeBreton denied it, that the officer had purchased the property because of what he had overheard during the dinner party in Richmond, and had tried to reap an atrocious profit at government expense. Instead of buying the LeBreton Flats, Dalhousie purchased a tract from Hugh Fraser, a resident of Three Rivers, in 1823, land which fronted on the Ottawa River east of the LeBreton and Sherwood properties. The tract extended to the Rideau and was backed by Nicholas Sparks's 200 acres.

On September 26th, 1826, Dalhousie reached Hull, accompanied by Colonel Durnford, and to the governor-in-chief's delight, Colonel John had chosen a bay on the land bought from Fraser for the entrance to the canal. To His Excellency's greater satisfaction, the Superintendent also informed him that for £2,000 he could build a bridge over the Ottawa River and a timber slide at the Chaudière Falls. The governor authorized £1,000 so that Colonel John could begin, and funds would be separate from those intended for the Rideau Canal project, for they would be paid through money collected in timber dues for the use of the slide. Next, Dalhousie informed the government agents at Perth and Richmond that Crown reserves in the neighbourhood of the proposed canal route should not be sold until further notice, so that Colonel By could select the parts he would need. Enormous quantities of timber had to be cut, and no one could predict how much land would be flooded once the necessary dams had been erected.

After surveying the terrain and the kind of labourers he could hire in Canada, Colonel John wrote to General Gothar Mann asking to be allowed four companies of Royal Sappers and Miners but only received two companies to work under the direction of his Royal Engineer officers. Enthusiastically he reported that locks 100 feet long would suffice, because the Rideau had strong natural banks, and the shorter locks would still be adequate for steamboats. He planned to start work at three places: the entrance on the land Lord Dalhousie had purchased which he called the Military Reserve, at the summit on Rideau and Mud (Newboro) Lakes, and at Kingston. He would need 2,000 men, and at each work point a staff surgeon. The Inspector General of Hospitals at Quebec City agreed to provide the surgeons, but storms were brewing when Colonel John sent substantial requests for material and tools to the Commissariat Department. The officers in that organization were reluctant to comply until Colonel Durnford stepped in, for the first but not last time. The other problem that would dog the Superintendent's steps was land acquisition.

While Lord Dalhousie could place restrictions on Crown lands, he had no jurisdiction over other land in Upper Canada. The best he could do was allow Colonel John to compensate owners for damage done when the men making the first surveys cut down trees and made diggings on private property. The governor was eager to assist in any way he could, and he helped establish a supply depot at Hull. The material had to come from the Commissariat, and His Excellency made sure that an officer of that department was sent to administer a good supply of cash. Colonel John would need all the backing he could get in the trying years that lay ahead.

New Edinburgh, from the west or Bytown side of the Rideau River above the Falls, 1845 by Thomas Burrowes. (Ontario Archives).

8. The Founding of Bytown

John By, the canal builder, was destined to plan a town and govern a settlement by serving as a magistrate. After crossing the Ottawa River from Philomen Wright's village, the Colonel found a forested site downstream from the Chaudière Falls, with the store, tavern and few cabins at Richmond Landing. East of the LeBreton Flats and Mount Sherwood was the tract Lord Dalhousie had purchased in 1823—the Military Reserve—where the Parliament Buildings now stand. In Colonel John's time it would have a wooden barracks. At the mouth of the Rideau, farther down the Ottawa was Green Island, with the twin waterfalls on either side that resembled curtains, and whose presence made a separate entrance canal necessary. On the right bank lay a triangle formed by the Rideau and the Ottawa known as "Letter O" from the designation on the early survey of Nepean Township. Part of this land was set aside for a fortress, although none was ever built upon Letter O, and in time Thomas Mackay, a contractor who built part of the canal, would found a mill complex and the village of New Edinburgh.

In 1826, when the Superintendent arrived, most of the surrounding land was held by absentee owners, some of them sons and daughters of loyalists. Letter O was the exception, for in 1808 Rice Honeywell, Ira's father, had leased it for 21 years. Rice was from the Mohawk Valley and had served in the rebel army during the revolution, but his wife's family had been loyalists, which gave him an aura of respectability. A lease of such short duration gave Colonel John the hope that he could use some of this property.

Although the colonel brought some officers of the Royal Engineers with him, he was soon joined by many half pay officers who left their inland farms in quest of employment. Several became his contractors, and all rented lots on the Military Reserve. The prospect of jobs also lured eager civilians, many of them Irish immigrants who were too poor to acquire any land. Two obvious places for housing were available. The first lay on a wedge of land between the Military Reserve where Colonel John planned to build the entrance to the canal, and the Rideau's left bank. Workers built their cabins and the area soon became known as Lower Town. It was bounded approximately by today's Sussex Drive to the west and north, Rideau Street along the south, and the Rideau River to the north and east, now part of downtown Ottawa. The other spot was Upper Town, west of the Military Reserve towards Richmond Landing, land now bounded by Wellington Street on the north, and Bank Street on the east. The Military Reserve separated the communities physically and mentally. Lower Town was mainly Roman Catholic; Upper Town Anglican and Presbyterian.

Colonel John built a comfortable house for Esther and his daughters on the right bank of the canal, now the south side of MacKenzie Avenue, half a block from Rideau Street, tucked behind the Chateau Laurier Hotel. Its thick walls were of rubble stone—small pieces picked out of the soil—and plastered with clay mixed with straw, surrounded by verandas and trellis-work which one visitor, Captain Alexander of the 42nd Regiment, described as a "cottage ornée, tastefully decorated."

At first the burgeoning village in two parts was known as Rideau Canal, until at a lively and convivial social gathering of Royal Engineers, half pay officers and important civilians, the guests decided to call their community Bytown in honour of the founder. One who visited the village and left a personal glimpse of the By family was Mrs. George Simpson, who, after travelling with her husband from Montreal, reached the ornate cottage on May 4th, 1830:

> Near this is situated the village of "Bytown" deriving its name from Colonel By of the Engineers with whom Mr. Simpson is well acquainted. He laid the first stone here, and is the principal superintendent of the great Rideau Canal, which connects the St. Lawrence and the Uttowas Rivers: . . . He was away from home when we arrived, but we were very kindly received by Mrs. By (a very agreeable and accomplished young woman) who insisted upon our stopping to breakfast with her.
> The house which stands in a good garden, overlooks one of the most beautiful spots I have seen in the Country; it commands an extensive view of the river, on the opposite side of which is the little village of Hull, The spires of the three Churches are visible through the trees, several bridges (one of which is very handsome) are thrown over the different channels of the River, formed by the islands and projecting banks of the Falls; from the upper storey are to be seen the fine and romantic Kettle Falls and beneath runs the Rideau Canal, Mrs. By has resided here 4 years, and is to remain 2 more, until the works which are under the superintendence of

the Colonel be completed; at the expiration of which time they return to England."

By Kettle Falls Mrs. Simpson meant the Chaudière. Her description of the road which her party used after taking leave of Mrs. By bears repeating:

> The road was so rough that it required some exertion to keep our seats, as the carts were without springs, indeed on rattling over a 'Stripe of Corduroy' here, we narrowly escaped cutting a Somerset over the Horse's head, into a deep slough through which we plunged.

Colonel John managed to keep his family in comparative comfort at Bytown, despite the newness of the place. He also opened a school, a necessity for the two girls. By 1828, the village had two schools, one conducted by a Miss Napp, the other, and probably the one Colonel John started, was called the English Mercantile and Mathematical Academy. The master was James Maloney, and he taught until 1879, by which time it had been taken into the public system. Another man of enterprise drawn to Bytown was Dr. Alexander James Christie, who founded the village's first newspaper, the Bytown Gazette. His print shop stood in Upper Town at the site of the Garden of the Provinces on Wellington Street.

From these slender beginnings at and around the Military Reserve arose the town that would be chosen as Canada's capital by good Queen Victoria, on the grounds that it was a safe distance from the United States. A few climate statistics showing the extremes of hot and cold might have given the old lady second thoughts.

9. Colonel John Gets Down to Business

Superintendent John By decided to build three separate barracks on Barracks Hill and upon the completion of these three buildings, two buildings in the Entrance Valley were constructed, one which was to be his office. He hired Contractor Thomas Mackay to erect a stone building which was not finished until 1827, and for the remainder of the autumn Colonel John worked from Hull. Thomas Mackay was a reliable man, from Perth, Scotland, who had worked on the Lachine Canal before being hired for the Rideau project, and the foundations of the office he built may still be traced in the ground near the Bytown Museum to the east of Parliament Hill.

As November of 1826 was drawing to a close, the timber slide at the Chaudière Falls was finished, but the first span of the bridge had collapsed, and Thomas Mackay was rebuilding it. Colonel John decided that he and his family would spend that winter in Montreal, but before he took his departure he visited Kingston to consult with Samuel Clowes, who had made the preliminary survey of the canal route. When he left the scene of the works Colonel John was satisfied with the start his men had made. The gully where the first locks were to be built had been cleared, and Nicholas Sparks had given him permission to take 200 feet of his land on either side of the canal, which gave the Superintendent misplaced grounds for hoping that other landowners would be as co-operative. Yet he was nervous about the security of the materials assembled at Richmond Landing. Many would-be labourers had arrived, most of them poor Irish who were squatting in makeshift cabins, and on reaching Montreal he asked that a sergeant and 12 men be sent up the Ottawa River to patrol the stores, and also the largest trees, to prevent any being cut down for private building or firewood.

In the course of the winter, Colonel John turned his attention to land acquisition, and he found Sir Peregrine Maitland a stickler for legalities and leery of any form of expropriation in peace time. Instead, the lieutenant-governor recommended that the Superintendent proceed by private treaties with the landowners, and conduct his surveys as far as possible in secret. Both suggestions offended the straightforward and upright John By. Duplicity was foreign to his nature, and from what he had already seen of some farmers, he found it hard to imagine many of them surrendering land voluntarily. His staff's activities might go unnoticed in the less inhabited townships, but in Marlborough and Montague he feared bloody encounters between canal workers and local farmers. After Maitland's backhanded recommendations, the colonel appealed directly to Lord Dalhousie, who far from showing his usual co-operation, referred him back to Sir Peregrine.

In February, 1827, the Upper Canada Legislature passed the Rideau Canal Act, giving the Superintendent the power to explore and to enter lands regardless of ownership, and to decide which pieces of land his pro-

Material requisition list October, 1826.
(Public Archives of Canada—RG8, C Series Vol. 44, p. 52-4).

Brewer's Lower Mill, view down the Cataraqui Creek with the clearing made for the Canal, 1829 by Thomas Burrowes. (Ontario Archives).

ject would require. He was allowed to do diggings and whatever else seemed necessary because the security of the province was at stake, but again Maitland urged him to make voluntary arrangements with the owners. Wherever disputes arose over payments, Colonel John was empowered to appoint an arbitrator. The people who lived along the canal route were to be allowed to use it for moving their cattle, and to have free access to all tow-paths, a measure the lieutenant-governor hoped would sweeten the effect of land purchases or damage to private property.

Colonel John felt that the legislation was not strong enough, but worse news was in store for him. His recommendations for a canal to accommodate steamboats had been shot down in London, with the help of General Sir James Carmichael Smyth, who was busy saving face. For military purposes, gunboats and supply boats were all that was necessary, and Colonel John's suggestion that even this work might cost four or five times Smyth's estimate of £169,000 was ridiculous. As an additional broadside, the general fired off the opinion that steamboat paddles would injure the canal banks and damage the locks! General Gothar Mann, his eye on the public purse and the danger of a blow-up in Parliament, was relieved to be able to agree with Smyth. A 20 foot wide canal was sufficient and must be built for the amount Smyth recommended in his report.

In due course Colonel By received his orders to proceed with the 20 foot wide canal, and furthermore, since the Superintendent had declared that he could build the larger canal in five years, he must now build the smaller one in four, and his budget would be Smyth's miraculous £169,000. Replying, Colonel John felt he could finish the work in the shorter time, but again he voiced his doubts that Smyth's estimate was in any way adequate. He repeated his argument on the need for steamboat passage, and if the paddles were placed on either side of the rudder, instead of at the sides of the boat, they could traverse a narrower canal. He referred to the old Macaulay Commission findings which stated that the route would be important for commerce, especially the trade in potash, flour and wood staves. Goods went down the St. Lawrence in scows and Durham boats, timber in large rafts. The Durham boats returned under their own power—oars—but the scows were towed by steamboats through calm waters. The new canal should accommodate the scows and rafts, and Colonel John felt he would be derelict in his duty if he did not recommend that the canal locks be 150 feet long, 50 feet wide and 5 feet deep. The depth was the same as in the Lachine and Grenville Canals, sufficient for the lumber trade, and the larger locks would add £50,000 to the cost of the Rideau Canal. Having sent off his rebuttal, Colonel By waited for word on how his compromise proposal would be received in London.

Unfortunately General Smyth was the man on the spot and able to defend himself, but in some instances the Board of Ordnance supported the man in the field. The members decided that Smyth's belief that all the work could be done by contract was impractical

Lower Bytown from the east bank of the deep-cut Rideau Canal, 1845 by Thomas Burrowes. (Ontario Archives).

because highly skilled stonemasons were not available in Canada. Colonel John received permission to employ two companies of Royal Sappers and Miners, names that require clarification. A sapper was a private serving under the Royal Engineers, trained as an artificer, who invariably had a civilian vocation such as a carpenter, blacksmith or cabinet-maker, even a tailor. A miner was skilled in the use of explosives and knew how to place gunpowder to blast through solid rock. Royal Sappers and Miners was the earlier name for the corps of Royal Engineers, and both names were in use during the construction of the Rideau Canal. The senior officer in command of these companies was Captain James Conway Victor, and he was assisted by a Captain Savage.

To overcome the problem of land acquisition, Lord Bathurst, the Colonial Secretary, authorized Lord Dalhousie on February 7th, 1827, to purchase the necessary tracts on behalf of the British government without delay. Now that word circulated that the canal was finally being built, land prices would soar. Meanwhile, in Montreal, Colonel John was planning his spring programme and he needed 1,500 to 2,000 daily rations for his soldiers and civilian workmen—pork, flour and spirits. He would have a temporary depot at Hull, but towards mid summer he would need a permanent one on the Rideau.

His decision to award the contract for two stone storehouses, each 70 feet by 30, led to a dispute with officers of the Ordnance and Commissariat Departments who were on duty in Montreal. Colonel John chose John Drummond, and the officers ob-

jected because this contractor had not submitted the lowest bid. The Superintendent argued that he preferred to employ contractors he knew well. Then in April he was embroiled in another controversy over tenders for the first eight locks up from the Ottawa River. Every offer was higher than he anticipated, and so were those for a barracks. Colonel John refused all of them and advertised a second time. To his consternation the lowest offers for the locks came from American contractors, and Lord Dalhousie assured him that he could employ them as long as they could be supervised carefully.

After negotiating, the colonel was about to accept a tender from Walter Fenlon, an American, when Thomas Mackay lowered his bid. Since he had already recommended Fenlon to Lord Dalhousie, the Superintendent sent Mackay to Quebec City to plead his case. Carrying a letter from Colonel John stating that Mackay was a skilled mason, while Fenlon was only an excavator, Mackay won the contract. In future, Colonel By and Lord Dalhousie agreed, each contract would be considered on its merits, not just on the lowest cost.

In April, 1827, when Colonel John was preparing to leave for Hull, he attempted to have bedding for labourers sent by steamboat from Lachine, to be paid for by gradual stoppages from the men's pay. This caused confusion in the Commissariat, but the Superintendent knew that many of his workmen had only poor rags to shield them from the early spring weather. He also arranged with George Simpson, of the Hudson's Bay Company, a personal friend, for the loan of an officer, ten men and two birch bark canoes so that he could make a three weeks' survey along the canal route. For this he needed men experienced at travelling through the bush. He hired Reubin Sherwood, the Brockville surveyor, to accompany him when the time came, at 15 shillings per day and expenses. All these details he duly relayed to Lord Dalhousie, whose reply was crusty. As governor-in-chief, he was too busy to be bothered with such trivia, and since Colonel John knew what he was about, he need not justify every action in his reports.

Soon the Colonel forwarded His Excellency a list of expenses: for the excavation of land in the gully where the first locks would be built, to determine where the bedrock lay and its configuration, the opening of five quarries, surveying and exploring the route, moving stores, artificiers and labourers from Montreal to Hull, and a small sum for canvas to back the paper on which important drawings were being prepared. Then he informed Colonel Durnford, the Commanding Engineer in Quebec City, that he would need more men than the Board of Ordnance and the Duke of Wellington had authorized. He wanted twice the number for the 1828 season, and as far as he understood the letters he had received from General Mann in 1826, he had the right to increase his work force.

On May 4th, 1827, the Colonel called for tenders to excavate five miles, from the first eight locks to Dow's Great Swamp, and from there to Hog's Back, plus a water channel, three more locks of 10 feet lift, and a 45 foot high dam at Hog's Back. He gave Walter Fenlon the contract to excavate for two years at 11½ pence per cubic foot. At the same time he awarded to John Pennyfeather the contract to excavate the first eight locks at the Ottawa end, to be completed by August 1st. (Pennyfeather fell behind because he found so many springs, and asked for an extension.) Administration prevented Colonel John from starting his journey with the Hudson's Bay Company men and Reubin Sherwood until the middle of May.

Early in June he had returned to Hull, very pleased with what he had seen. The route, he reported to Dalhousie, had been dictated by nature, and except for stretches of rapids, which he would eliminate by damming, and the portages and places where locks were planned, he found at least a five foot depth of water all the way to Kingston. Because much of the land was low and susceptible to flooding, or high and rocky, towpaths would be impracticable. The flood areas would require causeways that would be swept away by high water every spring. Also, paths were useless through the lakes. The route was shorter in midstream, the way along the shore nearly twice as long. Poling, too, was out of the question. The bottom was too deep in places, too muddy in others, and the boats would be powered by sails and oars.

Still praying the Board of Ordnance and the government would relent and allow him to make provision for steamboats, the Superintendent asked for permission to build one for £2,000, which would fit the 20 foot wide

Brewer's Lower Mill—masonry of the lock nearly complete, excavation for canal in progress, 1831-32 by Thomas Burrowes. (Ontario Archives).

*Lock and dam at Black Rapids,
1831—The men are pumping water out
of the lock to hang the gates, by
Thomas Burrowes.
(Ontario Archives).*

locks, to use for carrying materials. Then it could be a tow boat for barges when the works were opened to commercial traffic. This modest request was ignored, because an economy drive was on, and all government departments were curtailing their expenses. Back on the scene, the Colonel and his second-in-command, Captain Daniel Bolton, were arranging contracts, and the junior officers were at various sites.

In addition to the works under Messrs. Mackay, Pennyfeather and Fenlon, a Mr. Henderson was draining Dow's Great Swamp and working on a channel through it by building a watertight earth mound 1,128 feet long. Walter Fenlon had a contract to construct a 45 foot high dam at Hog's Back to drown the falls and seven miles of shallow rapids and turn them into a stretch of still water. Colonel John had expressed reservations about Fenlon's abilities as a mason, but he had no one else at that time to undertake the dam. At Black Rapids, Thomas Phillips was quarrying stone for another dam, 280 feet wide and 10 feet high with a lock of 10 foot lift, to create another five miles of still water. To complete the canal the forty miles to Burritts Rapids, the Superintendent planned three more locks, each of 8 foot lift, and with one 24 foot high dam, or three small ones, at Long Island.

At Kingston, directing construction were Lieutenant Edward Frome, Royal Engineers; Lieutenant Smith, Royal Artillery; and Ensign Wallace, 71st Regiment; John MacTaggart, the clerk of those works and Thomas Burrowes, the assistant overseer. Lieutenants Pooley and Dennison, and Captain James

*View of the Davis Mill lock
by Thomas Burrowes.
(Ontario Archives).*

Isthmus (now called Newboro) from an island in Mud Lake south of the lock, by Thomas Burrowes. (Ontario Archives).

Conway Victor were on the lakes between the Rideau and Cataraqui Rivers. Victor was supervising one company of Royal Sappers and Miners, who had reached Hull on June 10th.

Little is known about most of the officers and key civilians beyond their rank and surnames. Burrowes was from Worcestershire, England, a talented painter who left a valuable record of how the canal and the surrounding countryside looked during and after construction. John MacTaggart, a Scottish civil engineer, wrote a book entitled "Three Years in Canada" which was exaggerated in places, but which told certain episodes with a gusto that other sources indicate were reliable. He claimed that John By "encountered all privations with wonderful patience and good-humour". To illustrate further, MacTaggart observed:

> He could sleep soundly anywhere and eat any thing, even to raw pork. One night we lost ourselves altogether in Cranberry Lake, on our route through the waters from the Ottawa to Lake Ontario. There were two canoes of us, and the poor fellows paddled away lustily; but it was of no use; the more we sailed, the farther astray we went, and could not find the outlet of the river Cataraque.

Night fell, and the men clambered on the shore. They were without food because their canoe of provisions had been sent on to Brewers Mills, and they built a fire to raise their spirits. They continued their wanderings the following day, and found an Indian shooting ducks, who guided them into Loughborough Lake, and they found their

Lock, dam and blockhouse at the Narrows, Rideau Lake looking towards Kingston, by Thomas Burrowes. (Ontario Archives).

Lock and waste weir at Chaffeys Mill, 1833 by Thomas Burrowes. (Ontario Archives).

way to Brewers and the frantically needed canoe of food.

In December, 1827, MacTaggart recounted, he was travelling in the wilderness with Col. By and several others. They found the large house of an American settler. The ground floor was crammed with disreputable looking humanity, drinking heavily. "The back-slums of Holborn, London, where villains and vagabonds congregate, never were honoured with such a crew." Wanting to sleep and finding no space downstairs, the Superintendent and his followers climbed a frail, dirty staircase to a large room that was freezing cold. Few of the windows had any glass, and several people were asleep. On a table, covered with something resembling a sheet they found the body of a boy some fifteen years of age:

One side of his head seemed to be mangled in a shocking manner, and covered with clotted blood. "No; this place, indeed will not do," we all agreed, and down stairs we went. On coming below, we found the greater part of the company had "cleared out" as they say. Venturing to make some inquiries about the dead lad, we met with nothing but evasive answers, as much as to say, it might be better for all of s to keep a "caum sough," alias, make no noise about it.

The night passed in great discomfort on the ground floor of the house. In the morning, Colonel John learned that the dead boy was Irish, and had been killed two days before by a shot from the gun fired by a son of their American host.

the Father and mother of the lad came crying after us in great tribulation, wishing us to interfere, and bring, what they called the "murtherer of their dear child" to justice; but this was a

View from the upper end of the guard lock at Hogs Back—looking towards Bytown, by Thomas Burrowes. (Ontario Archives).

thing to us impossible, unless by engaging in an affair we had nothing to do with; and, after doing our best, the laws of the country would not probably have been exercised then, as we had often seen . . . There is something faulty in the administration of the criminal laws, no doubt; but energy and exertion lie dormant in Canada; humanity begins to be neither much felt nor talked about.

MacTaggart's book sheds light on what excavation in solid rock, often necessary, involved. Gunpowder was used to blast obstacles, with uncertain results. Despite safety routines, injuries occurred, often because of ignorance on the part of the workers. Those who failed to understand the danger were usually Irish:

It is my opinion that one-tenth of all the poor Irish emigrants who come to Canada perish during the first two years they are in the country; and when they will not amend their ways of their own accord, there are few will be found alive after being five years in the country . . . . On the public works I was often extremely mortified to observe the poor, ignorant, and careless creatures, running themselves into places where they either lost their lives, or got themselves so hurt as to become useless ever after. Some of these, for instance, would take jobs of quarrying from contractors because they thought there were good wages for this work, never thinking that they did not understand the business. Of

course, many of them were blasted to pieces by their own shots, others killed by stones falling on them. I have seen heads, arms and legs, blown about in all directions; and it is vain for overseers to warn them of their danger, for they will pay no attention. I once saw a poor man blow a red stock, and hold it deliberately to the priming of a large shot he had just charged. I cried out, but it was of no use. He seemed to turn round his face, as if to avoid the smoke; off went the blast, and took away his arm, and half of his head: he was killed in a moment. As the blocks of stone fell, one of them broke the leg of another poor man, who knew nothing of such a shot being fired.

The Scots engineer also concurred with Colonel John's opinion that General James Carmichael Smyth's estimates were too low:

It has been stated that the Rideau Canal has been estimated to cost £169,000: this is perfectly true, and, if the works were executed in a weak and unsatisfactory manner, might, probably, be found sufficient, but if British substantiality is required—and required it always is—three times the above sum will perhaps not be found too much. How can it be otherwise?

Once finished, MacTaggart acknowledged, the project would be unique:

The Rideau Canal, when constructed, will be perfectly different from any other in the known world, since it is not ditched or cut out by the

Smiths Falls, 1830 by John Burrows.
(Ontario Archives).

hand of man. Natural rivers and lakes are made use of for this Canal, and all that science or art has to do in the matter, is in the lockage of the rapids or waterfalls, which exist either between extensive sheets of still water or expansion lakes.

His summation was neat and to the point, and he added that with the help of dams, the Rideau was not one canal, but a series cut to join natural stretches of water.

10. Pomp and Progress

August 15th, 1827, was a red letter day in Bytown, as revealed in a report published in the Montreal Herald. The event in question:

> was no less than depositing of the first stone of the locks of the Rideau Canal. Yesterday evening at a late hour, Captain Franklin, the celebrated traveller, arrived at the headquarters of the detachment of the 71st Regt. now doing duty here, when Col. By decided upon welcoming this enterprising traveller to the Polar regions, with hospitality and civilization in a way that would identify his (return) with a grand undertaking so highly beneficial for the continent he had spent so long a time and labour in exploring, namely, the laying the first stone of the locks of the Rideau Canal . . . . Notwithstanding the briefness of the notice, a cause of disappointment to many, there was congregated on the occasion as large and respectable a concourse of spectators as had ever been witnessed in this place.

Captain John Franklin was returning from a journey to the Mackenzie Valley, and the Superintendent took advantage of the visit to hold the ceremony. (Twenty years later Franklin would perish while searching for the Northwest Passage.) Another celebration took place on September 29th, when Lord Dalhousie was on the scene inspecting the works. This time he laid the cornerstone in the entrance valley. After the honour done Franklin, Colonel John could do no less for the governor-in-chief, and besides, he enjoyed fanfare. Whenever he had grounds to let his hair down he seized the opportunity.

Meanwhile, he was making good use of his two companies of Sappers and Miners. Some were inland, and others were quarrying blocks of limestone, granite and sandstone near the Ottawa entrance, while a party cleared land to get rid of mosquitoes that were causing fever among the workers. He was satisfied, but a message from the Board of Ordnance in London expressed the fear that the soldiers, scattered throughout the wilderness might easily desert. The Colonel was quick to reassure the members. The sappers and miners were of good character, and anyway desertion was improbable. Philomen Wright's steamer Union came only twice a week from the Grenville Canal works to Hull, a journey of 60 miles, the roads to Richmond, Perth, Brockville and Kingston were nearly impassable, and the water routes a maze requiring a competent guide. The soldiers were not fools, and they knew they would perish in the bush consumed by black flies if they tried to escape from any of the construction sites.

Superintendent By was finding that he could not keep within his cost estimates. Apart from their being unrealistic in the first place, his workers were performing many tasks not envisaged in the original plans. The foundations of the locks requiring piling and planking, and weirs, coffer dams, lock gates, sluices, bridges, culverts and pumps, and drainage systems, were all on the grander scale than anyone ever anticipated. Everywhere more labour was needed, but he was delighted with the civilian skills of his Sappers and Miners. Most important, some were experienced in arched key work, competent at building the sweeping, concave faced dams where each huge block acted as a keystone. At first Colonel John thought stone dry-walling would be more durable, but he soon found that water seeped between the blocks, which caused them to work loose. For the rest of the stonework, his labourers grouted the blocks using cement extracted and burnt at a site on the far shore of the Ottawa River that is still a source of this material. He asked the Board of Ordnance for a third company of Royal Sappers and Miners, but was refused, and he had to make do with more civilian labourers. Many were Irish and very rowdy. John MacTaggart described some of the violence he witnessed:

> The Irish have frequent rows, and carry the spirit of party with them wherever they go; the orange and ribbon-men have often dreadful rencounters. A man was murdered in one of these riots on the banks of the Ottawa; a fellow knocked him on the head with the knotty root of a tree, and stove and his skull. The poor man died in an instant; the murderer fled away above 60 miles, was pursued, caught, brought to trial, and acquitted. The saying is, that "it takes great interest to hang a man in Canada," which is, indeed, true.

That convictions were rare was not surprising. The courts were conducted by magistrates who were the more affluent settlers. In a scantily populated land where a magistrate was either the friend of, or intimidated by, the accused, he naturally seized upon the flimsiest of excuses for dismissing the charge.

Another episode—a donnybrook—is still remembered as the Battle of Merrickville, although the fight took place downstream at Clowes Lock, named not for Samuel Clowes, but for James, who operated a quarry and did some of the contract work. When this lock was under construction, timber was appropriated from a farm belonging to a Mr. Mosher. When he was not paid at once, he summoned Sheriff Adiel Sherwood, Reubin's brother, from Brockville, who planned to arrest the men responsible for trespassing.

After eyeing some of the contenders the sheriff hastened back to Brockville for reinforcements, and returned with a dozen newly sworn deputies. Even this force was quickly put to flight by a gang of pick swinging Irishmen. The next move was up to Stephen Burritt, then a lieutenant-colonel of the Grenville Militia, who called out a company, arrested the miscreants, and escorted them to Brockville. If it was hard to hang a man in Canada, as John MacTaggart maintained, it was equally hard to make a charge of trespassing stick. At the ensuing trial, no prisoner would testify against his fellows, and no local farmer recognized any of them. They were released for lack of evidence, ending one more instance of an unbridled breach of good taste during the construction of the Rideau Canal.

As John MacTaggart averred, some of the Irish trouble stemmed from the Orange-Roman Catholic feud. The first immigrants from the Emerald Isle could not forget the conflict, because most were Protestants and included a number of devotees of the Loyal Orange Lodge. At Perth, some half pay officers belonged to the order, among them certain magistrates, while Alexander Matheson, also a member, was a deputy-sheriff. When, in 1823, a group of Roman Catholics from Cork settled in the area, the fun began. The fact that these arrivals had been given assisted passage and free rations, which the earlier Scots had not, was a sore point. On April 23rd, 1824—St. George's Day—following a muster of the militia that included settlers of both persuasions, a brawl ensued. Afterward, when a party under the Orange

deputy-sheriff, Alexander Matheson, went to the Roman Catholic settlement of Shepherd's Falls to discipline the culprits, shooting started. One constable was wounded, and one of the Irishmen was killed and two were wounded.

An investigation ordered by Sir Peregrine Maitland brought to light the fact that the men who started the shooting were probably Orangemen in the deputy-sheriff's party. Later Matheson was dismissed, but the damage was done, battle lines drawn. Irish Catholics were horrified to discover they were in the same situation they thought they had left behind when they emigrated, and Protestant sympathies were aroused. The first Loyal Orange Lodge was formed in Brockville by the militant Ogle Robert Gowan, who arrived from County Wexford in 1829. The second lodge formed at Kingston, and the seventh in the province at Perth, in part under the guidance of the deposed deputy-sheriff, Alexander Matheson. In the interval, many of the brawls involving construction workers were of a religious, though unholy, nature.

When in 1827, Orangemen attempted to parade on July 12th in Kingston, they were attacked by a large mob of canal workers, and three constables and a bystander were wounded by pistol shots. Through jury-rigging, most of the Orangemen were acquitted, while the Catholics were jailed. The latter were freed after Levius Sherwood, then a district court judge, suggested they be released because the cells in Kingston were low and damp and pneumonia should not be part of the punishment. Sherwood was an Anglican—with a Catholic wife.

Reporting on the work done in 1827, Colonel John informed the Board of Ordnance that he had spent £32,622. The first eight locks were nearing completion, as was a temporary dam 200 feet long and 10 feet high at the first lock. The inverted arches of the foundations and part of the side walls had been laid, and above the eighth lock a stone bridge with a 56 foot span was under way. Two stone storehouses, each 70 feet by 30 feet, had been completed on either side of the canal entrance by Thomas Mackay. That on the west side was the commissariat. One of the oldest buildings still standing in Ottawa, it now houses the Bytown Museum and many personal effects of Colonel By and his officers. The other, on the east side of the

*First eight locks of the Rideau Canal with the two stone storehouses, Barrack Hill
and steamboat wharf, by Thomas Burrowes.
(Ontario Archives).*

canal, which has not survived, was the engineers' storehouse and office. Three other stone buildings, long gone, each 108 feet by 70 feet, served as living quarters for the soldiers, and four log buildings housed workshops and the officers' quarters. Two wooden barracks sheltered civilian workers, a butchery and bakery. Quarries near the canal entrance and across the river at Hull furnished cut stone blocks for the locks and canal walls. Above the first eight locks, towards Hog's Back, land had been cleared, wood piled and burnt. The earth mound at Dow's Great Swamp was growing, and a rough road fifty feet wide extended twenty miles from Bytown to Long Island.

Other quarries were at Black Rapids, Long Island and Smiths Falls, and work on locks at all these places had begun. Land had been cleared at the connecting points between Rideau, Mud (Newboro), Clear and Indian Lakes. Colonel John travelled along the entire line, inspecting, and he noted that eight miles of clearing remained to be done at Cranberry Marsh by the party of axemen there, and that they had some yokes of oxen to haul the logs. At Kingston Mills, Robert Drummond had received the contract for four locks, each of 9 feet lift, and a dam 18 feet wide and 10 feet high. He employed 20 stonecutters who were shaping blocks for the dam. Farther up the Cataraqui, James Clowes was excavating to straighten out a curve in the river.

At Jones Falls, Thomas Mackay and John Redpath were to build the 45 foot high dam and six locks, each of 10 feet 2 inches lift. John Redpath was a skilled stonemason from Berwick, Scotland, who emigrated to Canada in 1816, and was one of the contractors on the Lachine Canal, gaining the experience he needed to work on this, the most challenging portion of the Rideau Canal. The six locks turned into four, each with an average lift of 15 feet, after Colonel John decided that the dam should be raised to 60 feet. John Redpath carried out the work without any setbacks, which was not the case with the second highest dam at Hog's Back. The contractor built a mansion in the wilds to house his family, and two single story log buildings as barracks for his workers. Following the rebellion of 1837 log guard houses were built at Whitefish Dam and Jones Falls for defense purposes. When the canal was finished John Redpath moved to Montreal and on the profits earned he established among a variety of business ventures, a sugar refinery on the bank of the Lachine Canal.

Locks at Jones Falls from the rocky hills southwest of the locks, by Thomas Burrowes. (Ontario Archives).

At Smiths Falls, the contracting firm of Rykerts and Company had the 23 foot high dam two thirds finished, and were to build three locks, each with a lift of 11 feet, 2 inches. A Mr. Lever was in charge of building the lock at Davis's Mills. A Mr. Thomson was at Maitland's Rapids, building what was later named the Kilmarnock Lock, while Messrs. Andrew White and Thomas Phillips were at Long Island and Black Rapids. Philomen Wright and Sons were at Burritts Rapids, Dow's Great Swamp and Hog's Back. At the latter place 36 feet of the planned 45 foot high dam had been raised. The Wrights had taken over Mr. Henderson's contract when he withdrew for reasons not specified. Nor did James Clowes's work satisfy the Superintendent, who broke the contract in January, 1828, on the grounds of inferior workmanship.

During the winter of 1827-28, Colonel John was growing uneasy. The time was fast approaching when he would be committed to locks 20 feet wide, inadequate for all but the smallest steamboats. In November he had written Colonel Durnford pointing out another compelling argument for having the waterway large enough to take the steamers then in service on the St. Lawrence and Lake Ontario. A steamboat could travel the 180 miles from Quebec City to Montreal in 22 hours. From Montreal to Lachine by canal boat required 3 hours to cover 9 miles. Then from the Ottawa River to Kingston through

Dam at Jones Falls, when nearly completed showing the last temporary passage provided for the surplus water, by Thomas Burrowes. (Ontario Archives).

the Rideau Canal by steamboat—133 miles—needed only 25 hours, as against 45 for a canal boat.

In an emergency a 24 pounder gun could be moved to Kingston by steamer in half the time and at a lower cost. Also, the local people were asking to have a steamboat on the 27 mile stretch of still water between Burritts Rapids and Long Island which was called the Long Reach, to meet the road the canal workers had built from the Chaudière Falls. Again Colonel John begged for permission to build a government steamboat, because the village of Bytown was the logical place for a military depot, a site much safer than Kingston, where supplies valued at £1,000,000 were stockpiled and poorly protected.

Colonel Durnford was less impressed by the argument for a steamboat route and Kingston's vulnerability than by the size of Colonel John's estimate of his expenditures for 1828. The Superintendent was asking for £100,000, and insisting that General Gothar Mann in London understood that the estimate of £169,000 was woefully inadequate. Busy in his wilderness, John By was not aware that the members of Parliament favoured stringent economy, and a committee of Royal Engineers was already investigating the very future of his project. All Durnford dared to do was order him to abide by the rules laid down by the Treasury Department with respect to the payment of expenses.

At that critical time luck intervened in the form of Contractor Robert Drummond, who had a meeting with Commodore Robert Barrie, Royal Navy, at Kingston. In the course of conversation, the Commodore wondered why Colonel By was building locks for such small vessels. They should be 50 feet wide and 7 feet deep, or they would not meet the needs of the military, and Barrie promised to inform the home government of his opinion. Drummond reported the matter to Colonel John, who wrote to Barrie and then sent a letter to Sir James Carmichael Smyth, warning him that the Commodore had said that small locks would be useless. The junction of the Ottawa and the Rideau, he told Smyth, was the logical place for a shipyard, safe from attack, and since steamboats then on Lake Ontario were as much as 48 feet wide, a 50 foot wide canal was imperative. Furthermore a 7 foot depth would drown more of the swamps, reducing the amount of fever and ague that was carrying off so many of his workmen. He then dealt with Smyth's argument that steamboat paddles would damage the works by stating that spring floods were a greater menace. Stone canal banks that could withstand that punishment had nothing to fear from the turbulence caused by mere paddles. The letters to Barrie and Smyth on their way, Colonel John went to Montreal for a visit, and no doubt a much needed rest.

Beckett's Landing and ferry, Long Island Reach or still-water, looking towards Long Island and Bytown, by Thomas Burrowes. (Ontario Archives).

11. Turning Point

True to his word, Commodore Robert Barrie wrote to the Lord High Admiral in London, and things began to happen. The Duke of Wellington, so anxious to have the canal for defence, was now Prime Minister, and a committee of Ordnance engineers, including General Smyth, met in January. They found Colonel By's plans sound, although they wondered whether dams as high as those planned for Hog's Back and Jones Falls might be expensive to maintain. After some debate the members decided that the Superintendent, the man on the spot, should use his judgement. Then they turned their attention to the costs, and to see whether these could be cut. The 36 locks not yet started might be of wood, and temporary against the day when steamboat navigation would warrant enlarging them.

As for making the 11 locks under construction 50 feet wide, while Colonel John had advanced compelling arguments, the added expense was beyond the capacity of either Britain or Upper Canada to contemplate. Smyth, predictably, maintained that a 20 foot wide canal was sufficient for military purposes, in the face of Commodore Barrie's letter. As for Smyth's estimate of £169,000, the committee agreed with Colonel John that the amount was too conservative. On January 2nd, William Huskisson, the Secretary of State for War and the Colonies, wrote to Lord Dalhousie, informing him that a commission would soon be sent to Canada to conduct in inquiry, and in the meantime the Superintendent was to suspend all operations that were not absolutely necessary. The chairman of the commission would be Sir James Kempt, the lieutenant-governor of Nova Scotia.

This news was sent on January 5th, 1828, by General Gothar Mann to Colonel John, who received it in Montreal with considerable consternation. Many new contracts had been let on February 1st, some weeks before Mann's letter had reached him. He dismissed his civilian carpenters, blacksmiths, labourers and squad-masters, and asked some contractors to extend their deadlines for completing and to curtail expenses. Many refused, for even if they slowed down work wages must be paid and their margin of profit would be reduced. Colonel John confided to General Mann that he feared lawsuits, especially from the American contractors. Lord Beresford, who had succeeded the Duke of Wellington as head of the Ordnance Department, wanted to live up to the terms of the contracts, lest the funds so far expended be wasted. The government must come to a decision on the future of the canal project without delay. He dispatched Colonels Fanshawe and Lewis, who had reported once on the canal, to join Sir James Kempt's commission, and they reached Montreal in June, 1828.

During the winter months, Colonel John was unaware of these developments, but again he warned General Mann that his contractors would sue him if he was prevented from honouring his end of the bargain. With the spring he found that the partly finished dam at Hog's Back had been damaged, and repairing it was keeping construction behind schedule. When Sir James Kempt and the two other commissioners reached Bytown, Colonel John prepared to take them to inspect the entire route accompanied by John MacTaggart. His clerk of works refused to leave Bytown, pleading illness. A surgeon went to examine him and reported that what ailed MacTaggart was a drinking spree. The Superintendent dismissed him and he returned to Britain to write the story of the three years he had spent in Canada. Later Colonel John derided some of the book as fiction, and maintained that MacTaggart's contribution was less than claimed.

After viewing the works all the way to Kingston the three commissioners returned to Bytown and reported that the completion of this important project in a manner that would protect Upper Canada could not be carried out with the funds General Sir James Carmichael Smyth had estimated. Secretary Huskisson speculated that Samuel Clowes, who had come up with the same estimate, had deliberately kept his figures low to entrap the British government into starting the canal, which, once embarked upon would leave no choice but to complete it. In fact, General Smyth had had more influence in the decision to proceed, but Clowes was a useful scapegoat.

The Kempt Commission had orders to stop the work should the project seem impracticable, or exceedingly expensive, but the members were also to study the route with an eye to permitting a 50 foot wide canal and locks. If they agreed with Colonel John, they were to recommend the larger canal. Gradually the Superintendent was winning his case. For the current year, Huskisson agreed to ask Parliament to approve £120,000 to cover existing commitments. Sums for the next three years' work would be considered in due course.

On July 3rd, 1828, from Bytown, Sir James Kempt, Colonels Fanshawe and Lewis, reported that they had reached a solution. The locks should be 5 feet deep, and broad enough to allow the passage of 30 foot wide steamboats. According to Kempt, this compromise was necessary, otherwise all the work done and the money already spent would be wasted. He rejected a 50 foot wide canal as involving too much expenditure. In advance, Colonel John had prepared three sets of estimates, all for locks of 5 foot depth; the first was £544,676 for locks 20 feet by 108 feet; the second, £576,757 for locks 33 feet by 134 feet; the third, £597,676 for locks 50 feet by 150 feet—the last his choice. The commissioners decided on the median estimate, and recommended that the Superintendent be allowed to spend £105,000 for the 1828 season, and with that he had to

be content. At least his position was no longer untenable and he could pay his contractors.

The commissioners were not through. For better supervision and a more careful accounting, officers and professional civilians were to be distributed along the canal, conducting daily inspections and keeping diaries. The lockmasters' houses, when such were built, were to be fortified, and Bytown would be a depot for 5,000 troops. Their work finished, Fanshawe and Lewis returned to London. Sir James Kempt was setting out for Halifax when he learned that as of September 1st he would be the governor-in-chief of Canada, to succeed Lord Dalhousie. This change would not affect the canal, for both men believed in its importance. The Kempt Commission's recommendations were accepted by Parliament and the Board of Ordnance, but they were not a panacea for Colonel John's troubles, not the end of crises that disrupted his most carefully laid plans.

12. Sickness, Suits, Setbacks, Success

Some contractors were sued for trespassing and cutting timber on private property,

Edmonds Station, No. 11—59½ miles from Bytown, by William Clegg, 1828-32.
(Public Archives of Canada—C1211).

on the grounds that the Rideau Canal Act passed by the Upper Canada Legislature allowed Colonel By this latitude, but it did not give him the right to delegate trespassing to his employees. Also, the summer work was almost halted through illness among all levels of personnel. Smallpox and malaria were rampant, and Colonel John reported that many of the sick were casual labourers, impoverished Irishmen who had come independently to the Rideau in search of a livelihood and had been discharged because of budget restrictions. Dr. Tuthill, one of the staff surgeons, travelled from Bytown to Kingston handing out his own medicines, giving freely of his services to alleviate some distress. The Superintendent ordered smallpox vaccine from Montreal which his several surgeons used to immunize 500 men and children. Later Surgeon Tuthill was repaid for his time and supplies.

The malaria, which Colonel John called swamp fever, was not native to North America. It had been introduced over several generations by British regular soldiers who had been on duty in India. They caught the disease there, and once they had had it, mosquitoes who bit them in other parts of the world became carriers who could infect others. The completion of the canal helped eradicate the fever, for it raised water levels and turned swamps, notably Cranberry and Dow's, into lakes.

Late in August, Captain Savage toured the work camps, and in September he reported on conditions to the Superintendent. At Kingston Mills, Lieutenant Henry Briscoe, in command of some Sappers and Miners, his assistant overseer, the contractor, his clerk and foreman, and 100 men were unable to work, and 13 labourers had died. At Brewers Mills the work was at a standstill, while at Chaffeys Mills, contractor John Haggart was not fit to supervise the few who were able-bodied. The same situation prevailed at Davis's Mills and Jones Falls, but from Rideau Lake to Bytown fewer workers had been stricken and had made some progress. By September 20th, the fever was subsiding and Colonel John hoped to see more accomplished before winter set in. He was especially pleased with the Hog's Back dam, but in October heavy rains struck. The men on the spot were unable to close the gap against the heightened flow of the Rideau and he moved in both companies of Sappers

Brewer's Upper Mills, 1828-32, Station No. 20—11 miles from Jones Falls, 1828-32.
108¼ miles from Bytown, by William Clegg.
(Public Archives of Canada—C1220).

Dam at Hogs Back, showing the breach in the stonework in 1830, by Thomas Burrowes, 1828-32. (Ontario Archives).

and Miners to strengthen the existing wall.

In November he fired Walter Fenlon, for the American contractor was unable to cope with finishing the dam at Hog's Back, and replaced him with Philomen Wright and his sons. Soon after this capable entrepreneur took charge he was asking for more help. Although Colonel John had assigned most of his Sappers and Miners and 300 civilian labourers, Wright felt he needed 200 more or he might not have the dam high enough to withstand next spring's floods. The same month the Chaudière Bridge, destroyed by last spring's flooding, was reopened, and the watertight mound at Dow's Great Swamp had converted it into a placid lake. Of all the works, the Superintendent was proudest of the Hog's Back dam, and he confidently expected that his labourers and soldiers could build it to the necessary 45 feet by the end of the 1829 season. He complained, however, that he needed more troops for guard duty. His Military Chest, which held the supply of British silver coins to pay the soldiers and workmen was not secure and he was afraid of a break-in.

In January, he upset the Assistant Commissary General at Montreal by asking for provisions to feed labourers working for contractors who were on the verge of bankruptcy. Civilians, that gentleman maintained,

should not be nourished on stores intended for troops. The Commissary General at Quebec City agreed with Colonel John, and his men got their relief supplies. By February, 1829, the Superintendent was having more difficulties with landowners, this time two who objected to workers who had put up cabins and cut trees for fuel. The Colonel settled the matter by purchasing the land in question outright.

The previous autumn the Hog's Back dam had been built to a height of 41 feet, and linked by a bridge to the quarry where the stone for the work was cut. The men had placed three booms at the weirs to prevent them being blocked by stray timber. At each boom Colonel John mounted a guard when he discovered that raftsmen passing downstream found them a nuisance and had taken upon themselves the removal of these obstacles. On February 17th, the Superintendent went to visit Jones Falls, after Lieutenant Briscoe notified him that some of the work had not been carried out according to instructions. On his return to Bytown he recommended that the contractors at Kingston be paid by cheque to save transporting large quantities of coins from the Military Chest.

The Commissary General at Quebec City objected. Contracts made in Montreal were payable in dollars, and the cash at Bytown was British silver. When cheques for the equivalent in sterling were cashed in Montreal the contractors could collect a premium of 8 to 9 percent, a profit that was unwarranted. Then on March 28th, Colonel John was called to the Hog's Back dam, which was leaking through the arch key work, and on April 3rd, disaster struck. He was standing on the middle of the dam directing 40 workmen when he felt what he described as an earthquake. Shouting a warning and dashing for safety, he got off the dam. No lives were lost but the arch key work crumbled 15 feet above the foundations and fully one third of the rocks at the centre were swept away.

Colonel By knew immediately that the calamity might have been prevented had his workmen had time to build the dam to its full 45 foot height before the Rideau reached its spring crest. Analysing, he discovered that freezing and thawing, a phenomenon new to his experience, were responsible. Water trapped in the stonework above the surface of the river had frozen. The exposed portion of the dam had separated from the foundations beneath the water, and when the spring floodwater struck, it pushed the upper structure away from the lower, causing the collapse. Two solutions presented themselves, build the dam to 45 feet before next

years' floods, or find an alternate route at Hog's Back.

After exploring thoroughly, Colonel John admitted he could not bypass the Rideau at that spot, and he resolved to have his workers fill the space in the dam with timber if the arch key work were not completed before the following winter. Then he asked that 30 soldiers be sent from Montreal, as his Sappers and Miners were doing guard duty, a waste of their talents. Next, Lieutenant Pooley reported that the dam at Smiths Falls was leaking through the arch key work. Fortunately it held, and the dam four miles downstream at Old Sly's was standing up well. Colonel John was relieved, for he had doubts about the lower dam, and had ordered a waste weir added to carry some of the excess spring runoff. The setback at Hog's Back, he informed Governor Kempt, was to be expected, since the dam was an experiment. When his men began building it, he did not have a single worker who had ever done arch key work before. Now, however, he knew he had the men to finish the job, to create a dam that would stand for generations.

That season two men who had received contracts for the Welland Canal visited Bytown. After viewing the Hog's Back dam, they confessed they were afraid to attempt

Old Slys Station, No. 12—60½ miles from Bytown, by William Clegg, 1828-32.
(Public Archives of Canada—C1212).

anything similar on their own works. Then, without warning, Colonel John collapsed with what may have been a heart attack, and an alarmed Dr. Tuthill cared for him. John By was convinced that his illness was brought on by detractors in London who thought him a fool for attempting the Hog's Back dam. Early in May, Colonel Durnford reached Bytown, eager to inspect the works all the way to Kingston. Although not fully recovered, Colonel John insisted on accompanying his superior and friend, and he intended to continue on by steamboat to Muddy York to confer with Attorney-General John Beverley Robinson on some legal problems.

As the Superintendent had feared from the outset, his land dealings had embroiled him in several lawsuits. Owners were challenging his right to expropriate land for a reservoir to serve the first eight locks at the Ottawa end, Walter Fenlon and other contractors he had fired were demanding compensation. In August, the courts agreed that Colonel John had not exceeded his authority, but he was unhappy over the amount of time being squandered. Furthermore, his visit with the Attorney-General had done nothing to simplify the complex methods he had to use for taking pieces of land. John Beverley Robinson maintained that the Rideau Canal

Act which the Upper Canada Legislature passed in 1827 was adequate, but his legal mind contrived a devious solution repugnant to the upright John By. Robinson, the golden haired boy of the Family Compact, suggested that whenever the Superintendent found that he had to enter private property, he should be attended by a committee of officers. That way the owner would not know whom to sue! Colonel John retorted that he would use a certificate signed by Colonel Durnford showing his right to be on any land close to the canal route. When he left York he was in no stronger a position than before he arrived.

Following his tour of inspection, Colonel Durnford reported that Colonel John had performed miracles, and his greatest handicap was a shortage of labourers. The contractors had done a fine job, competing among themselves to see who could produce the best quality stonework, and Durnford was convinced that the dams would stand up to spring floods, provided that these were finished to their prescribed heights before the snow began to melt the next spring. In future Colonel John intended to use thicker arch keystones, and lower waste weirs that were turned farther from each dam to lessen the water pressure on the structures.

The Superintendent found that he had to

NAME OF LOCK	MILEAGE FROM OTTAWA	NUMBER	LIFT OR DROP IN FEET
OTTAWA	—	1 to 8	79.00
HARTWELLS	4.17	9 & 10	21.50
HOGS BACK	4.25	11 & 12	14.50
BLACK RAPIDS	9.25	13	9.16
LONG ISLAND	14.25	14 to 16	25.33
BURRITTS RAPIDS	38.93	17	9.00
NICHOLSONS	41.83	18 & 19	14.50
CLOWES	42.50	20	7.58
MERRICKVILLE	44.65	21 to 23	24.66
KILMARNOCK	52.81	24	2.00
EDMUNDS	56.22	25	9.16
OLD SLYS	57.72	26 & 27	16.00
SMITHS FALLS, COMBINED	58.52	28 to 30	26.00
SMITHS FALLS, SINGLE	58.88	31	8.50
POONAMALIE	60.98	32	5.75
BEVERIDGE	66.10	33 & 34	25.00
NARROWS	80.02	35	3.00
NEWBORO	84.74	36	7.75
CHAFFEYS	90.00	37	10.75
DAVIS	92.15	38	9.00
JONES FALLS	96.45	39 to 42	58.50
UPPER BREWERS MILLS	107.28	43 & 44	18.00
LOWER BREWERS MILLS (WASHBURN)	109.06	45	13.00
KINGSTON MILLS	118.81	46 to 49	44.99

purchase several mills after the canal works damaged them or put them out of business through changing the water levels, and he paid these amounts:

Chaffey's mill	£2,000
Brewer's Upper mills	2,000
Smith's Falls sawmill	1,500
Damage to Merrick's mills	1,000
Davis's sawmill	700
Long Island sawmill	700
Damage to Lock's distillery at Clowes quarry	500

Colonel John asked for permission to purchase 5,000 acres, of which 55 were under cultivation, for fear portions of it would be drowned. He was finding that more land than he anticipated was being flooded, and he wanted to avoid further litigation.

Soon after the mosquitoes appeared, and throughout the hot weather of 1829, work slowed down when many labourers departed leery of "Lake Fever". In July Colonel John went to Montreal to attend to business matters and after his return to Bytown he took Sir John Colborne, the new lieutenant-governor of Upper Canada, on a tour of the canal works. He found only four men at the excavation site between Rideau and Mud Lakes, where many had died, and he resolved to send some officers and 300 men there in September, as soon as the mosquito season had passed.

Late in August, the Superintendent himself, bitten many times while escorting Colborne, succumbed to malaria, and he was unfit for duty until October. At that time Colonel Durnford arrived from Quebec City for another tour of inspection, and Colonel John insisted on getting up to brief the Commanding Engineer. When he returned to Bytown, Durnford pronounced himself well pleased with what he had seen. The Superintendent had recovered sufficiently to accompany Durnford to Mud Lake, where the weather turned frigid and their party spent a night "frozen in the lake on an uninhabited island", something the recent victim of malaria did not need.

When the season of 1829 closed, Colonel John had possession of the land around every works site, and had begun work on every lock and dam, with one exception. He was still negotiating for the land at Whitefish Falls, near Morton, where his men had put up a temporary dam that had collapsed. No wonder Colonel Durnford was pleased when he reached Quebec City. But his report on

Colonel By's health alarmed Governor Kempt, who sent him an assistant of equal rank, Lieutenant-Colonel Richard Boteler, Royal Engineers. Colonel John sent Boteler to take command of all the works between Rideau Lake Narrows and Lake Ontario, and ordered him to survey for defence sites at Kingston.

In his year end report on the condition of his finances, the Superintendent stated that three-fifths of the entire canal and waterway improvements had been completed, and he had spent £349,264, roughly three-fifths of the £576,757 approved by the Kempt Commission and accepted by the British government. The remaining £227,493 should be enough to finish the project. He expected to spend £200,000 in 1830, and the other £27,493 for finishing touches in 1831. The canal would probably be in operation ahead of schedule, because his contractors were eager to complete their work. The longer the job dragged on, the more lake fever and other complications cut into their margin of profit. The dam at Hog's Back was 45 feet high and perfect, and at Black Rapids he had "thrown back 6 feet depth of water into the Lock."

In London, the Board of Ordnance was perturbed when Colonel By's report arrived. He had been authorized to spend £296,666 between 1826 and 1829, but he had in fact spent £349,264. In reply to a query from General Gothar Mann, the Superintendent explained, not for the first time, that contractors had to receive some money in advance, to purchase their supplies and move them to the site of their operations. At that time Colonel John appeared to be within his budget, but evidence on unforeseen costs which he enumerated in March, 1830, suggests that in the long run he could not avoid spending more than the Kempt Commission had recommended. Extra masonry had been needed for the highest dams, extra excavation at many sites, stronger foundations at some of the locks, lower waste weirs, and the necessity of cutting through longer stretches of solid rock had added substantially to his costs. He had overspent by these amounts:

Between 1st 8 locks and Hog's Back	£15,299
Jones Falls	15,164
Long Island	13,801
Smiths Falls	13,095

Locks at Kingston Mills, 1830, by Thomas Burrowes.
(Ontario Archives).

Rideau Lake, Mud and Clear Lakes	7,852
Hog's Back to Black Rapids	6,327
Old Sly's Rapids	5,597
Nicholson's	3,939
Merrick's Mills	3,371
Kingston Mills	2,892
First 8 locks from Ottawa River	1,418

All told Colonel John had spent an excess of £123,866 on these and some minor items, but he had also saved £10,018 through modifications, and the real excess was £113,848, still a staggering amount.

When this news reached London, Colonel Durnford felt compelled to send an explanation to General Gother Mann. The contractors had to be paid in advance. If they approached the courts, a procedure within their rights, the British government might have to pay enormous settlements. Nonetheless, despite loyal backing from prestigious officers, trouble was brewing in London for Colonel John By.

Meanwhile, he was involved in financial and legal tangles over land acquisition, and he tried again to get some amendments to the Rideau Canal Act from the new attorney-general, Henry Boulton. Like John Beverley Robinson, Boulton was convinced that the act gave the Superintendent all the ammunition he required. He expected Colonel By to behave moderately—even though confronted by immoderate owners—for he had the right to appeal to the King's Council. Yet Boulton did give him one useful tool, by asking that the names of those resisting parting with land at a reasonable price be given to him so that he could "file an Information" against them. Land values were inflated, Colonel John insisted, because the canal was being built, and owners should realize that they would benefit from its presence soon. The Rideau Canal Act specified that the prices paid should be those existing before the work started. The owners backed down when they heard of Boulton's list, and were soothed when the Superintendent offered to lease back to them for one shilling per acre per annum any lands he found he did not need.

On May 19th, 1830, Colonel John reported to both Governor Kempt and General Mann that owners were no longer demanding ten times their lands' real value, and were agreeable to leasing it back. He had also taken the precaution of retaining Christopher Hagerman of Kingston as his lawyer. Before each purchase was made, he had Hagerman look over the agreement to protect himself from further legal actions. At last Colonel John had an established procedure to follow. After he arranged for purchases and leases, with Hagerman's endorsement, he sent them to Sir James Kempt for his perusal, and the governor forwarded them to the Board of Ordnance for final authorization. This took time, but the onus was no longer entirely on the Superintendent's head.

At Kingston Mills, the Royal Navy threw its own wrench into Colonel John's operation, by purchasing a property he had tried to acquire. Commodore Barrie, so helpful over the question of steamboat navigation, informed him that the Ordnance Department should pay any damages done there, which irked the Superintendent. He had made some improvements prior to the sale, and felt that the navy should pay its own way, not compete for Ordnance funds.

By midsummer of 1830, Colonel John had spent £441,183, and soon 50 miles of waterway from Bytown would be opened. He expected to be finished with the two companies of Sappers and Miners by June, 1831, and to return to England with his family for a holiday by August or September. As in the two previous summers, 1830 was dogged by lake fever which slowed down the work. Conditions were worst at Brewers Mills and between Rideau and Mud Lakes, despite extra clearing to provide a "current of air" to destroy the mosquito habitat. Nevertheless the work did progress and it was of good quality. Colonel Durnford admitted that he had found some slippage in the banks at the entrance locks in Bytown, and at Dow's Lake an embankment had sunk. This last did not matter for it made the foundations more solid. At Long Island some clay soils had washed away near the waste weir, but Colonel By would soon have this shored up.

The ironwork for the lock gates was not being fashioned to keep pace with the woodwork. Iron was brought from the forges of St. Maurice, the most important source since the Seven Years' War, and delivered it cost £22. 10s per ton. Chains for the gates were sent from the Naval Dockyard at Kingston, and the coal for smelting from Newcastle, England. Of timber there was of course no shortage. The lock gates were built on the spot by carpenters working under contract, the iron bindings and fittings hammered out by blacksmiths. Even with the government providing the lumber and iron, each pair of gates, when hung, cost £100. One man could operate the winches, nicknamed crabs—geared wheels with handles installed at either side of each pair of lock gates—to reel the chains in and out to open and shut them. (On the much smaller wooden locks of the Erie Canal, the gates were operated by long oars mounted on top of each lock and required two or three men to push them open and shut.)

Colonel John turned his attention to the running of the canal, and he informed Governor Kempt that this work would mean 20 lockmasters and 35 labourers stationed along the route. There were 47 locks, but most were in series, close enough together for one lockmaster to attend to several. He recommended that the positions go to deserving men who had served him well during the construction. The appointments of the lockmasters should be for life, at 7 shillings and sixpence per day. Many writers have tried to express costs and wages in terms of present dollar values, but such comparisons have little meaning. In 1830, $5.00 was approximately £1 sterling, and 25¢ equalled 1 shilling. A correlation may be made through examining wages paid for different kinds of skills.

The lockmaster's 7 shillings and sixpence equalled $1.88 per day, while a stonemason earned 7 shillings, ($1.75); a blacksmith 6 shillings, a carpenter 5, and a labourer 2 shillings and sixpence—63¢. By this comparison, Colonel John's suggestion for the locksmiths' wages was generous. He also recommended that Captain Daniel Bolton, long his loyal subordinate, was the best man to take over the canal when he was on his leave of absence in England. He passed on to Sir James Kempt advice on caring for the waterway, the cleaning of the canal, the raising and lowering of the water levels, and on when to close the waste water weirs. The governor, aware that he would shortly be recalled, passed all Colonel John's letters to his successor, Mathew Whitworth-Aylmer, 5th Baron Aylmer, who would assume his duties in Quebec City early in 1831.

With the cost of the canal in mind and its benefit to the populace, the Superintendent drew up a schedule of tolls, but one that led to indignant squawking. A captain of a vessel should purchase tickets from the Commissariat for £5. Each crew member should pay 5 shillings for every trip through the waterway, a passenger the same, and 3 shillings per hundredweight of baggage under one ton. Assuming that 8,000 persons would pass through per year, Colonel John calculated the revenue at £2,000, but the real profit would be the freight. If dry goods and flour, spirits and wines were charged at the rate of

View of the west end of Wellington Street, Upper Bytown looking east, 1845, by Thomas Burrowes. (Ontario Achives).

£1 per ton, assuming 20,000 tons the income would be £20,000. Potash might fetch another £5,000, and grain, carried at 1 shilling per bushel would yield another £500. Soft woods would go for 3 shillings fourpence per ton, and assuming 9,600 tons would yield another £1,600. Hardwoods shipped at 6 shillings eightpence per ton, assuming 3,000 tons, would produce another £1,000. Staves, more valuable, would cost £1 per ton, and assuming 1,000 tons fetch another £1,000.

Livestock would yield less, and 2,000 cattle and horses at 5 shillings per head meant a further £500. Sheep, calves and pigs could be charged at 1 shilling, threepence each, and if 1,000 travelled would fetch £62, 10s. The total income from commerce per year might be £41,762. 10s, and the canal would still be able to carry all the military, naval and commissariat stores for which it was intended. The revenue would do little to defray the enormous cost of construction, but it would more than cover the cost of operating and maintaining the system.

Unfortunately, trouble was brewing in London. This time in the form of Mr. H. Howard Burgess, an Irishman whom Colonel John had hired when he arrived in Bytown in 1826, armed with a letter of recommendation from Jacob Mountain, the Anglican Bishop of Canada. In the spring of 1830, the Superintendent discovered that Burgess was a drunkard and dismissed him. The rascal departed for England, taking with him

Chaudière Falls, Ottawa River with wire suspension bridge from west end of Upper Bytown, May 1845, by Thomas Burrowes. (Ontario Archives).

vouchers stolen from the canal office to use in a slander campaign. This scalawag and ne'er-do-well reached London at a time when defamation of Colonel John By's character was exactly what certain politicians and newspapermen, complaining at the appalling cost of the canal, wanted to hear. Burgess charged that the Superintendent had mismanaged funds and falsified his accounts, information that fell upon receptive ears and made glaring headlines.

Colonel George Nicholls, who had superceded Colonel Elias Walker Durnford as the Commanding Engineer in Canada, was dispatched to Bytown in November, 1831, to set up a board of enquiry. He soon ordered Burgess to return to Canada as a witness, but Burgess hedged, claiming that if he showed his face in Bytown the Superintendent's friends would have him murdered. He would go if the site of the hearing were moved to Montreal, and if he were forced to go to Bytown he demanded guards—all very melodramatic. No one would have given Burgess the time of day, but for the fact that the Lords of Treasury were disturbed that the canal was costing so much more than General Sir James Carmichael Smyth's mystical £169,000, that still stuck in their minds as a reasonable sum to invest in so unimportant a colony as Upper Canada.

When Colonel John became aware of Burgess's behaviour, he admitted in a letter dated November 22, 1830, to General Gothar Mann, that some irregularities had, inevitably occurred, but none were serious. The probing into the costs continued, and in December the British Cabinet decided that the Ordnance Department should assume full control of the canal and watch expenditures more carefully. Nor were the members reassured by Colonel John's assumption that the tolls he proposed would be acceptable to the populace.

For the Superintendent the first hint of opposition to the tolls came through a request from Peter McGill of Montreal, a tycoon and member of the Lower Canada Legislative Council, who was also the chairman of the Ottawa Steam Boat Company. McGill wanted to put a steamer on the Rideau Canal, but he asked Colonel John to exempt it from tolls for the first season, on the grounds that it could not operate at a profit. The Colonel was perplexed and reluctant, but he agreed, provided that McGill bring up the iron needed for lock gates at "a liberal price", and only until the canal had been opened to the public. McGill had no right to assume he could have a monopoly.

In June, 1831, Lord Aylmer, the new governor-in-chief, arrived in Bytown on a tour of inspection. After he departed Colonel John informed Captain Airey, Aylmer's acting secretary, that the work would eventually cost £710,199. When this bad news reached London, the Board of Ordnance announced that it would be responsible only for the £576,757 agreed upon by the Kempt Commission, and Upper Canada must pay the difference. The assembly stoutly refused, and the matter hung fire for a time.

Kingston Mills, 1855, by Thomas Burrowes. (Ontario Archives).

83

Towards the end of July, Lieutenant-Colonel Richard Boteler was posted to Nova Scotia and Colonel John had lost another valued friend. With Sir James Kempt and Colonel Durnford both back in Britain, he now had to contend with changes in routines which Governor Aylmer and Colonel Nicolls would impose. Not only that, from London came rumblings that the Board of Ordnance was not giving him the support he deserved. For one thing this body disliked By's recommendation that Captain Daniel Bolton be his successor, and chose instead Captain James Conway Victor, who had commanded the companies of Sappers and Miners, probably on the suspicion that Bolton was tarred with the same brush as his superior. Then in August, just as the stage seemed set for the grand opening of the canal, the water level, mysteriously, began to drop.

Investigation soon revealed that the culprit was William Merrick, who had constructed a private dam so that he could repair his mills. By August 19th, the water was too low to permit the passage of a steamboat, and Colonel John protested that individuals must not be allowed to alter the levels. Crown law officers should be empowered to take action against anyone who did so. When this news reached the Board of Ordnance, it ordered Governor Aylmer to take these steps, and to avoid complex legal proceedings that would interfere with navigation. Then on October 9th, Philomen Wright's steamboat *Union of the Ottawa* penetrated the waterway as far as Nicholsons Locks, half way between Burritts Rapids and Merrickville. The first steamer had used the canal, but the official opening was delayed until the spring of 1832. For John By this was a disappointment. He had decided to honour his best contractors, and had ordered commemorative silver cups inscribed with the date August 21, 1831. Now these awards could not be presented at the time he predicted for he had planned the ceremony as part of his grand celebration.

With the coming of Governor Aylmer and Colonel Nicolls, and the departure of Colonel Durnford, the squabbles the latter had smoothed over broke out afresh. The Commissariat challenged many of Colonel John's requests, while the Ordnance officers had to placate that body. Then, too, as though not to be outdone, the public was upset when the notices of the projected tolls

Silver cup awarded to John Redpath. Photo by Mary Beacock Fryer. (Redpath Museum, Toronto, Ontario).

for the canal were posted. In the absence of any instructions from the Board of Ordnance in London, the Superintendent posted the tolls he had worked out, which caused an immediate hue and cry that they were far too steep. They should be lowered by 1 shilling in every 5, and by 1 penny for every twopence. Besides, many people would ship their goods only along parts of the route, especially to and from Oliver's Ferry (Rideau Ferry) or Rideau Lake Narrows, important crossing points. Those using half the route should pay only half the toll. The greatest pressure came from lumbermen, who claimed they had purchased timber rights on the understanding that they would have cheap transport. The posted rates would ruin them, thereby destroying the trade on which the local economy depended. The Ordnance officers at Quebec City ordered Colonel John to consult with the lieutenant-governor of Upper Canada, Sir John Colborne, to work out a compromise.

For the moment the Superintendent could not make the arrangements, because Colborne was busy in York. In the interval more petitions poured in. One from certain businessmen in Kingston to Governor Colborne stated that the high tolls would discourage trade, the very thing Colonel By had advocated as a vital reason for building the works to accommodate steamboats. They pointed out that the toll on a barrel of flour on the Rideau Canal would be 1 shilling, with additional charges laid for the use of

84

the canals of the Ottawa River and at Lachine. That same barrel could be sent via the St. Lawrence by Durham boat for 2 shillings threepence—a saving. Who would use the Rideau route unless it was more economical? What they did not admit was that a barrel sent by the St. Lawrence had a good chance of being smashed en route. On paper at least, their argument looked convincing. They also avoided mentioning that the Grenville Canal was not finished, and goods had to be unloaded into small canal boats and reloaded at the exit from that canal.

By the middle of May, 1832, Colonel John had met with Sir John Colborne and they agreed to lower the tolls, although the Superintendent soon commented that forwarders along the St. Lawrence were lowering their rates to avoid losing too much trade to the Rideau. This, he maintained, was proof that the tolls he first proposed were not as ruinous as the merchants and lumbermen had pretended. His opinion aside, the competition between the St. Lawrence and the Rideau was healthy, and the public was the winner. At Kingston, enthusiastic businessmen were delighted and talked of taking oxen and ropes to speed the passage of Durham boats and barges through the Grenville Canal in order to compete more effectively with the Erie Canal, in the expectation that American shippers would send their goods to Montreal instead of along the Erie route to Albany.

13. Adulation and Blows for John By

At last the grand opening was at hand, but a severe epidemic of cholera that year overshadowed the great event. Many Irish immigrants were coming inland by way of the St. Lawrence and Ottawa Rivers, spreading the dread disease as they went. Workers on the Grenville Canal succumbed in droves, slowing its progress even more.

In the spring of 1832, Colonel John admitted that his final estimate of the whole Rideau Canal project was a staggering £803,744! This amount included £46,615 to complete the finishing touches, £14,000 for more land purchases and compensation for parcels taken, £7,750 for blockhouses and bridges, and £20,000 to pay off more property owners whose land or mills had suffered damage. Upon receipt of this report Gover-

nor Aylmer was alarmed, but a more detailed statement from the Superintendent placated him. The Treasury Board in London was another matter, but while storm clouds gathered across the Atlantic, Colonel John had few detractors in Upper Canada. On March 13th, the men of standing in Kingston paid tribute to him by a testimonial dinner at Carmino's Hotel. On the 17th, the Kingston Chronicle carried its story entitled "Public Dinner for Col. By":

> Tuesday last being the day on which Col. By accepted the invitation of the principal inhabitants of Kingston to a public dinner, upwards of 70 persons, including the military heads of departments, Commodore Barrie, and several others, who were invited to meet the Colonel, sat down to a most sumptuous dinner, prepared in Mr. Carmino's best style . . . .

> After the cloth was removed, the President, the Hon. John Kirby, who filled the chair with his usual good temper and honest beneficence, proposed the health of the King and Queen, both of which were received with an enthusiasm, the deafening effects of which are still resounding in our ears. The next toast, which was received with an equal exhibition of feeling was, "Our distinguished guest, Colonel By". When silence was with difficulty procured, the Colonel in a short, manly and spirited style, returned his sincere thanks for the honour conferred upon him, and although evidently labouring under the influence of those feelings which occasionally stifle all human utterance, proposed, "Prosperity to the Town of Kingston", to which every glass was filled to the brim by the happy multitude, who appreciated his unwearied exertions to promote the object of his toast by several years of unparalleled difficulties and most disheartening obstructions . . . .

> The occasion, combined with the stimulating influences of copious Champaigne libations, rendered many a tongue loquacious, which only through that medium was taught to believe it possessed the powers of eloquence . . . . only one speech was delivered to us for insertion. Upon questioning the oration, we discovered that it was the one he intended to deliver, but neither himself or his friends could recollect whether in the hurry of the occasion he had not forgotten the most necessary ingredient. However, we give it as he furnished it to us, and have no doubt it would have been most suitable and appropriate, had it not been unluckily called for after the bewildering influence of a few bumpers of Champaigne and Madeira had rendered the recollective faculties rather imperfect."

The band of the 66th Regiment, the newspaper continued, played fitting tunes for the merrymakers. Afterward Colonel John returned to Bytown, no doubt nursing a hangover shared by 69 others. By mid May he was back in Kingston with his wife and daughters for the first official journey through the entire waterway by steamboat. The vessel was the *Pumper*, owned by Robert Drummond, rechristened *Rideau* for this one occasion, which gave rise to argument in later years as to the name of that first steamer. The *Pumper* was 80 feet long with a 15 foot beam and a 12 horsepower engine. She derived her name because she was used to pump water out of coffer dams that were erected to hold back water while masonry was put in place. Drummond built another vessel in 1831, which he named the *John By*, 110 feet long with a 26 foot beam, intended to draw only 3½ feet of water. When launched she drew much more and could not travel on the canal. Ironically the boat named after the Superintendent had to be placed in service on the St. Lawrence and Lake Ontario.

On May 22nd, the *Pumper*, temporarily the *Rideau*, left Kingston towing two barges and preceded by the naval cutter *Rattlesnake*, and the By family, crew and guests began a week-long revel. At Jones Falls the cutter tied up and the barges were cut loose, allowing the unencumbered *Rideau* to proceed under full steam, but still the progress was slow. Everyone wanted at least to see her, and preferably join in the fun. H. MacGregor, a passenger on the steamer, described what followed in a letter to the Kingston Patriot dated June 5th, 1823:

> After leaving Chaffey's Mills, we beheld a party of Indians drawn up rank and file on the beach in front of their encampment having two Chiefs & Union flags floating among the dark green foliage of the clustering pines. On our approach, they saluted the boat with a fue-de-joi in most regular order, and in a style that would not discredit a regularly organized corps. We immediately returned the compliment by firing a cannon several times and making a shear out of the direct course, passed in front of the men, women & children, who went on to the Isthmus with us, their boats and canoes towed astern of the steamer, ten in number—here we were again received with shouts of applause, from the numerous body of people ready on the rock to receive us:"

The *Rideau* docked at Smiths Falls at six o'clock the following dawn, and more friends of the canal came aboard. Now the steamboat was top heavy with exuberant guests and moving gingerly. On May 29th, she

locked down the final steps in Bytown to the Ottawa River. The next event was the anticlimax, the big letdown. To Colonel John's mortification, for three weeks the western end of the waterway was shut down owing to more private enterprise. Some unidentified person at Ansley's Mills, near the southeast outlet of Loughborough Lake—one not directly affected by canal building that drained into Cranberry Lake—had put up a flimsy dam of boards in order to operate a sawmill. The dam washed away, and in the rush of water through Cranberry Lake to the Cataraqui River the coffer dam at Brewers Mills had been damaged. Yet good news softened the blow. While the western end was being repaired, 35 cribs of timber, each of more than 2,000 cubic feet, passed down the Long Island Locks without doing a scrap of damage.

At last Colonel John was able to award the four ornate silver cups which he had ordered made for the purpose in England, all of which are still accounted for. Two are 17 inches tall, 12 inches in diameter at the brim, and 7 inches at the base. The other two are half the size. The large ones were awarded jointly to John Redpath and Thomas Mackay, and to Thomas Phillips and Andrew White. In the engraved dedications Colonel John had the works these contractors built listed. The other two cups went to Robert Drummond and Thomas Mackay, the latter for works he carried out separately from John Redpath. At the time of writing the Drummond cup is in the Bytown Museum in Ottawa; the Mackay cup is in the possession of a descendant at Victoria, British Columbia; the Phillips-White cup is in the Chateau de Ramezay in Montreal; and the Redpath-Mackay cup is in the Redpath Museum in Toronto.

The canal opened from end to end, Colonel John took his wife and daughters to New York State for a holiday. Returning by sea they reached Quebec City on August 7th to a gloomy welcome. The gilt was off the gingerbread. John By had orders to return to England at once and appear before the parliamentary committee enquiring into the ultimate cost of the Rideau Canal. He went to Bytown to pack and attend to last minute administration, and Governor Aylmer and Colonel Nicholls decided that Captain Daniel Bolton, not Captain Victor, would take over his duties as Superintendent. At least, with

Head Quarters,
Royal Sappers & Miners,
Woolwich 28 July 1834.

Nominal List of Non Commissioned Officers, Privates and Buglers of the Companies of Royal Sappers and Miners, disbanded at the Rideau Canal, Upper Canada, in December 1831. —

Rank	Names	Company	Rank	Names	Company
Serjeant	William Addison	7th	"	James Murdoch	"
Corporal	Thomas Jenkins	"	"	John Smith	"
"	William Clyma	15th	"	Samuel Patrick	"
2d Corporal	Archibald Sands	7th	"	John Ayres	"
"	George Hay	"	"	Hugh Patrick	"
"	Daniel McDonald	"	Bugler	Thomas Duffy	"
"	John Rickard	15th	Private	William Adam	15th
"	John Jones	"	"	William Howers	"
"	William Mitchel	"	"	Thomas Dickson	"
Private	Thomas Jones	7th	"	Robert Peets	"
"	Alexander Burns	"	"	Robert Snowdell	"
"	Henry Hay	"	"	John Newman	"
"	John McDonald	"	"	Philip Clogge	"
"	Thomas Green	"	"	David Mitchell	"
"	George Webbs	"	"	Thomas Newman	"
"	Charles Taylor	"	"	William Smith	"
"	Robert Neay	"	"	Michael Rowe	"
"	Cornelius Connor	"	"	Roderick McKay	"
"	Andrew Gray	"	"	Henry Bullen	"
"	William Mushmore	"	"	William Fielding	"
"	William R. Broad	"	"	James Dykes	"
"	Thomas Finn	"	"	Robert Clements	"
"	Robert Gillocar	"	"	Edward Pascoe	"
"	Henry Davis	"	"	George Sims	"
"	James Hume	"	Private	Patrick Pattew	15th
"	John Fraser	"	"	Robert Jones	"
Private	James Bromley	7th	"	Stephen Simmonds	"
"	Thomas Little	"	"	James McEvoy	"
"	Joseph White	"	"	John McLaren	"
"	Robert Mitchell	"	"	Thomas Smith	"
"	David Nesbitt	"	"	James Coll	"
"	James Callaway	"	"	John Burgoyne	"
"	William Fraser	"	"	John White	"
"	John Serjeant	"	"	George Hamilton	"
"	William Fleming	"	"	John Porteous	"
			"	Samuel Spry	

The following men returned to England on the disbandment of the Companies

Rank	Names	Company	Remarks
Color Serjeant	John Eads	7th	Now serving at Gibralter
	John Johnston	15	" " " " at Woolwich
Serjeant	Joseph Coombs	"	Discharged 9th March 1832 & gone to Canada,
Corporal	George Roff	7	Now serving at Chatham
"	Denis Ryan	15	Discharged 31 Jany. 1832 & reside at Thurles Ireland
"	Thomas Simmonds	"	Now serving at Purfleet
Private	James Burrel	7th	Disc.d 31 Jany 1832 & to reside at Dumfermlin
"	Andrew Kinross	"	" Do " " Do " " at Sterling
"	Charles Turner	"	" Do " " Do " " at Haywood
"	Edward Connielle	"	" Do 31 March 1832 " at Dublin
"	William Smith	"	" Do 31 Oct. 1833 " " at Forres
"	William Bond	"	" Do 31 Jany 1832 " " at Probus
"	Thos. Edrington	"	Now serving at Woolwich
"	James Burlace	"	Disc.d 31 March 1832 to reside at Davenport
"	George Cook	"	" Do 14 Jany 1832
"	William Kemshaw	"	Now serving at the Mauritius
"	John Milford	"	" Do " " at the Cape
"	Arthur Kelly	15	Disc.d 31 Jany 1832 to reside at Omagh
"	William Frusk	"	} Now serving at the Cape
"	John Cooke	"	
"	William Colwell	"	" Do " " at Woolwich
"	Owen McGrath	"	Discharged 16 January 1832
"	William Harris	"	} Now serving at Woolwich —
"	Henry Sobey	"	
"	John Baird	"	Discharged 7th September 1833.
Bugler	William Cameron	"	Now serving at Bermuda

List of Soldiers of the Corps of Royal Sappers and Miners, disbanded at Bytown, December 1831. (Public Archives of Canada—RG8 C Series, Vol. 632—pp. 178-81).

respect to a successor Colonel John got his way.

Colonel By wrote to Lord Aylmer asking him to come and inspect the works before he had to depart, anxious to have the governor-in-chief's endorsement when he faced that parliamentary committee. Aylmer was coy, unwilling to take sides. His military secretary informed Colonel By that His Excellency could not grant the request for the moment, but he would visit the canal at his earliest convenience. Meanwhile, with Bolton, Colonel John tried to complete a set of estimates for all remaining expenditures which he planned to take with him, ammunition when he had to defend himself. These were not finished by September 1st, the day Aylmer wanted the Colonel to leave Bytown for Quebec City. Bolton promised to forward them as soon as possible.

When Colonel John had planned his leave of absence in England after the canal had opened, he apparently expected to resume his duties in Bytown. A few months before his recall he had purchased 600 acres south of Nicholas Sparks's property for £1,200—the area now bounded by Bronson Avenue on the west, the Rideau River on the east, Laurier Avenue on the north, and Gladstone Avenue on the south. When he set out for Quebec City with his family he must have suspected he would never again see the village he had founded, nor the canal he had sacrificed his good health to build.

He waited three weeks, hoping that the estimates would come. Then, disappointed, he went aboard ship after sending a message to Bolton to send them as soon as they were ready. He left Canada apprehensive, sorrowing that his great achievement was shaded by the enquiry. Instead of a knighthood, his due, he would suffer a reprimand from politicians who refused even to try and understand either the methods he had had to use in order to pay his contractors, or the fact that the Rideau Canal had been a great experiment upon which he had embarked with so many questions unanswered. He was a broken, discouraged man, under a cloud, weakened by privation and disease, a man whose days were numbered.

He settled his family in Shernfold Manor, which Esther had inherited at Frant, in the lovely Sussex countryside not far from Tumbridge Wells. In London the enquiry launched by spurious letters from H.

Howard Burgess to members of Parliament, droned on as witnesses for and against Colonel John's expenditures came and went. Under the title of the British Select Parliamentary Committee on Papers Relating to the Rideau Canal, it had begun on March 21, 1831, under the chairmanship of John Nicholas Fazakerley. Several officers who had served in Canada were examined, and all agreed that Colonel By's expenditures for the project were within reason. On June 25th, 1832, Colonel Elias Walker Durnford's turn came, and he had no criticism to offer on his friend's performance.

In his own letters to the enquiry—he never appeared in person because his health was failing fast—John By asserted that he had built a canal with 18 dams, 17 waste weirs, 46 locks (there were 47) and all the other works, at a cost 15 percent lower than any similar construction in Canada. In that last he erred—there was no construction of that scale as a basis for comparison in either Canadian province. He reminded the members that he had said, before he ever left for Canada to be the superintending engineer, that General Sir James Carmichael Smyth's estimate of £169,000 was so much pie in the sky, and that the work might cost five times this amount. He cited the support of General Gothar Mann, who had agreed that it would be impossible to estimate accurately the sum required, and indeed had urged Colonel John to use his own judgement.

The committee of enquiry was unimpressed, and the Board of Ordnance, numbed that so extravagant a work had been permitted in an unimportant colony, was standing back, so that many observers saw John By as a scapegoat. The age of reform had begun, when all public servants would be accountable year by year to the politicians. While the officers stood by him, they were powerless. On February 28th, 1833, Colonel Durnford wrote to General Andrew Pilkington, a friend of Commodore Barrie:

> The expenditure has certainly far exceeded the estimate, particularly the original one; but I must state at the same time, where it possible for any of His Majesty's ministers or members of the House of Parliament to have seen the country lakes and swamps, etc., etc., through which this water communication has been carried agreeably to the orders given to Lieut.-Col. By, and could now see the stupendous chain of works that have been constructed, that the outlay of money would not be wondered at, or

given unwillingly, as a record of British ability and munificence."

Some weeks earlier, on January 23rd, Colonel John had written Durnford:

> I was never ordered to stop the works until I was so unjustly recalled; when, thank God, they were all finished, and the Canal had been open to the Public for some months, or I should have been robbed of the honour of building the magnificent erection.

John By lived in seclusion at Frant, a disappointed man. Like most officers who had sacrificed themselves in outposts of empire, he expected to win distinction. Without that hope few would have ventured abroad to undertake such arduous work. Although the committee of enquiry exonerated John By of misusing public funds and failing to obey his instructions, he never received any recognition from the British government for his fine contribution to the security of Upper Canada. He died on February 1st, 1836, after a series of strokes, at age 53. On the monument still standing in St. Albans Churchyard at Frant, erected by "his afflicted widow in remembrance of every virtue that could endear a husband, a father, and a friend," Esther By asserted that his death had been hastened by "his indefatigable zeal and devotion in the service of his King and Country, in Upper Canada."

Others, at disparate ends of the social spectrum, were as lavish, given a lower level of emotional involvement. Sir Richard Bonnycastle, of the Royal Artillery, who foiled William Lyon Mackenzie's attempt to capture Kingston by his efficient martialling of the Frontenac Militia, wrote in 1841, that if any man deserved to be immortalized "in this utilitarian age," it was Colonel John By. Mackenzie, who regarded Bonnycastle as an intimate of Satan, visited parts of the Rideau works in September, 1831, and wrote:

> Such locks as I saw are noble monuments of the skill and experience of the masons and architects who planned and built them . . . . are the equal, if not superior to the locks at Lockport, and on the Lachine Canal; and being upon a grand scale, and built of beautiful hewn stone, have a very imposing and durable appearance, looking as if they would last for ages.

The people who have lived near the waterway often expressed their gratitude to John By. The public dinner at Kingston stands as an early testimonial to the man and his fortitude. The citizens of Brockville, who did not benefit as directly, held a public

The gravesite of Lt. Colonel John By at St. Alban's Churchyard, Frant, England. (Historical Society of Ottawa).

meeting in November, 1832, and passed a series of resolutions, some expressing gratitude to the mother country, but nearly all singling out Colonel John for special mention. A typical eulogy drafted by the Reverend William Smart, the Presbyterian minister, read:

> That the termination of the great work by Col. By, and his persevering and successful efforts in overcoming the many difficulties presenting themselves during its progress and which to an ordinary mind would have appeared unsurmountable, entitle him to the lasting gratitude of the people of Upper Canada."

In the interval between the time when Colonel John had returned to England in near disgrace, to the present, his memory, at least in the vicinity of the canal, is still treasured. From the members of the Historical Society of Ottawa has come the most recent tribute. In September, 1979, as a token of their lasting gratitude, a tablet of Welsh slate which they paid for was unveiled at the foot of Colonel John's monument at Frant. The Canadian High Commissioner officiated, and the event was close to the 200th anniversary of the superintending engineer's birth. This ceremony culminated three years of work by the historical society. Beforehand, also financed by the members, the monument had been restored and the paving stones surrounding it repaired. For many years the grass was cut regularly by a retired Commander of the Royal Navy and churchwarden of Frant whose son lived in Ottawa for a time. His name—poetic justice—was Burgess. The tablet at the base of the monument reads:

Bytown 1826   Ottawa 1855
Colonel By founded the City
which became the
Capital of Canada
This Tablet was erected by
The Historical Society of Ottawa

JOHN BY
LT. COLONEL ROYAL ENG'RS
1779 — 1836

BUILDER OF THE RIDEAU CANAL
1826 — 1832

FOUNDER OF BY-TOWN, 1827
NOW OTTAWA, CAPITAL OF CANADA.

Lt. Colonel By Monument at the Rideau Locks, in Ottawa.

91

The members had long been concerned that the monument mentioned only Colonel John's sufferings, not the work he had done for Canada. They concentrated on his role as the founder of their city, which still leaves a gap, the opportunity for friends of the Rideau Canal to add a second tablet commemorating that tribute to John By's engineering genius.

14. Finishing Touches

By the summer of 1832, the Rideau Canal was in operation all the way from Bytown to Kingston, but several works had yet to be done before it could be called completed. Daniel Bolton, now a major, was soon pre-occupied with the water levels of Loughborough Lake, a threat to the Upper Brewers Lock. On October 19th, Bolton's full-time staff included 3 officers, 7 specialist civilians—blacksmiths, carpenters and stonemasons—22 lockmasters, 33 permanent labourers and 32 temporary ones. As well, 4 soldiers were on guard duty at each of the isolated locks and the 22 stations. To maintain the structures and keep the wooden lock gates well painted, Bolton requested the sum of £7,247. In addition, Colonel Nicholls recommended to Governor Aylmer that £5,418

be set aside, as Colonel By had suggested, for repairs, additions and alterations that might prove necessary in a structure so new and untested.

In December, 1831, 71 Royal Sappers and Miners were discharged since their work was finished. Some months before, Colonel John had offered each private 100 acres, an inducement not to desert—this despite his earlier assurances that the men would not contemplate such a move. Of these, 41 accepted the offer and remained in the neighbourhood, while the other 30 returned to Britain. As well, some of the senior employees whom the Superintendent had hired in Montreal settled along the canal route. Notable among them was the overseer, Thomas Burrowes, who built a fine house at Kingston Mills and was on the canal's permanent staff for some years. He was also the artist, and to his paintings we owe a debt of gratitude for the detail he showed and the record he left on how the countryside looked in his day.

Major Daniel Bolton remained as superintending engineer until 1843, and during that time the canal was fortified. Four blockhouses were constructed. Two, those at Newboro and the Narrows, were built by Benjamin Tett at a cost of £104 each. The

Thomas Burrowes house at Kingston Mills as it is today.
(Dennis Wallace).

Blockhouse at Newboro.

Defensible lockmaster's house, Jones Falls.

Defensible lockmater's house at Chaffeys Lock.

Blockhouse at Kingston Mills.
(Public Archives of Canada—PA888A).

other two located at Kingston Mills and Merrickville, all of them were built in 1831-32. A fifth was started at Burritts Rapids but was never completed. Defensible lockmasters' houses were constructed following the 1837-38 troubles.

All the defensible lockmasters houses were one storey. The second stories were added between 1890 and 1924. Kilmarnock has a stone second storey added at the turn of the century. Eleven defensible lockmasters houses are still standing; Lower Brewers, Upper Brewers, Jones Falls (still original one storey in height) Davis (still one storey high), Chaffeys Lock, Poonamalie, Old Slys, Smiths Falls, Nicholsons, Clowes and Hartwells. There were others, one at Ottawa Locks destroyed when the Chateau Laurier Hotel was built. Lastly, the two barracks that John Redpath had built at the base of Jones Falls and at Morton completed the chain of posts, and were later called log guardhouses. In time of peace certain of the

blockhouses served as residences for the lockmasters. The other improvement during Superintendent Bolton's term was a bridge at Kingston Mills, built by the contractor, Robert Drummond, for £520.

Colonel John By's work was as durable as he could have wished, requiring only anticipated maintenance, with one notable exception. On June 8th, 1836, the timber overflow dam which he had built at Long Island washed away, weakened by erosion. Major Bolton rebuilt the dam and had the canal open by August 1st, a remarkable feat. Otherwise all the dams and locks did their duty.

The modern traveller is told that there are 49 locks in the Rideau system, while Colonel By remembered building 46 when in fact the correct tally was 47. The two Beveridge Locks on the Tay River that link Perth to the waterway through Port Elmsley, a short distance east of Oliver's Ferry, were added later. As the name of the latter implies, a

93

White Fish River and wooden dam with log guard house, built 1838-39 for protection, by Thomas Burrowes. (Ontario Archives).

ferry boat was operated by a man named Oliver, who lived in a cabin close by. The boat was a good size, for it would carry not only pedestrians over this narrow point between Big and Lower Rideau Lakes, but horses and wagons as well. Out of wisdom, or malice, Oliver did not make crossings after dark. Once in a while, so the story goes, a stranger would arrive too late, and the hospitable Oliver and his good spouse maintained a spare bedroom for such emergencies.

The ferry seemed lucrative, for Oliver and his wife always had plenty of food and presentable clothing. There was just one small catch. The overnight guests, whom Oliver said he took across the water at first light, were never heard of again. Some years later, when men were dismantling the old cabin for firewood, they made a grisly discovery. Thinly concealed beneath the earthen floor were many human skeletons. Was our Oliver a thrill killer, or a native Sweeney Todd? Small wonder the local people soon changed the name of the landing to Rideau Ferry.

Even before the canal opened the citizens of Perth wanted to share its benefits, but such a link had no military value and would have to be financed by private or provincial means. Under the leadership of one of the two sitting members of the legislative as-

Rideau Ferry, 1832, by John Burrows.
(Public Archives of Canada—C3991).

*Jones Falls Barrack,
later called log guardhouse.
(Public Archives of Canada—PA89827).*

Restored blockhouse at the Narrows.

*Defensible lockmaster's house
at Davis Lock.*

sembly, the Honourable William Morris, a group of businessmen set up the Tay Navigation Company in 1830, and began raising funds. The settlement was only 14 years old, and the sum required put a strain on its slender resources. Notwithstanding, four small wooden locks and a canal needing only earth excavation were designed by a builder named John Jackson, and the first two locks were finished within a year.

In the meantime the company had appealed to the government of Upper Canada for assistance, and in January, 1832, received a grant that raised its capital to $10,000. A sale of public land on April 27th, added another $1,500—an occasion still remembered as the day the town lost its greenbelt. The Bank of Upper Canada loaned the company another $5,000, and with this financing most of the project was carried out. The first two locks were built with alacrity, the others after a political hassle. Donald Fraser, the other sitting member, accused the directors of the Tay Navigation Company of feathering their own nests. The Executive Council of Upper Canada conducted an enquiry which exonerated Morris and the company. In the scuffling Fraser lost his seat in the legislature, after two indignant voters discovered that he did not meet the property qualification and filed a petition with the assembly.

With the help of further loans the other two locks were finished in 1834, and for the Tay service the small steamer *Enterprise* was built at Perth. She operated between Bytown and Kingston, and her captain, William Richards, was Irish. He had served in the Royal Navy during the War of 1812, and settled for a time in New Brunswick before making his way to Perth. He sailed the waterway only for a few years. The Tay Canal proved to be dangerously shallow, and before long only barges moved up and down, carrying square timber, potash and consumer goods. The tolls did not yield enough revenue to keep the canal in repair, and in time the federal government came to the rescue. In 1886, when, coincidently, another local politician, the Honourable John G. Haggart, was the Minister of Railways and Canals, the four wooden locks were demolished. These were replaced by the two stone ones which match the others in the waterway. Thus, including the Beveridge Locks, the modern system comprises the 49 locks.

The other construction of importance to the Rideau Canal was at Kingston, the vulnerable outlet that could be threatened from the American naval base at Sackets Harbor,

View from Barriefield, U.C., 1839-41 by W.H. Bartlett.
(Metropolitan Toronto Library Board).

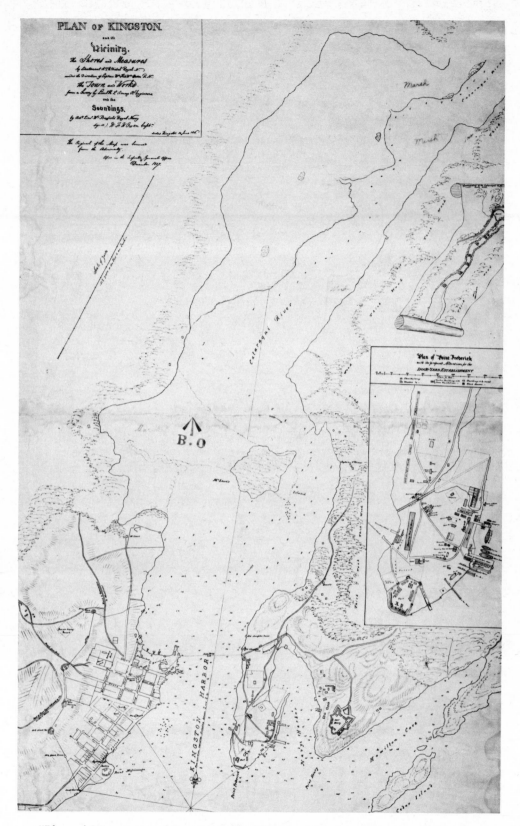

"Plan of Kingston and its vicinity"—The shores and measures by Lieutenant A.T.E. Vidal Royal N. under the direction of Captain Wm. Fitz Wm. Owen R.N.: The town and works from a survey by Lieut. H.L. Renny, Rl Engineers, and the soundings, by Actg. Lieut. Wm. Bayfield Royal Navy. signed W.F.W. Owen Captn. dated Kingston 14 June 1816. Copied by L. Pereira March 1908. (Public Archives of Canada—C4247).

Point Frederick, 1860—The wooden blockhouse of 1812 burned down in 1820 and the Martello Tower was built between 1846-47. The centre building, built 1819-21 is the Stone Frigate. Its construction was supervised by Sir Robert Barrie. It housed ordnance and stores after the war of 1812. (By permission of the Commandant of the Royal Military College).

across Lake Ontario. Work at Fort Henry began in 1832, on the high promontory which earlier had had, first a wooden blockhouse, and later a small stone stronghold to protect the Naval Yard on Point Frederick. The new fort's main purpose was the protection of the navy and its all important dockyard, but incidently it would guard the canal entrance. In fact, the new fort's most formidable armament faced inland, rather than towards Lake Ontario. This gave rise in later years to speculation that Fort Henry had been built the wrong way round, and that its plans had been intended for a site in Kingston, Jamaica. This was not true, and the

heavy armament was so placed to protect the harbour, dockyard and shipping as well as the entrance to the Rideau Canal. Besides, there was always the possibility of an enemy disembarking some distance away and approaching the fortress by land.

Planning for the new fort commenced in 1825, when Lieutenant Colonel Ross Wright of the Kingston garrison received instructions to prepare estimates on the cost of improving the city's defences. At that time Wright was authorized to spend only £5,000 for quarrying stone. Three years later, Colonels Fanshawe and Lewis, of Sir James Kempt's commission, recommended a chain of five strong

Fort Frederick and the Royal Military College, 1979.

Kingston defenses viewing south to Lake Ontario. Left to right—Fort Henry, Navy Bay, Fort Frederick and Royal Military College, Shoal Tower and the City of Kingston, 1979.

British troops at Fort Henry, Kingston, Ontario—ca. 1867.
(Public Archives of Canada—C55511).

99

redoubts along Kingston's perimeter, to prevent an attack overland, and to protect the dockyard and the entrance to the Rideau Canal. They included a plan to build a chain of Martello towers at half mile intervals to check a naval attack. The old stone fort on Point Henry was to remain as part of the overall defence system.

In October of 1829, a committee of the Board of Ordnance in England approved the preceding plans, but decided that the fort on Point Henry should be replaced by a larger, stronger structure. However, no funds for this construction would be forthcoming until the Rideau Canal was completed. Therefore, in 1832, with the waterway functioning, Colonel Wright received orders to begin demolishing old Fort Henry, and whereas that structure had been built by soldiers, its replacement would be undertaken by contractors. Under the direction of Colonel Wright and his assistant, the then Captain Richard Bonnycastle, the contractors and their labourers quarried limestone along the road leading from Kingston towards Gananoque. By 1836, the main, six-sided portion of the fort was completed, in time to house prisoners during the upcoming rebellion. The first garrison consisted of the 24th Regiment of Foot, and two batteries of Royal Artillery. This building cost £70,000 sterling.

The plan for the new Fort Henry included a sea battery—an indication of location rather than water quality—as well as two parallel rows of Commissariat store houses, tying the battery to the main fortress. This battery, overlooking Lake Ontario, and the store houses, were begun in 1841 and completed in November, 1842, at a cost of £10,632 sterling. A modern visitor enters the courtyard enclosed by the Commissariat buildings, the Advance Battery (formerly the sea battery) and the southwest wall of the hexagonal building that is perforated by the main gate with its drawbridge.

On the walls of the main building, originally, were twenty-seven 24 pounder guns, mounted on traversing platforms, so that each could be swung round and aimed. This main structure was enclosed with a dry ditch 50 feet broad and 30 feet deep, in turn surrounded by a wall called a counterscarp and containing galleries to be used as reverse fire chambers. Reached by tunnels from the fort, from these galleries the soldiers could sweep the ditches with rifle bullets and with six 18

pounder carronades, should an enemy penetrate past the counterscarp. East and west branching side ditches extending down each side of the small peninsula completed the defences for the time being.

In 1845, work commenced on two Martello towers on the shore below Fort Henry, at either end of the east and west side ditches. By the time these were under construction, the name implied a squat, round tower of thick masonry topped by a parapet below a rather flat, conical roof, usually from 30 to 35 feet high and 35 to 55 feet in diameter at the base, a few feet less towards the top. These round towers, a relatively inexpensive substitute for a fort, were named, inaccurately, after a tower on Cape Mortella in Corsica, which was bombarded by the Royal Navy in 1793-94. Martello towers were erected along the south coast of England during the Napoleonic Wars, and a few were built in the colonies. The East and West Ditch Towers were 30 feet in diameter at the base, 45 feet high, and the walls were 8 feet thick on the water side. Mounted on top of each beneath the roof was a 24 pounder gun.

Before these two towers were completed, the Oregon Boundary Dispute threatened to endanger peace between Britain and the United States, and in 1846, work began on four more Martello towers. Two would guard the entrance to the Rideau Canal directly, while the other two overlooked the approaches to Kingston. The Murney Tower, on Murney Point, was built on what was then the western extremity of the town. It was 56 feet in diameter at the base and 36 feet high, with two 32 pounder guns on top and two 32 pounder carronades inside. The Cathcart, or Cedar Island Tower, stood on the island of that name guarding the naval base from the east. This one was 54 feet in diameter and 36 feet high, with the same armament as the Murney Tower.

Of benefit to the security of the canal were the Fort Frederick and Shoal Towers. The first was built on Point Frederick in front of the dockyard, across Navy Bay from Fort Henry, and its dimensions and armament showed that it had the dual role of protecting the naval establishment and the canal. It was 60 feet in diameter and 45 feet high, with two 32 pounder guns on top and six 32 pounder carronades within. The Shoal Tower was placed on the west side of the harbour in front of the Kingston market

Aerial view of Fort Henry, Kingston.
(Ontario Ministry of Industry and Tourism).

house, and it was the most difficult to construct because the base was submerged. It was 65 feet in diameter, rising 30 feet, and both measurements were made at the high water level. Like those at Murney Point and Cedar Island, Shoal Tower had two 32 pounder guns on top, and two 32 pounder carronades inside. A foreman on the Martello tower works was a stonemason named Alexander Mackenzie, later a Prime Minister of Canada.

Lastly were added two gun batteries, sited to protect both the town and the canal. One stood behind the Shoal Tower, on the shore in front of the market house. The other was on Mississauga Point, now the location of the Kingston Yacht Club.

The five large redoubts recommended by the Kempt Commission in 1828 were never started, nor was the fort Colonel John By advocated for the Ottawa end of the canal ever built. Fort Henry seems oddly oriented, partly because it was to have been a cog in a grander scheme that was never realized. The guns of the fort have never fired a shot in anger, and only on two occasions has the Rideau Canal been required to rush troops to the front. Both fort and waterway stand today as splendid testimonials to the beneficence of the British taxpayer, for the amusement of the Canadian—and American —tourist.

II

A Century of Commercial Navigation

The Rideau Canal functioned as a commercial waterway until the 1930s, and the busiest period was from its opening until the construction of the St. Lawrence canals. The locks on the rival system—9 feet deep, 55 feet wide and 200 feet long—were open by 1848, except for a stretch near Cardinal. Even beforehand, forwarders—the modern name would be shippers—preferred to send cargo down the St. Lawrence, and passengers liked that route because it was faster, with reasonably comfortable stagecoaches to carry them around the stretches of rapids. The small steamboats, barges and rafts could slide down the rapids, but it was nearly impossible for boats to move upstream. Thus a triangular traffic evolved, many boats sailing from Kingston to Montreal and returning by way of the Ottawa River to Bytown and back to Lake Ontairo through the Rideau Canal.

Once the St. Lawrence canals were operating, the Rideau carried mainly local traffic between Kingston and Bytown and timber rafts and barges loaded with the produce of the region. While the canal never did live up to Colonel John By's expectations by attracting trade from the Great Lakes ports, it was a boon to the population along its course. When it first opened the countryside was being settled rapidly, because the townships facing the St. Lawrence were nearly filled up, and cheap land was no longer available there. In the last quarter of the nineteenth century a new dimension was added. The towns and cities were growing, and the number of people employed in industry and commerce grew with them. The custom of

taking a summer vacation came into vogue, and people with the time and the means were looking for places to spend both. The many lakes accessible from the Rideau Waterway were a perfect playground, and passenger steamers a fine way to travel to what was becoming cottage country, or to take a holiday aboard ship.

All over the continent canal traffic declined when the railway era began, but some goods still moved more economically by water. Heavy and bulky low value items such as lumber, grain and potash, and the coal the trains required, where time was not a factor, moved cheaply by water. Canals could compete successfully for that kind of trade. With the invention of the automobile, road transport, the gradual change-over from coal to diesel fuel for trains, and the depletion of local resources, commercial navigation on the Rideau Canal ground to a halt.

The pretty waterway never did carry the trade volume anticipated and wearied of the unprofitable investment the Ordnance Department offered the canal to the Province of Canada in 1845, as an outright gift, but received a negative response. Again the department made the offer in 1848 amidst considerable dissent, since that body wanted to retain the ownership of the land along the canal. Finally, by Order-in-Council dated October 1st, 1853, the province accepted the Ordnance offer on the grounds that it would be wise to keep the waterway open a while yet. As long as the rates were kept low it would compete with the railways and continue as an alternate route to the St. Lawrence. The operation of the canal passed to the Board of

Schooner in Foster's (Davis) Lock, Rideau Canal, ca. 1800.
(Public Archives of Canada—PA8818).

Works of the two provinces, formerly Upper and Lower Canada, united in 1841 as Canada West and Canada East.

During the Great Depression of the 1930s, the Canadian government wanted to close the waterway to curb expenses. It was immediately apparent that this measure would cause more problems than it solved. If the locks and embankments fell into ruins the water levels would revert, resulting in untold damage to the surrounding country-side. The canal had to stay. The stonework that had always been well maintained would not require vast sums to keep it in good repair, with its lock gates renewed. The government would pay the modest amounts necessary, and all for the enjoyment of pleasure boat owners.

1. Schooners, Puffers, Barges and Rafts

The first ships on the St. Lawrence that had steam power were sailing vessels with tall spars. The engines installed in them were for auxiliary power to enable these large freighters to combat the current and the prevailing wind, both from the west. At the same time most freighters, until towards the end of the nineteenth century, were unpowered topsail schooners. By the time the Rideau Canal was under construction some steamboats were powered only by engines. They carried passengers, small quantities of freight, and towed barges and rafts. However, about one third of the freight carried through the waterway in its heyday was aboard schooners with draft shallow enough to negotiate the locks. Wherever a crossing point was required, the Ordnance Department built a swing bridge to accommodate the masts of the sailing vessels.

The very name steamboat conjures up an image of a small puffer with one or two smokestacks, side or stern paddle wheels, a rounded, stubby hull and one or more decks where gentlemen and ladies stroll. This craft has become the symbol of the early steam-boat era, which obscures the fact that as a freight carrier it was in the minority. The records of boats and traffic on the canal are sketchy for the first decade, but the bateaux and Durham boats—a larger form of bateau—carried sails. Four of the vessels on the canal were described as sloops, two as schooners, and one as a rigged barge.

The little steamboats that carried passengers and freight and towed barges were built at Kingston, Bytown, and at many points along the Rideau system, as well as at towns along the St. Lawrence. Passengers were allotted none too comfortable bunk beds at first, and the bulk of the freight went in the barges the steamer towed. Barges, sometimes open, were pointed at either end or squared. Where they were decked they resembled Noah's Ark, and were sometimes called arks. They included living space for the crew and occasionally passengers. Users of the Rideau Canal, whether passengers or sailors, evolved their own terminology owing to the unique nature of the route. The steamers were called canal boats, whereas on other waterways the name implied an unpowered barge, scow or ark. On the Rideau the steamer was really a river boat, because it had to be able

Portaging boats at Portland, Ontario.
(Public Archives of Canada—C8966).

104

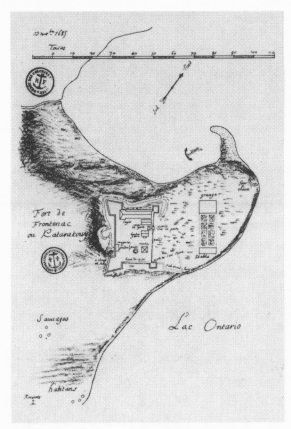

Fort Frontenac, built in 1673 by Cavelier de La Salle and Count Frontenac.
(Public Archives of Canada)

Cataracoui or Fort de Frontenac, 13 November, 1658. Located at the present site of Kingston, Ontario. 1 inch to 15 toises (100 ft.).
(National Map Collection, Public Archives of Canada)

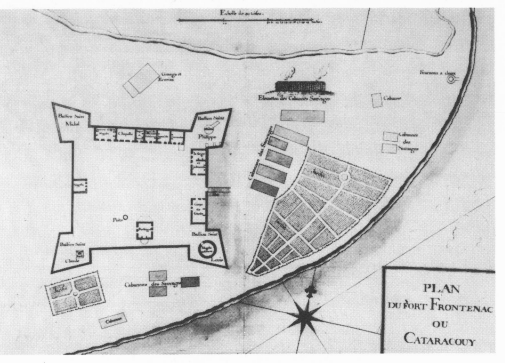

Fort Frontenac in 1720 at Kingston.
(National Map Collection, Public Archives of Canada)

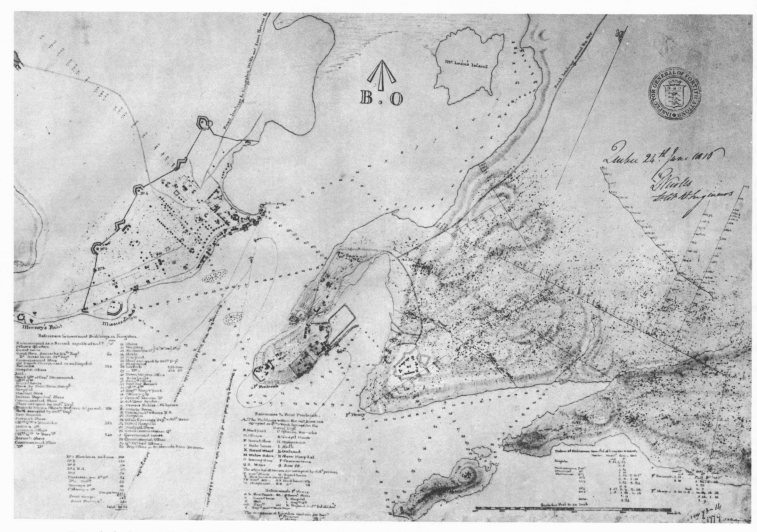

*Detailed plan of the fortifications at Kingston by J. B. Duberger; signed and dated, Quebec, 24th June, 1816;
Approved by G. Nicholls, Lt. Col. R^C. Engineers.
(National Map Collection, Public Archives of Canada)*

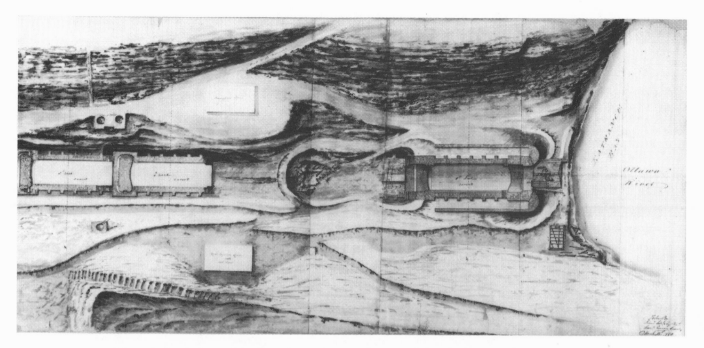

Plan of the Rideau Canal Locks at Ottawa River while under construction in 1830.
(National Map Collection, Public Archives of Canada)

Detail of the Sluice Valves at Kingston Mills and Jones Falls.
(National Map Collection, Public Archives of Canada)

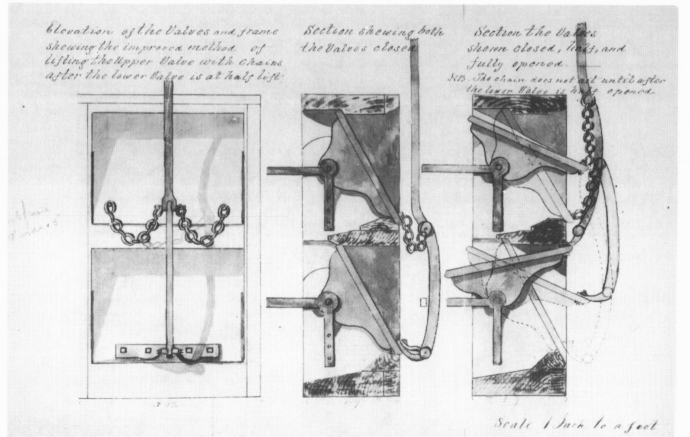

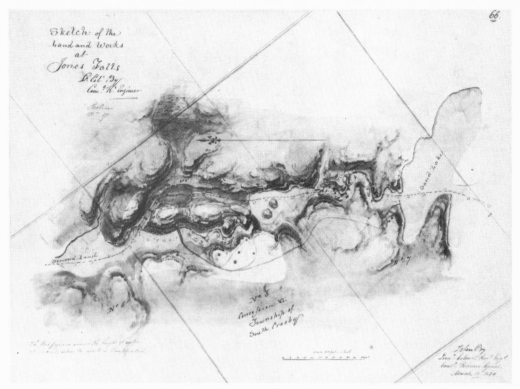

Sketch of the land and works at Jones Falls, Rideau Canal, March 18th, 1830.
(National Map Collection, Public Archives of Canada)

The dam at Jones Falls, preparatory to turning the water from sluice-way 1 into sluice-way 2, from whence it was turned into the regular channel to the locks, the waste water then running off through the permanent waste channel.
(National Map Collection, Public Archives of Canada).

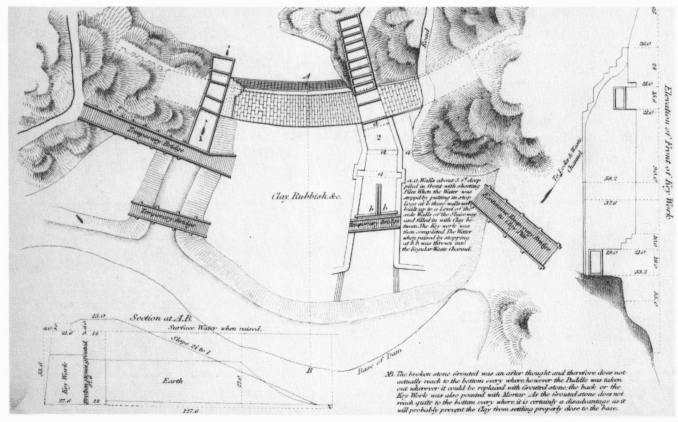

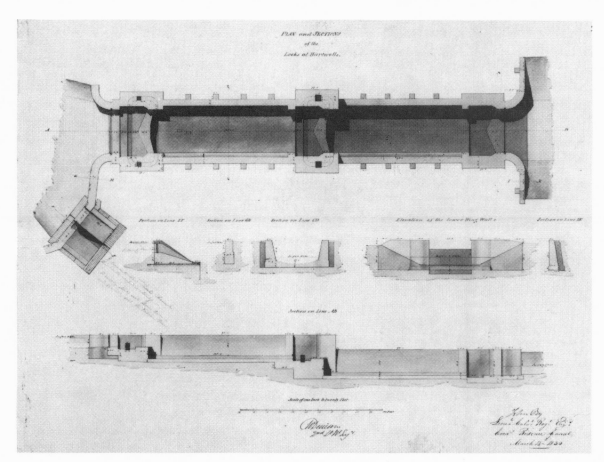

Plan and sections of the locks at Hartwells, Rideau Canal, 1829-30.
(National Map Collection, Public Archives of Canada)

Plan, elevation and section of large locks, Rideau Canal, 1827.
(National Map Collection, Public Archives of Canada)

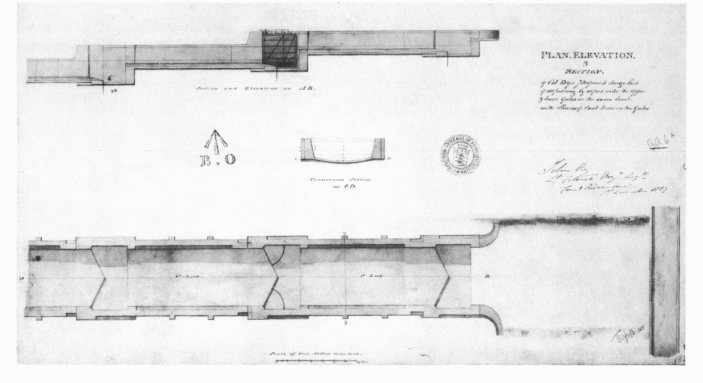

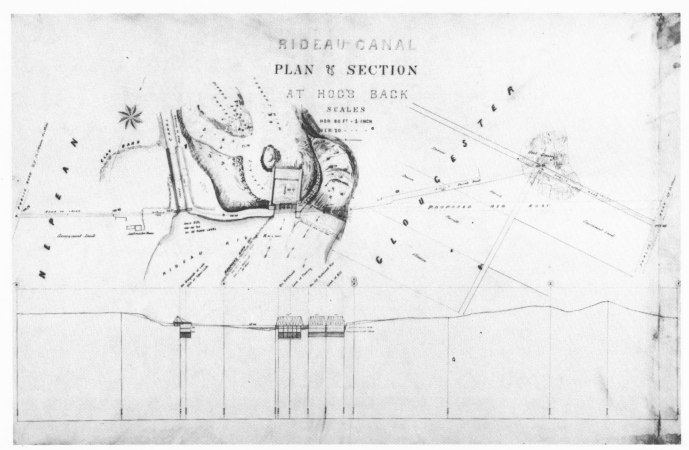

Plan and section at Hogs Back, Rideau Canal.
(National Map Collection, Public Archives of Canada).

Plan of the dam and locks at Black Rapids, Rideau Canal.
(National Map Collection, Public Archives of Canada).

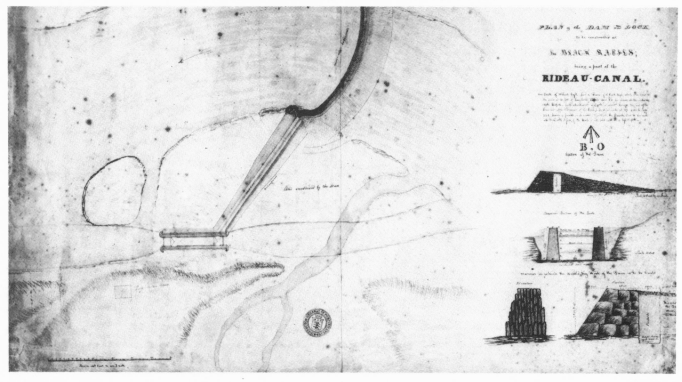

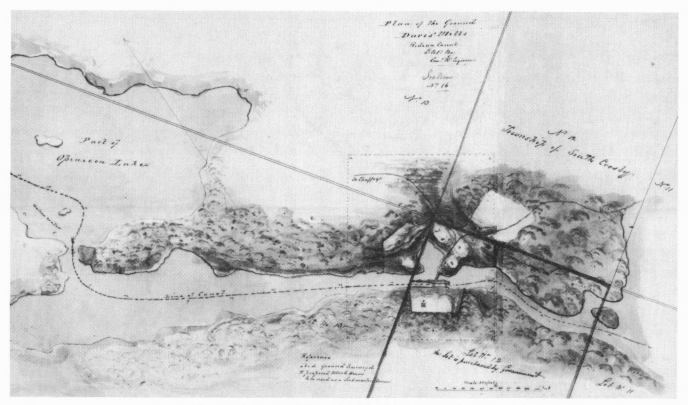

Plan of the ground Davis' Mills, Rideau Canal, 1830.
(National Map Collection, Public Archives of Canada)

Survey of the works of the Rideau Canal and adjacent ground
Smiths Falls, 1830.
(National Map Collection, Public Archives of Canada)

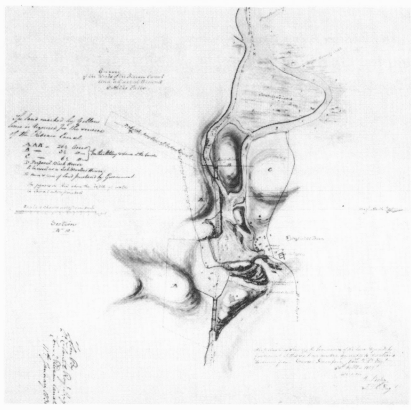

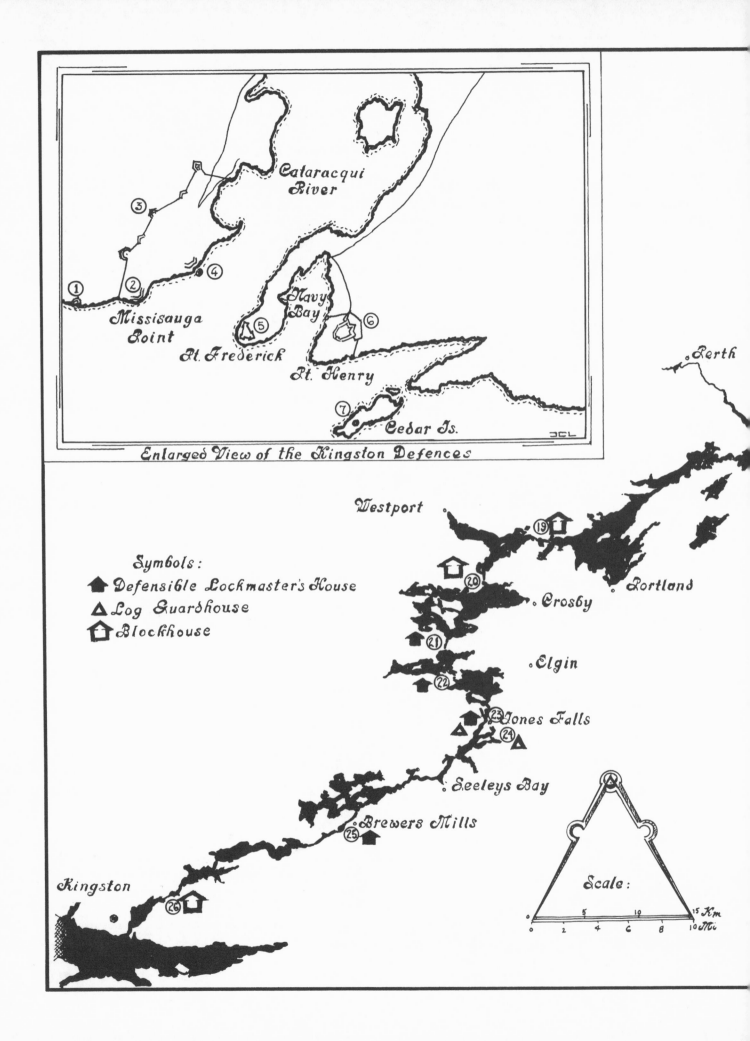

Enlarged View of the Kingston Defences

Cataracqui River

Missisauga Point

Navy Bay

Pt. Frederick

Pt. Henry

Cedar Is.

JCL

Perth

Westport

Portland

Crosby

Elgin

Jones Falls

Seeleys Bay

Brewers Mills

Kingston

Symbols:

🏠 Defensible Lockmaster's House

△ Log Guardhouse

⌂ Blockhouse

Scale:

0   5   10   15 Km
0   2   4   6   8   10 Mi.

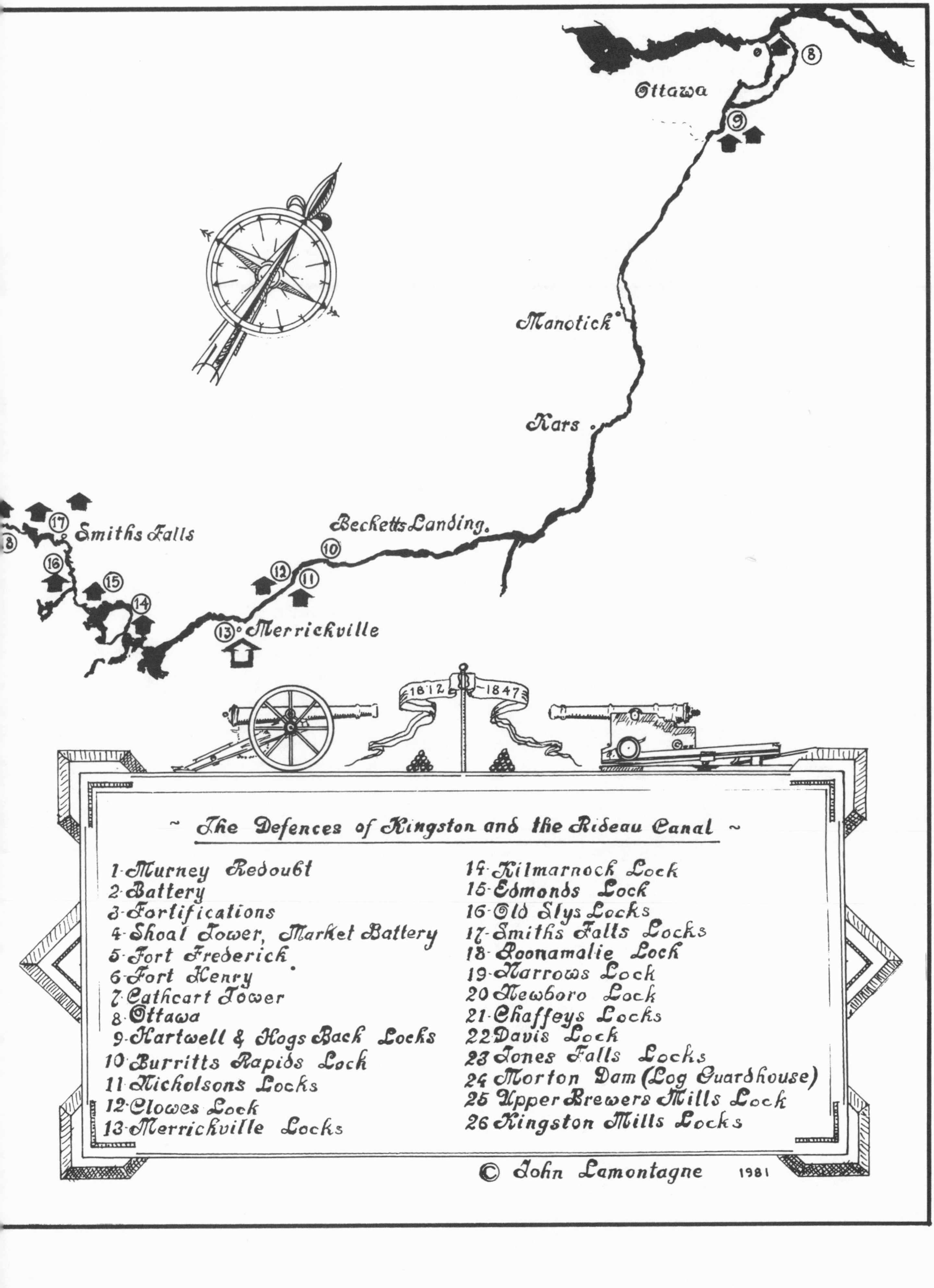

Ottawa

⑧

⑨

Manotick

Kars

⑰ Smiths Falls   Becketts Landing.

⑧   ⑩
⑯   ⑫ ⑪
      ⑮
            ⑭
            ⑬ Merrickville

1812 — 1847

~ The Defences of Kingston and the Rideau Canal ~

1·Murney Redoubt
2·Battery
3·Fortifications
4·Shoal Tower, Market Battery
5·Fort Frederick
6·Fort Henry
7·Cathcart Tower
8·Ottawa
9·Hartwell & Hogs Back Locks
10·Burritts Rapids Lock
11·Nicholsons Locks
12·Clowes Lock
13·Merrickville Locks

14·Kilmarnock Lock
15·Edmonds Lock
16·Old Slys Locks
17·Smiths Falls Locks
18·Poonamalie Lock
19·Narrows Lock
20·Newboro Lock
21·Chaffeys Locks
22·Davis Lock
23·Jones Falls Locks
24·Morton Dam (Log Guardhouse)
25·Upper Brewers Mills Lock
26·Kingston Mills Locks

© John Lamontagne   1981

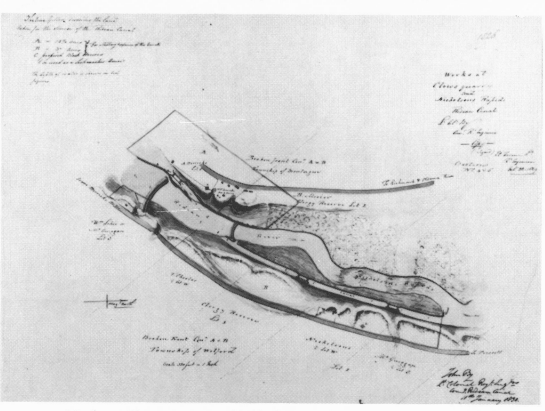

Works at Clowes quarry and Nicholsons Rapids, Rideau Canal, 1830.
(National Map Collection, Public Archives of Canada)

Survey of Long Island, Rideau Canal; showing the land to be purchased, 1830.
(National Map Collection, Public Archives of Canada).

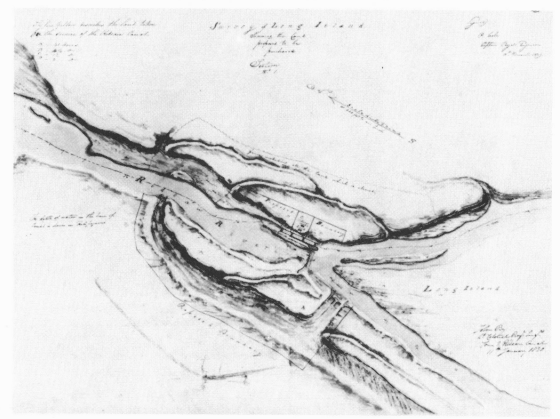

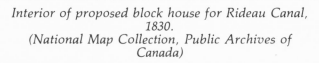

Elevation of proposed block house for Rideau
· Canal, 1830.
(National Map Collection, Public Archives of
Canada)

Interior of proposed block house for Rideau Canal,
1830.
(National Map Collection, Public Archives of
Canada)

Works at Merricks Mills, Rideau Canal, 1830.
(National Map Collection, Public Archives of Canada)

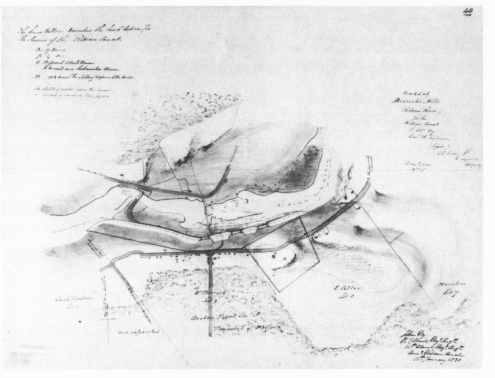

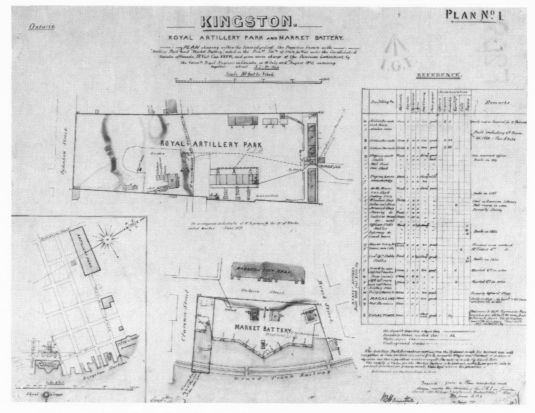

Royal Artillery Park and Market Battery, Kingston, 1871.
(National Map Collection, Public Archives of Canada)

Market Battery, Kingston, Ontario, 1851.
(National Map Collection, Public Archives of Canada)

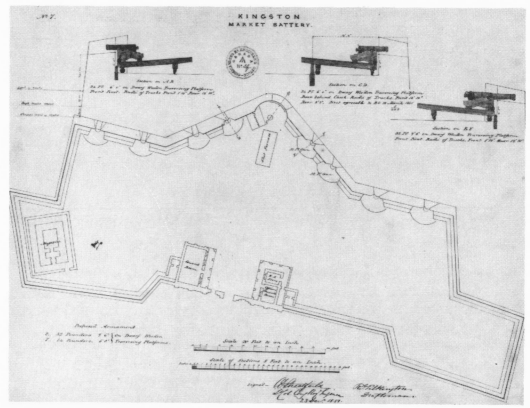

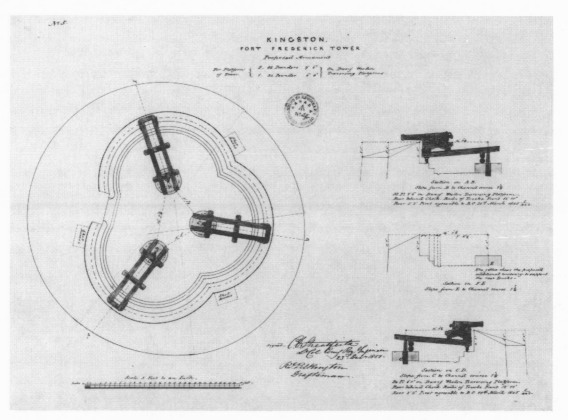

Proposed armament for Fort Frontenac Tower, Kingston, 1857.
(National Map Collection, Public Archives of Canada)

Interior and exterior of Murney Redoubt, Kingston.
(National Map Collection, Public Archives of Canada)

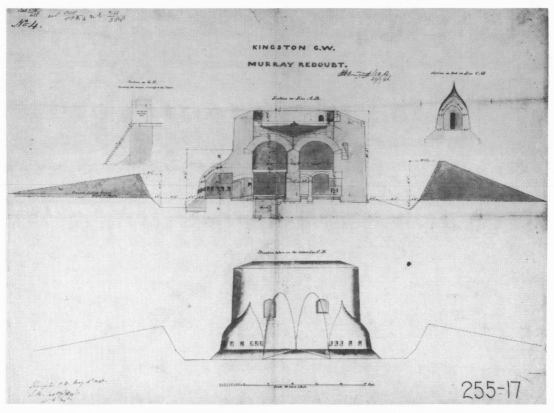

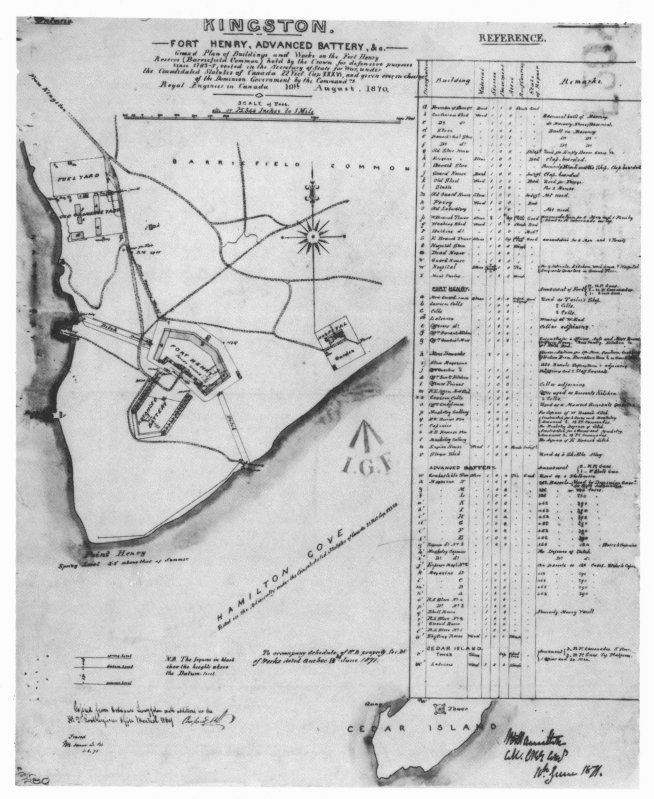

*Ground plan of buildings and works of Fort Henry, Kingston.
(National Map Collection, Public Archives of Canada)*

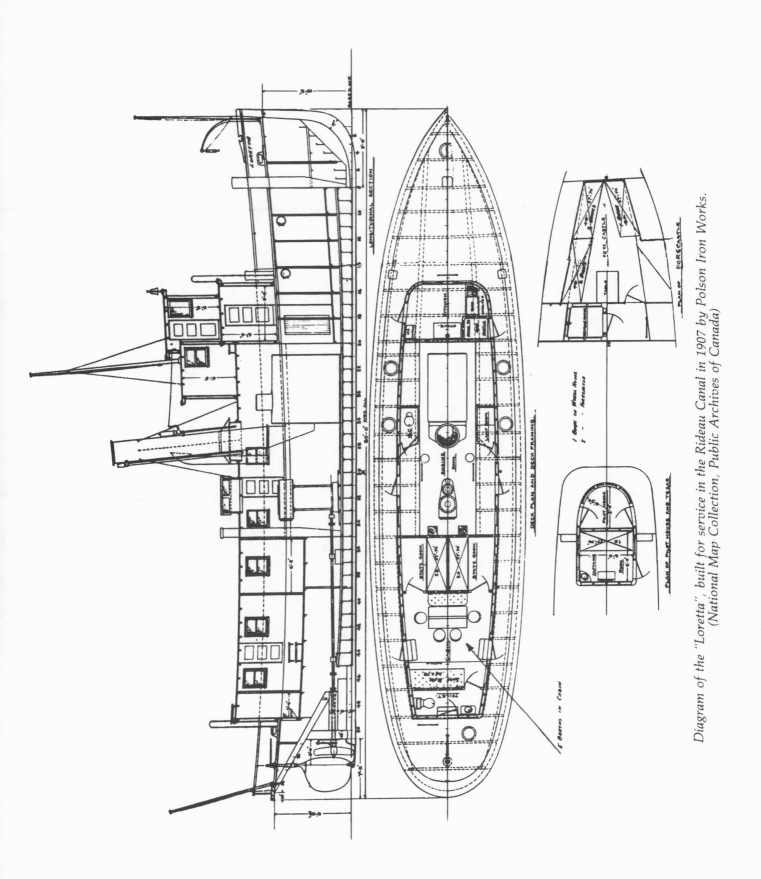

Diagram of the "Loretta", built for service in the Rideau Canal in 1907 by Polson Iron Works. (National Map Collection, Public Archives of Canada)

The Anatomy of a Lock

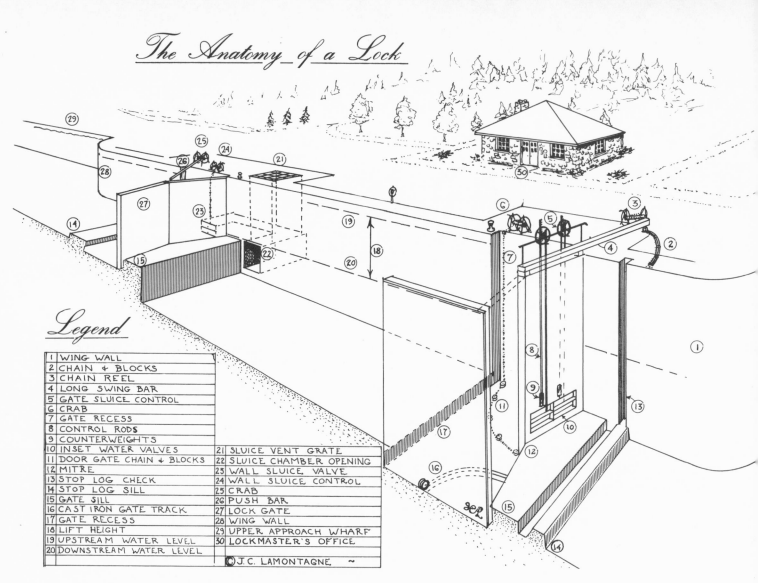

Legend

1	WING WALL
2	CHAIN & BLOCKS
3	CHAIN REEL
4	LONG SWING BAR
5	GATE SLUICE CONTROL
6	CRAB
7	GATE RECESS
8	CONTROL RODS
9	COUNTERWEIGHTS
10	INSET WATER VALVES
11	DOOR GATE CHAIN & BLOCKS
12	MITRE
13	STOP LOG CHECK
14	STOP LOG SILL
15	GATE SILL
16	CAST IRON GATE TRACK
17	GATE RECESS
18	LIFT HEIGHT
19	UPSTREAM WATER LEVEL
20	DOWNSTREAM WATER LEVEL

21	SLUICE VENT GRATE
22	SLUICE CHAMBER OPENING
23	WALL SLUICE VALVE
24	WALL SLUICE CONTROL
25	CRAB
26	PUSH BAR
27	LOCK GATE
28	WING WALL
29	UPPER APPROACH WHARF
30	LOCKMASTER'S OFFICE

© J.C. LAMONTAGNE ~

Anatomy of a Lock.

Workings of a Lock.

LOCKING DOWNSTREAM

1. LOCK GATES CLOSED
2. LOWER GATE VALVES OPENED
3. WATER LEVEL DESCENDS

LOCKING UPSTREAM

1. LOCK GATES CLOSED
2. SLUICE VALVES OPENED
3. WATER LEVEL RISES

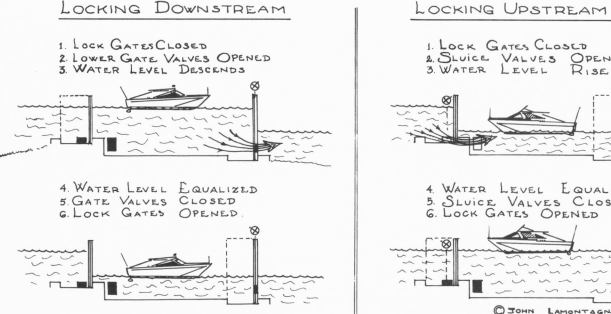
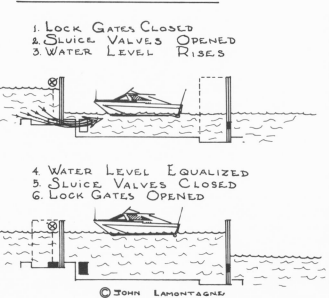

4. WATER LEVEL EQUALIZED
5. GATE VALVES CLOSED
6. LOCK GATES OPENED.

4. WATER LEVEL EQUALIZED
5. SLUICE VALVES CLOSED
6. LOCK GATES OPENED

© JOHN LAMONTAGNE

Rideau Falls, Ottawa, Canada West—1864.
(Public Archives of Canada—C18683).

Bytown.
(Public Archives of Canada—C2813).

to navigate the Rideau and Cataraqui Rivers, the intervening lakes, as well as the sections of man-made canal.

The classic Rideau steamboat had a wooden hull, one watertight deck and a rounded stern. The frame was also of wood, although in some of the later ones it was of iron or a composite of both, and still later of steel. All were sidewheelers, as opposed to a stern paddlewheel. Over the years 52 steamboats were built in Kingston, Portsmouth, Battersea, Wolfe and Garden Islands for the Rideau service. A few came from yards in Montreal, and 15 from Ottawa and Hull. Another seven were built at Brockville, while 12 steamers and 74 barges were built along the waterway proper. Of these, eight steamers and 46 barges came from boatyards at Bedford Mills, on Devil Lake, which flows into Newboro Lake.

The engines tended to come from farther afield. A few were built at Kingston or Bytown, but more often they were imported from American port cities, Montreal or Toronto, and at least one came from Scotland. The earliest to be installed in Canadian steamboats were built in England. These were low-pressure engines and not very powerful, with a single cylinder and popular until technology improved, for they were quiet and fairly safe. The first boilers were merely water tanks encased in brickwork and susceptible to explosion. The engines were the low-stroke type with low-speed piston action. A walking beam with vertical connecting rods protruded above the deck. Although a screw propellor had been developed by 1827, these were not used for some time on the Rideau. The paddle wheels had a shallower draft, and, an added advantage, wheels could operate as well in reverse as forward.

Lock at Parliament Hill, Ottawa, ca. 1870.
The lock is being used as a drydock.
(Ontario Archives).

Tug "Ranger" built in Kingston in 1888, in the Rideau Canal.
(Ontario Archives).

Lower Lock Rideau Canal, Kingston Mills, Ontario, ca. 1880.
(Public Archives of Canada—PA8883).

Little is known about the earliest steamboats on the waterway, because the lockmasters were not required to keep complete records until the mid 1840s when safety standards, inspection and registration came into force. By 1837, however, a craft operating an hour before sundown or dawn was required to show a bow light.

Once the canal was open, Philomen Wright's steamer *Union of the Ottawa*, built in 1819, cruised along the Rideau, joining Robert Drummond's *Pumper*. In 1840, at the boatyard of Macpherson and Crane in Kingston, the *Beaver* was launched and assumed bi-weekly service between Kingston and Bytown. She measured 104 feet long and 17 feet wide, weighed 55 tons, and was retained by the firm who built her for the forwarding business. At least two boats were named *Bytown*. One was built at Kars at the mouth of Stevens Creek by Richard Garlick, before 1840; the other at Montreal in 1842, by Macpherson and Crane, which had a boatyard there as well as the one at Kingston and another at Prescott. Other steamers mentioned were the *Hunter* and the *Mohawk*.

All these steamers towed barges. One report showed the *Hunter* pulling 24 on a trip through the canal, but the usual number was from 6 to 16. Barges were locked through in pairs, and from the opening until 1840, traffic increased steadily, even though it did not draw off as much trade from the St. Lawrence as Colonel John By had hoped. Immigrants were the exception among passengers, because the rates were lower. A person could go by the Rideau for four shillings, while the fare from Kingston to Niagara through York, in 1819, was £3, and from York to Niagara £1. Those who could afford to pay extra preferred the larger steamers of the St. Lawrence, and the stagecoaches that carried them past the sets of rapids.

The Rideau was of greatest value to the lumber trade at a time when settlers were clearing their lands in the adjacent townships, and lumbermen were cutting trees on land leased for the purpose. Rafts passed through the locks to Bytown, or to sawmills along the canal route, and many were built large enough to fill an entire lock. Sawn lumber exited from the Rideau country

Steamer "D. C. West" at Jones Falls, ca. 1880. Built 1874 in Clayton, New York.
(Public Archives of Canada—PA8829).

through Kingston and the Ottawa River to markets in the United States, Montreal and overseas. Lumber continued an important source of wealth until on into the twentieth century, and in the early days of the canal, potash provided cash income to farmers clearing their fields. Despite the stimulus the canal gave the lumber trade, it was apparent even before the St. Lawrence canals were in operation that the British government would never recoup the cost of building the Rideau Canal. While the volume of trade was a disappointment, the same could not be said of the waterway's other unfulfilled purpose. Only for a brief time was it pressed into military service.

Before Colonel John By left Canada he recommended 22 lock stations, each supervised by a lockmaster at a salary of 7 shillings sixpence per day. Later the stations were classified according to the amount of work involved in running them. Only Kingston Mills was considered a first class station, and the lockmaster received 4 shillings sixpence per day, far short of what Colonel John felt appropriate. Those at Bytown, Long Island, Merrickville, Smiths Falls, Jones

Falls and Brewers Upper Mills were second class, the lockmasters paid four shillings per day. All other stations were third class, and at these the lockmasters received three shillings sixpence per day.

Each lockmaster was provided with a house—the blockhouse if a station had one. At the lock stations that were not fortified, he occupied a more modest dwelling. At all stations he was also permitted to plant a small garden on government property. In 1847, the lockmasters were issued with the military uniforms to give them an aura of authority, in keeping with the potential defence function.

This uniform consisted of a blue jacket with scarlet collar and cuffs, a crown emblem on the right sleeve, grey trousers, blue cap with a scarlet band, and a blue greatcoat with a scarlet collar. The entire outfit was valued at £2. 19s. 8d., and the following year it became compulsory. That suited many of the lockmasters, who were either retired canal workers or disbanded Royal Sappers and Miners. Later the wearing of the uniform was not mandatory, and in time the practice was discontinued.

Tug "Hiram Easton" at Merrickville where it was built.
(Public Archives of Canada—C54508).

The life of a lockmaster was very demanding when the waterway was open. He was on duty round the clock, depending on the traffic. When heavy he and his labourers napped while the locks were filling, and had their meals brought to them. For hours on end they manned the crabs, opening and closing the wooden gates from early spring until late fall—seven to eight months. They must have looked forward to the quiet of winter, although there is some doubt as to whether their pay continued when the waterway was icebound. The grace and favour dwelling may have been deemed sufficient remuneration by the Ordnance Department and later the Board of Works.

The building of the canal had another beneficial side effect on the surrounding countryside. Many of the stone cutters and masons who had emigrated from Scotland remained after the work was finished. These skilled craftsmen and the Canadians they had trained built most of the fine stone houses and public buildings that date from the 1830s and 40s. Because of slow growth in the

towns and villages of late, most have not been demolished to make way for more modern premises, and the rich architectural heritage remains intact. The finest buildings in Kingston and Perth, and the smaller villages, and the neat, symmetrical farmhouses dotted about the townships are a tribute to the men who fashioned the huge blocks of the Jones Falls dam and the many lock walls. Contractors Phillips and White returned to the Montreal area once the canal was finished, but Thomas Mackay settled near Bytown, and built the first Court House there.

The canal gave birth indirectly to a distinctive urban landscape, one that like the locks themselves and the steamboats built to navigate them, was on a small scale. The setting was serene, the politics and participants rowdy, and the atmosphere warming up as quarreling in the Legislative Assembly of Upper Canada between the Conservatives and Reformers mounted. The behaviour of the rebels, and certain interfering Americans, set the stage for a defence which the Duke of Wellington had foreseen.

2. 1837-1840: a Time of Crisis

When the fiery topped diminutive William Lyon Mackenzie engineered the rebellion that opened with his march down Toronto's Yonge Street in December, 1837, the Rideau country was not in the line of fire, with one exception. Little Mac's wife had relatives at Barriefield, and in Kingston was an enthusiastic band of reformers. Notable among the leaders were the Bidwells—Marshall Spring and Barnabas—and Dr. Edward Barker. The last named ran a newspaper called the British Whig, which came to the same end as Mackenzie's Colonial Advocate. Supporters of the Family Compact—the ruling clique—smashed Mackenzie's press in Toronto, and the same kind of arrogant young bucks destroyed Barker's in Kingston. Their opposition to the reformers was organized by Colonel Sir Richard Bonnycastle, of the Royal Artillery.

He martialed the Frontenac Militia to keep order, because the regular troops of the Kingston garrison had been sent to Lower Canada, where the rebellion had broken out earlier. In February, 1838, Mackenzie, who had fled to New York State following his unsuccessful attempt to take over the government in Toronto, plotted to capture Kingston. He went to Hickory Island, near Clayton, New York, where he expected to be joined by 600 Americans calling themselves Patriots—as the rebels had done during the American Revolution. The Patriots had formed secret societies called Hunters' Lodges, whose avowed intent was the liberation of Canada from the tyranny of British rule. When word of Mackenzie's presence reached Kingston, Bonnycastle and his militia were ready. Meanwhile, on Hickory Island, the members of the Hunters' Lodges showed that they had more bark than bite, and when scarcely 300 showed up, Mackenzie, aware that he would meet some opposition, called off the attack in disgust, and the emergency ended.

Inland along the Rideau Waterway, although grievances were as irksome as elsewhere, and many people favoured reforms, few were ready to resort to force of arms. Two-sevenths of all the land had been set aside for the support of the clergy and Crown, leaving blank spots among the farms. Since 1824, many of the Crown reserves had been sold off, ending that source of irritation, but the clergy reserves remained a thorn in the flesh of the settlers. Yet the nature of the people and their situation both decreed that they look with disapproval at Mackenzie's rebels. Some residents, notably the lumbermen, were doing well, and the half-pay officers in the military settlements kept their own followers unswervingly loyal. As the Duke of Wellington had predicted, these officers raised militia companies and stood ready to quell uprisings in other parts of Upper Canada, or to chase out the American Patriot Hunters. Another element was the Yankee population that believed in government by discussion and insisted on reform through the political process.

Lastly, the frontier itself helped prevent a local uprising. In mythology, families who had been loyal during the American Revolution have been credited with exercising a moderating hand on affairs, but this assumption is only half true. If they were contented they remained steadfast, if not they were rebels, and many sons and grandsons did join Mackenzie. During the American Revolution, frontiersmen on the fringes of Pennsylvania and New York were usually loyalists, and the same applied to most of the frontiersmen in the Rideau country. Busy establishing themselves, they had more immediate concerns than the nature of their provincial government. A few Americans who did feel strongly left the country.

Only in one place was there evidence of Patriot Hunter activity. Members of the Hunters' Lodges in the northern United States were convinced that an epidemic of lodge forming was taking place in Upper Canada. One of the few communities known to have members in that secret society was Kemptville, but all kept their heads down. When the trouble ended, the paymaster used lodge funds to build a stone house which he operated as an inn.

At Richmond, predictably, the half-pay officers formed a militia company under the superintendent of the settlement, Colonel George Thew Burke. At Bytown, where some British regulars were stationed, a company of volunteers was formed and drilled by Sergeant Law, of the 60th Regiment, while at Fort Henry, Sir Richard Bonnycastle commanded the Frontenac Militia. The militia companies of Leeds and Grenville were also mustered, and Thomas Mackay became a Colonel in the Russell County Militia. The

Blacksmith's forge and residence, erected 1832, Burritts Rapids, Ontario. June 15, 1925.
(Public Archives of Canada—PA26976).

onetime contractor had founded the mill village of New Edinburgh, in Gloucester Township, at the mouth of the Rideau River. At that time Gloucester was part of Russell, although it was later placed in Carleton. Mackay's was the only unit that was moved out of the Rideau area, to do duty on the St. Lawrence front.

Shortly before the alarm perpetrated by Mackenzie, Mackay had begun work on a fine stone Regency villa, which he completed in 1838. For a time it was called Mackay's Castle, and it stood on a tract of bush which he owned. Later he changed the name of his home to Rideau Hall. Today, after many alterations, it remains the residence of Canada's governor-general, and Mackay's Bush has become the fashionable Rockcliffe Park, the best address in Ottawa.

The uprising Mackenzie fomented is still known as the Rebellion of 1837, but the crisis did not subside until 1840, owing to the interest of the American Hunters' Lodges of New York and Vermont. The members caused a number of border incidents. The most serious was the Battle of Windmill Point, near Prescott in November, 1838; the

silliest and last, when they blew the top of General Brock's monument at Queenston Heights in 1840. Because of the activities and schemes of the Canadian rebels and American Patriots, for nearly three years the Rideau Canal was used to rush troops to the front.

Sir John Colborne ordered the blockhouses garrisoned at Kingston Mills and Merrickville, lest the rebels or any of their American compatriots attempted to damage the canal works. Detachments of regular troops and militia occupied all the blockhouses, while more militiamen kept watch at Chaffeys Lock. In 1838, two gunboats passed along the canal, and Durham boats or large row galleys carried British regulars between Bytown and Kingston. In May, 1840, the record shows that the steamboat *Bytown*—the one built at the mouth of Stevens Creek—carried some of the 65th Regiment to Kingston. Other records indicate that detachments of regulars travelled between Kingston and Montreal through the Rideau Canal following the start of the rebellion. Thus, the Duke of Wellington's plan for the waterway was, briefly, fulfilled.

Isthmus 25th December

Major Loppor

Sir   According to your Orders
I have musterd the Company at the Isthmus
and have Called for Volenters, In behalve
of Mr Ogle R Gowan, the general part of
they Company do not like Mr Gowans
principles, but are all mostely willing
to Volenter for the _Queen_ and _Conectitution_
     the foling are the names of Mr Gowars
       Volenters

Hugh Stevenson	The.
Richard Grothen	Number of North Coosbery
William Bell	Comy is One hunderd
James Green Junr	and five Ithony. the
John Bennot	were all present but one
Abraham Brine	person the name of
Abraham Bell	Charals Reid, miller
John Molton	105
Patrick Dovany Sor	
Joseph Barker	I am Sir your most
Arthur Clendening	Obdt Servant
Charals Kennedy	Servt James Bilton
Robert Barker	
John Mc Alister	
Timothy Cavanor	
Isaac McCartheny	
James Conely	
Thomas Littel	
John McDonald	
Obidiae Reid Senr	

*Muster roll of the men living near the
Isthmus on the Rideau during the
Rebellion of 1837.
(Public Archives of Canada—Charles
Jones Papers, Vol. I).*

Kingston Mills Grist Mill.
(Queen's University Archives).

3. Settlement at Mid Century

The opening of the Rideau Canal corresponded with the era when the townships along the St. Lawrence and Lake Ontario, which people called the Front, were nearly filled up. The Rideau country was the next place where settlers began applying for grants of land. Along the Canadian Shield portion between Kingston and Smiths Falls the land fit for cultivation was spotty, and a short distance eastward lay a limestone plain, the soil thin over the bedrock. Both conditions prevented the development of a farming community comparable with the lower Rideau River. At the same time, among the granite rock knobs in the western half of the waterway there was no shortage of waterfalls for powersites.

Some of the new arrivals were second or third generation loyalists whose families had been living in the front row of townships since 1784. Others were a mix of American and British stock, but by far the largest single group were Irish people, assisted to emigrate because of the great potato famines of the 1840s, the majority Roman Catholic. A less severe famine in 1821 had resulted in the emigration of a few families who came into the Rideau country, a forewarning of events to come. Following the more serious crop failures, the half starved Irish were herded aboard every conceivable sailing vessel, many quite unfit for human conveyance, even for a short time, let alone weeks on storm-tossed seas. The poorest and most wretched came into the neighbourhood as labourers, but those better off took up the remaining lots throughout the townships. The Census of 1861, which gives the religious affiliation opposite each person's name, shows a substantial increase in the number of Roman Catholics over 1841, a guarantee that the Loyal Orange Lodges would be no less militant than they were earlier. In their eyes, the Italian Pope's flock was a threat to the security of the state, the imperial connection, the monarchy itself.

Throughout the townships the settlers sold timber and grain at first, but they soon discovered that their land was more suited to grazing, with some fodder crops where the soil was deep enough. Elsewhere they grew hay and pastured cattle and sheep. Wool and milk were important cash crops, and since the markets were small and remote, production of cheese and woollen cloth became vital local industries. Soon each village had at least one cheese factory, and at many of the powersites, carding, fulling and woollen mills were to be found.

The first industry in any township was

Log cutting near Westport in winter.
(The Roberts Family, Westport).

usually a sawmill at a waterfall, to square timber and cut boards for local settlers and the lumber trade. Next, an entrepreneur built grist mills to grind wheat that was the first cash crop grown. Next in the sequence were carding mills. Homespun cloth was woven in the settlers' cabins, and this process prepared the wool for spinning, eliminating one unpleasant task. Later mills took over the whole operation of cloth making, and some specialized in a variety of wood products, such as shingles. Another business likely to be present in the mill villages was a distillery, or a brewery or two. At every farm, as logs were cut, the members of the household made potash, a valuable source of cash, and each spring farmers boiled maple sap for sugar to last all year. Also present in small quantities were phosphate, mica and iron deposits, which were exploited for a short time.

Commencing at the Frontenac County end of the waterway, in Pittsburgh Township, Barriefield, named for the commodore, stood high on a hill overlooking the Cataraqui River. The other population centre was Kingston Mills. The first was oriented towards Lake Ontario, the second attracted attention early because of the powersite, and the mills were erected by the government to serve the earliest loyalist settlers. Kingston Mills was the exception that proved the rule.

Because it was so close to Kingston, a thriving commercial centre, this millsite did not attract many tradesmen and craftsmen. Most preferred to locate in the larger community.

In Storrington, which was part of Pittsburgh, Kingston and Loughborough Townships until 1850, settlers had begun taking up land twenty years earlier. The only urban place was Battersea, at first called Van Luven's Mills after the miller Henry van Luven. A boatyard supplied barges for the Rideau Canal, and when the township was established, Henry van Luven was the first reeve. As he prospered he hired stonemasons, recently retired from work on the canal. to build him a fine house. Most of the settlers and tradesmen who located in the village were from second and third generation loyalist families who had been living in the front townships.

In Leeds County, in the rear of the township of the same name, the first port of call on the waterway was Seeleys Bay. The founder, Justus Seeley, was a drummer boy in Captain Justus Sherwood's company, Loyal Rangers. An item in Sherwood's account book for the winter of 1783, when he commanded a blockhouse on an island in Lake Champlain, showed that he purchased "1 pr skaits" for Seeley so that he could travel more rapidly along the ice. In 1784,

131

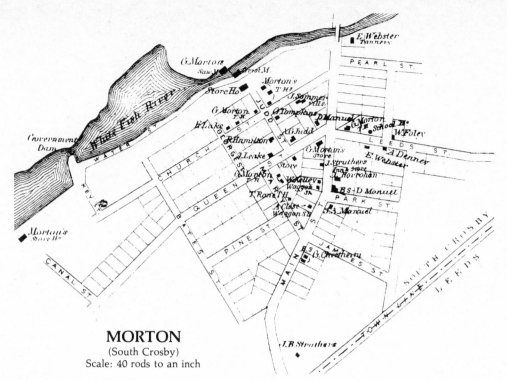

MORTON
(South Crosby)
Scale: 40 rods to an inch

From H. F. Walling's map of the Counties of Leeds and Grenville, C.W., 1861-62.

Seeley settled in Augusta Township, on the St. Lawrence, and he moved to the shore of Little Cranberry Lake, above the marsh, in 1825. Seeley set up a trading post, and for a time his only customers were Indians. He died in 1828, and his family continued operating the store. By 1839, Seeleys Bay had become a lumber port, and a place where potash was trans-shipped from the canal to wagons for the road journey to the St. Lawrence. The village also boasted a school somewhat earlier than was usual in a new community.

Just inside the Township of South Crosby was Morton, originally called Whitefish Creek because it grew beside a stream that flows into Whitefish Lake. (Disease wiped out this species of fish in 1888.) Later the village was named in honour of George Morton, who operated a cheese factory and had a farm nearby. Like most other villages Morton had a powersite and mills. Elgin, a short distance inland, was a crossroads community which boasted a cheese factory, as well as a potash works, churches and a school. For a while the village was called Nauvoo, after the Mormon community founded by Joseph Smith in Illinois in 1839. (This religion enjoyed brief popularity among certain local people, because of its exclusively new world roots.) The modern name derived from the

first man appointed Governor-General of Canada, James Bruce, the 8th Earl of Elgin, who arrived in January, 1847, at Montreal, the capital city at that time. On the shore of Mud (Newboro) Lake, still in South Crosby, was Singleton's Corners, named for William Singleton, on whose land it developed. Later the name was changed to Crosby. On the main road between Brockville and Upper Rideau Lake, the village was a port on the waterway.

Towards the west end of Opinicon Lake around another powersite a village had grown. There John Poole built a sawmill and was soon followed by Thomas Cook, who put up a flourmill. Named Opinicon, this community's prosperity was enhanced by a nearby phosphate mine which belonged to the Canada Company. That organization was better known for land development in the more westerly parts of the province, but it had purchased the Crown reserves everywhere after 1827, and brought some settlers in to occupy the scattered lots along the Rideau Waterway. With the opening of the canal, Opinicon flourished as a port from which barges carried phosphate, timber and flour to Kingston. For a time the village was the home of a commercial fishery, and the catch was also exported through Kingston.

Due north, at the west end of Devil

Morton dam and guardhouse with the patrol boat "Shanly" built by R. G. Waters of Ottawa in 1890, owned by the Department of Railways and Canals.
(Parks Canada).

Chaffeys Mill at Chaffeys Lock.

Lake, which empties into Newboro Lake, the interesting community of Bedford Mills was a hive of activity largely owing to the enterprise of Benjamin Tett, his sons, and the Chaffey brothers of Brockville. (The family is best known for Benjamin Chaffey's work on the Victoria Bridge in Montreal and the Brockville Court House, and for George Junior's designs for irrigation works at Ontario, California, and the Murray River in Australia.) Until 1835, when the village got a post office, it was known as Buttermilk Falls, and the newer name commemorated the Duke of Bedford. Here the Chaffey brothers, John, George, William, Benjamin, Samuel and Elswood, built mills and opened a shipyard that built steamboats and barges for use on the canal.

Benjamin Tett, who had built two blockhouses, and whose home was in Newboro, had leased the land from the government in 1831, and he sublet it to the Chaffeys for their sawmill. Colonel John By had purchased the sawmill at the site of Chaffey's Lock for £2,000 as it was damaged during canal construction. At Bedford Mills the Chaffeys added a flourmill, and in 1834, they sold their mills to Benjamin Tett and retained the boatyard. Later Samuel Chaffey left Bedford Mills and built a woollen mill near the lock bearing his name, not far from the site of the mill his family lost. Bedford Mills was also a lumbering centre, and the Chaffeys opened a store, ran a boarding house and built rental houses for workers. Later mica was extracted from the rocks in the vicinity.

On the border of the Township of North Crosby the village of Newboro was growing. It was first called The Isthmus and later New Borough, on the portage between Newboro Lake and Upper Rideau Lake. Canal workers cut a channel across this stretch of land, thereby linking the watershed of the Cataraqui River with that of the Rideau. At the Narrows between Big Rideau and Upper Rideau Lakes, Colonel John By had constructed the dam to raise the water level of the latter lake by nearly four feet. This reduced the amount of excavating his workers had to cut at The Isthmus. During canal construction Newboro had 60 buildings, and a hospital for the victims of lake fever. Like the village of Crosby, Newboro was on the stagecoach road, and it had a tollgate where each vehicle was charged 10¢ per journey.

Newboro had no powersite, and it grew as a convenient focal point for the canal workers on the lakes. Several of the carpenters' and blacksmiths' shops located there. In 1833, the population was 300, larger than most of the hamlets, and the property owners had held their first town meeting two years before. Elswood, Benjamin and John Chaffey owned two small iron mines in the neighbourhood. One was on an island in Newboro Lake, a mile from the village and linked to the mainland by a causeway. The other, called the Yankee Mine because of a former American owner named Fitfield, was on a farm the Chaffeys had bought. Bog iron was removed from a number of sites in Leeds County, but the quantities were so small that the operations were hardly economic.

Newboro

The settlement of this area was begun during the building of the Rideau Canal in 1826-32. In 1833 Benjamin Tett, owner of a nearby sawmill, opened a store and three years later a Post Office named 'Newborough' was established. A small community including several stores gradually developed as a trade centre for the region's lumbering industry and agriculture.

About 1850 a tannery was established and within ten years two iron mines had been opened in the vicinity. The ore was exported via the Rideau Canal to smelters in the United States. Growth was further stimulated by the erection of a foundry and a steam sawmill and in 1876 Newboro was incorporated as a village.

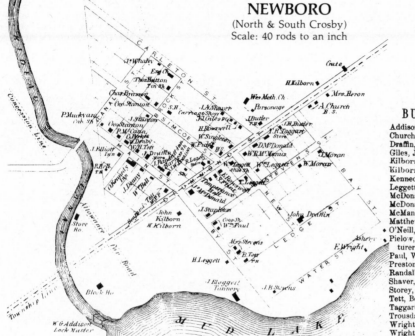

NEWBORO
(North & South Crosby)
Scale: 40 rods to an inch

NEWBORO BUSINESS DIRECTORY.

Addison, W. G., Lockmaster
Church, A., Blacksmith, N. Crosby
Draffin, John, Merchant
Giles, J. J., Post Master, Saddlery and Harness
Kilborn. John, Gent.
Kilborn. H., Clerk of 8th Div. Court
Kennedy, Owen, Hotel Keeper
Leggett, J. B., Tanner and Currier
McDonald, Daniel, General Merchant
McDonald, James, General Merchant
McManus, W. B., Tailor
Matthews, S. H. & Co., Miners, &c.
O'Neill, John, Blacksmith
Pielow, William, Saddle and Harness Manufacturer
Paul, William, Cooper
Preston, J. W., Saddle & Harness manufacturer
Randall, Jared. Inn Keeper
Shaver, J. A., Carriage Manufacturer
Storey, C., General Merchant
Tett, Benjamin, M. P. P.
Taggart, Thomas R., General merchant
Trousdale, J. D., M. D., Physician
Wright, Edward, Carpenter
Wright, S., Watchmaker and Jeweler

From H.F. Walling's map of the Counties of Leeds and Grenville, C.W., 1861-62.

Newboro, prior to 1900.
(The Roberts Family, Westport).

Bedford Mills

Bedford Mills flourished between 1830 and 1860 as a centre of lumbering and boat building. The village was first called Buttermilk Falls, after the cascade where a "squatter" mill was built in 1829 by two entrepreneurs, Barnet and Legg. This mill stood on Devil Lake above the falls, on Lot 12, Concession 14, a clergy reserve. On August 10, 1831, Benjamin Tett of Newboro received a government lease at £1,15s or 10½ bushels of wheat per annum. Tett employed Barnet and Legg as sawyers.

By 1834, the mill was using logs from 2,000 acres around Devil Lake, and in operation 24 hours a day. Tett introduced upright "gang" saws to keep up with demand. His brother William Tett rafted lumber to Montreal. Benjamin Tett opened a store, built a boarding house and sleeping annex for his workers, and enlarged the mill. In 1847, Tett formed a partnership with George Chaffey, and the two partners rented the Tett facilities at an annual rate of £500. The following year Tett built a new mill with circular and upright saws, and later he added a grist and flour mill near the east wharf. The contract for this mill went to William Chaffey, one of George's brothers.

In 1851, Benjamin Tett and George Chaffey disolved their partnership. The several Chaffey brothers renewed the lease and carried on. Although operations were reduced after the local timber was exhausted, the mills, boatyard and other commercial activities related to them continued until the first decade of the 20th century. For many

This version of The Bedford Mill was built in 1846-47, the building was used as a general store from 1945-1970 under the name of Ruby's Store.

years the building was used as a well known local store called Ruby's. Presently it is a private residence. As the mills closed down, the villagers left, and today Bedford Mills is one of Ontario's most picturesque ghost towns.
—From a paper by David Roberts, 1971.

Bedford Mills ca. 1890, left to right: General Store on the hill, Bedford Mill to left of pine tree, Tug Edmond (built 1879 on the right.)
(Howard G. Pain).

Bedford Mills c. 1890. General store on the hill, shingle mill, elevator and grist mill.
(The Roberts Family, Westport).

Bedford Mills 1907. Left to right: Boarding house, work bell, sleeping quarters, store, elevator, grist mill, lumber shed, Geo. Tett residence, lumber shed and St. Stephens Anglican Church.
(The Roberts Family, Westport).

Westport, Ontario with the tannery in the left foreground.
(The Roberts Family, Westport).

In the Township of North Crosby, Westport, between Upper Rideau and Sand Lakes, was surveyed in 1803, by Reubin Sherwood. A few settlers came after 1810, and in 1817, Sherwood, in partnership with Sheldon Stoddard, was operating a sawmill. Two other businessmen, Aaron Chambers and Gabriel Forrester, hired crews of French Canadians and Scotsmen to raft logs to the Ottawa River for the Montreal timber market. By 1827, three brothers, William, Peter and David Manhard, had arrived from Elizabethtown, on the St. Lawrence, and were building a sawmill on an island near the village. Joel Clark later operated a carding and woollen mill, while William Fredenburg was prominent in the early life of the community. Born in Bastard Township in 1822, Fredenburg later took over the Manhards' mill, opened a general store and other mills above Westport, and a second sawmill

on an island. He was also the first reeve of North Crosby, elected in 1850.

On Big Rideau Lake, in Bastard Township, was Portland, earlier called the Old Landing. One of the first roads to the Rideau country ended at that spot, and it had a wharf that may have been built by the Baptist elder, Abel Stevens, the township's founder, and as keen a businessman as he was a preacher of the gospel. With the opening of the canal, the village—named for the Duke of Portland—mushroomed as a lumber port, and the Chaffey brothers opened a boatyard similar to the one they ran at Bedford Mills. Downstream, on the north shore of the lake, Port Elmsley, up the Tay River, was stagnating. The construction of the side canal killed its reason for existing, by eliminating the need to break the journey and take a wagon around the rapids that stood in the way.

Stoness' grist mill, Upper Pond, Westport, ca. 1895.
(The Roberts Family, Westport).

Map of Westport.
(From H. F. Walling's map of the Counties of Leeds and Grenville, C.W., 1861-62).

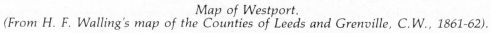

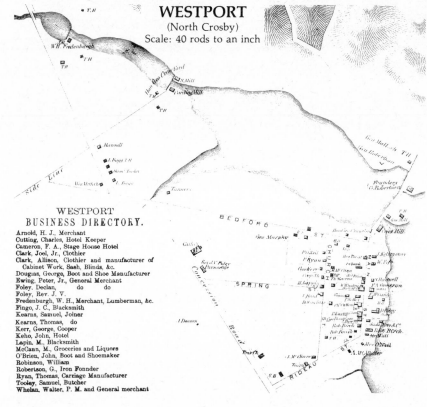

WESTPORT
(North Crosby)
Scale: 40 rods to an inch

WESTPORT
BUSINESS DIRECTORY.

Arnold, H. J., Merchant
Cutting, Charles, Hotel Keeper
Cameron, F. A., Stage House Hotel
Clark, Joel, Jr., Clothier
Clark, Allison, Clothier and manufacturer of
    Cabinet Work, Sash, Blinds, &c.
Douglas, George, Boot and Shoe Manufacturer
Ewing, Peter, Jr., General Merchant
Foley. Declan,   do   do
Foley, Rev. J. V.
Fredenburgh, W. H., Merchant, Lumberman, &c.
Fingo, J. C., Blacksmith
Kearns, Samuel, Joiner
Kearns, Thomas,   do
Kerr, George, Cooper
Keho, John, Hotel
Lapin, M., Blacksmith
McCann, M., Groceries and Liquors
O'Brien, John, Boot and Shoemaker
Robinson, William
Robertson, G., Iron Fonnder
Ryan, Thomas, Carriage Manufacturer
Tooley, Samuel, Butcher
Whelan, Walter, P. M. and General merchant

Lanark County, established as an electoral unit in 1824, was part of the Johnstown District until 1836. Then the District of Bathurst, basically Lanark and Carleton Counties, was set up by splitting Johnstown along the northern boundaries of Elmsley and Burgess Townships. In 1841, the south boundary of Bathurst was amended to follow the course of the Rideau Canal, which split these two townships roughly in half, creating four. South Burgess and South Elmsley remained in the Johnstown District, while North Burgess and North Elmsley were in Bathurst and then became part of the Lanark County electoral riding.

Perth was Bathurst's district seat, and supreme over rowdy, unrefined Bytown. Despite an atmosphere of gentility enforced by the half-pay officers, the little stone town on the banks of the Tay was something of a duelling capital, and the instigators were lawyers. The first such to set up practice in the town was James Boulton, a son of the Honourable Henry John Boulton, then the Attorney-General of Upper Canada. The second lawyer was Thomas Radenhurst, who, like Boulton, had studied law in Muddy York. Mrs. Radenhurst was a Ridout, which firmly tied her husband to the Family Compact, of which the Boultons were also members in good standing. This closeness, however, did not rule out quarrels.

In 1830, Boulton and Radenhurst agreed to fight a duel, but they decided on a change of venue since the gentlemanly procedure was illegal in Upper Canada. Off they went to New York State, and both returned unharmed, bragging over how narrowly each had missed the other. They had, unwittingly, set a bad example to students in their respective offices. John Wilson, the son of a North Sherbrooke Township pioneer, Ebenezer Wilson, worked for Boulton; Henry Lyon, whose father was Captain George Lyon of the Richmond settlement was also Radenhurst's nephew and worked for his uncle. Both young law students were in love, Wilson with Miss Elizabeth Hughes. She had been orphaned when her father, a Unitarian Minister, died of cholera in Lower Canada, and adopted by the Ackland family of Perth, which kept a school for young ladies. The name of the object of Lyon's affection was not of sufficient importance to have been set down for posterity.

The students were friends, until Henry Lyon made an ill-judged remark about Miss Hughes, which Wilson duly repeated to Mrs. Boulton, who spread it about. Whereupon, Lyon's own girlfriend rebuffed him for his rudeness. Enraged, Lyon attacked Wilson for being indiscreet. After consulting James Boulton on the matter, to assuage his honour John Wilson challenged Henry Lyon to a duel. The affair might have ended there, but for the vested interest of a third party, Henry LeLievre, who just happened to be attracted to Miss Elizabeth Hughes himself. Knowing that Lyon was an excellent shot who would probably eliminate John Wilson, LeLievre egged the two law students on.

Thus it came about that on June 13th, 1830, five men met on the banks of the Tay outside town in early dawn—Lyon with LeLievre as his second, Wilson supported by Simon Robertson, another law student, and Dr. Hamilton, the attending physician. Both Hamilton and Robertson tried to dissuade the contestants, but LeLievre, having brought them this close, would not let the dispute fizzle out. Lyon's shot went wide, perhaps deliberately, but Wilson's pierced the other's heart, killing him instantly. The body of 20 year old Henry Lyon was laid to rest in the Radenhurst family plot at the Craig Street Cemetery. Wilson and Robertson surrendered and spent three months in the district gaol in Perth, awaiting the next assizes that were held in the Brockville Court House. The two stood trial before Justice John Beverley Robinson—another well known member of the Family Compact—who informed the jury that Wilson had never wanted to duel and had been forced to take part by Lyon and LeLievre. Both Wilson and Robertson were acquitted.

Distraught over the sad affair, James Boulton decided to leave Perth and open a new practice at Niagara, where John Wilson agreed to join him and continue his studies. The night before Boulton departed, an angry mob marched to his house carrying a gibbet with an effigy dangling from it which they burned—an unsavoury parting shot. Henry LeLievre, the other instigator of the duel, fled to Montreal, and eventually found his way to Australia. Elizabeth Hughes, for whose honour, more or less, the duel was fought, married John Wilson, who later became a judge in London, Ontario.

The Wilson-Lyon duel is thought to be the last held in the province and it was certainly the last that ended with a trial. (What was probably the first concerned another man associated with the Rideau area. The Honourable John White, the first Member of the Legislative Assembly for Frontenac and Leeds Counties, was killed by John Small, the Clerk of the Executive Council. This duel was staged at York in 1800, and like John Wilson, Small stood trial and was acquitted. The reason behind the encounter was obscured at the time, but it may have been the conduct of Mrs. Small.

One of the Scots who emigrated to Lanark County in 1816, was Francis Allan who settled on the Scotch Line about six miles west of Perth. His son William acquired a piece of land to the south on both sides of Grants Creek, which flows into the Tay River. There William built a sawmill and a stone grist mill, and established the nucleus of another village. In due course he added a store and a blacksmith's shop, and not surprisingly this community was called Allans Mills. There were other good millsites on the same creek and several men emulated William. Meanwhile his village acquired a wagon maker and a shoemaker, and George Murphy occupied the blacksmith's shop. When a road of sorts extended to Perth and on to Westport, a stagecoach ran regularly through Allans Mills.

Smiths Falls and Burritts Rapids had mushroomed, while Merrickville was a thriving town. Before the canal was started, that village had 300 people, the largest community along the Rideau, and within 30 years the population had risen to nearly 1,200. A mile above Burritts Rapids, a new village had sprouted that was named Andrewsville, after Rufus Andrews, who obtained a lease for the site in 1843, and erected a large dam and a shingle mill. Like so many others, Andrews's community soon had a variety of small industries around the mill. Benjamin Tett, the Newboro entrepreneur, opened his own shingle mill and added a grist mill, and Henry Watts started a sawmill. The place soon had a carding mill, general store, blacksmith's shop, sawyers and labourers, and was served by the Kemptville-Merrickville stage.

Downstream were wharves at Becketts Landing, but this spot was close to Kempt-

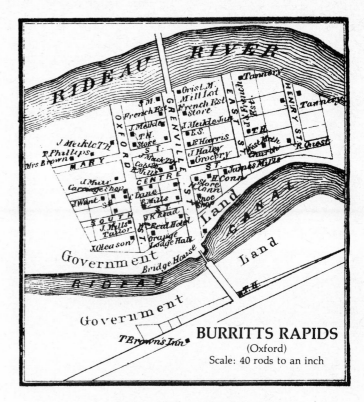

Map of Burritts Rapids.
(From H. F. Walling's map of the Counties of Leeds and Grenville, C.W., 1861-62).

ville, with its numerous industries, and the landing did not attract many enterprises. Three new villages had sprung up along the Rideau above Bytown. The first below Becketts Landing was Kars, in the Township of North Gower. For a time it was known as Wellington, which was confused with the town of that name in Prince Edward County. The later name commemorated the defence by the Turks against the Russians at Kars, Turkey, in 1855, during the Crimean War.

John O'Callaghan and his wife, Ellen O'Connor, settled at Kars as squatters in 1815, and later vanished. About 1822, Richard Garlick, a carpenter from the front townships, arrived and began logging along Stevens Creek. (There Roger Stevens, the earliest pioneer on the Rideau had drowned.) Garlick opened the first school in the township, and with two other settlers built a road along the creek. John Easton, of Eastons Corners, and James Lindsay, built a wharf and storehouse for the forwarding trade, establishing Kars as a river port. At the mouth of Stevens Creek Richard Garlick built the steamboat *Bytown*, the first of that name and probably the smallest. Farther down the

Mill at Burritts Rapids, Ontario, 1936.
(Public Archives of Canada—PA56986).

Aerial View of Burritts Rapids, 1980.

Rideau, 15 miles above Bytown, Manotick was developing on Long Island, at the junction of four townships—North Gower, Osgoode, Nepean and Gloucester, where sawmills had operated before the canal was constructed.

The first settlers were John Clothier, Richard Tighe, and William Doughney, and the community was called Long Island. The man who was to promote this village and change both its location and name had not yet appeared on the scene. Moss Kent Dickinson, the man known as the King of the Rideau, would move the village centre to the left bank and see that it was the only one on the waterway to have an Indian name. Manotick is an Ojibway word, for "manotic" means "island in the river." The last village before Bytown was Billings Bridge. Built by subscription among the settlers, the bridge spanned the Rideau. On the main route from Bytown, the village was called the gateway to Gloucester because of the roads that radiated from it. Close by stood the fine home of Braddish Billings, who had grown rich on the proceeds of the lumber trade.

Billings Home, erected 1828-29, Billings Bridge, Ottawa, July 1925.
(Public Archives of Canada—PA26917).

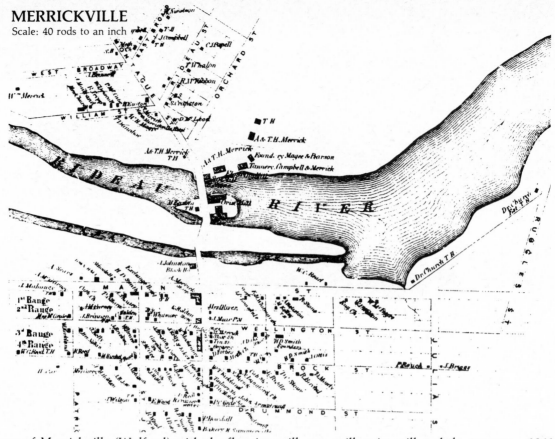

Town of Merrickville (Wolford) with the flouring mill, saw mill, grist mill and the tannery—1861-62.
(H. F. Walling, map of the United Counties of Leeds & Grenville).

Crowd watching the flood waters around the Chinese laundry in Merrickville, Ontario, 1885.
(Public Archives of Canada—C54505).

Bytown, still unruly, was in conflict with Nepean Township, of which it was nominally a part. With 1,300 people by the mid 1830s, the future capital of Canada was demanding separate status, at least where statute labour was concerned. The township officers could order able bodied men to do roadwork, a substitute for tax raising. The residents of Colonel John By's village took exception to orders from Nepean to turn out with picks and shovels, and appealed to the Attorney-General. That gentleman defined a town as "a Precinct anciently of ten families" and declared that Bytown, Perth (population 900) and Richmond (population 200) were towns. This implied that all three were separate from Nepean. What the Attorney-General had in mind is unclear, since none of the villages had any officers, elected or appointed, other than magistrates. In the townships along the St. Lawrence, several urban communities had become Police Villages, and could elect officers to oversee roadwork or fence viewing.

The three general elections held during the 1830s were notably rowdy in Leeds and Carleton Counties. In both, the Irish fomented trouble. Loyal Orange Lodges decided to champion the monarchy and support the Family Compact. (Since there were few Roman Catholics in Upper Canada until after the Great Potato Famines of the 1840s, the Orangemen could hardly pretend that such were a threat to the state.) The lodges tilted at the dangers of republicanism and maintained that all reformers were endangering the security of British North America.

Following the rebellions, which in Upper Canada were brought about in part by election rigging that kept the Conservatives in power, the British government dispatched Lord Durham, (nicknamed Radical Jack for his liberal views), as governor-in-chief, and to report on the causes of the uprisings. Returning to England, Durham recommended the union of the two Canadas under one Parliament. That way, the combined anglophone population would outnumber the francophones, leading in time to the assimilation of the French Canadians.

The home government resolved to accept Durham's advice, and in 1841, the united Province of Canada was born, with the first capital at Kingston. Durham and the British ministers failed to appreciate the staying powers of the French culture, but that was beside the point in the Rideau country. Parliament met at Kingston until 1843, when the governor-in-chief, then Sir Charles Metcalfe, and the honourable members were sick of the place and decided to move to Montreal.

Two pieces of legislation passed by the united Parliament instituted some control by local people over their affairs. One was the District Councils Act of 1841, which permitted each township to elect a representative to sit on the council and legislate such matters as secondary schools, roads and other municipal services, and to have limited powers of taxation to cover expenditures. The other was the Municipal Act, passed in 1849. Under its terms the counties, hitherto electoral ridings, replaced the districts in the more populated areas of the province as the units of local government. County councils assumed the functions of the old district councils. Kingston became the county seat for Frontenac, Perth for Lanark, and Bytown for Carleton. Leeds and Grenville, with smaller populations, were united, with the county seat at Brockville.

At the same time the old District Courts were taken over by the counties, the system still prevailing, although township councils, towns and cities have assumed most of the functions once performed by county councils. Among the members of Parliament in these formative years were the future Prime Minister of the Dominion of Canada, John A. Macdonald, representing Kingston, and, in 1858, Benjamin Tett for Leeds. Members of the Legislative Council were Levius Sherwood of Brockville, and Thomas Mackay of Bytown.

4. The Waterway on the Eve of Confederation

The canals along the St. Lawrence opened officially in 1851. Even before this event the Rideau Canal had felt the competition, because steamboats were able to come through the unfinished waterway. Yet, through lower rates, the Rideau route did not lose out entirely to the St. Lawrence. As the population at Kingston, Bytown and points in between grew, the number of small industries proliferated. The volume of agricultural produce increased, and the lumber

Rideau Canal Locks at Ottawa, 1861.
(Public Archives of Canada—C34001).

Falls at Hogs Back, 1892.
(Public Archives of Canada—PA33932).

Jones Falls blacksmith's shop still standing beside the locks. Any iron tools or fittings needed for the locks were made here by the blacksmiths.
(Parks Canada).

In the early 1900's a diver was brought to the lockstations to check for underwater problems. Air was pumped through the hose to the diver's helmet to allow him to breathe underwater.
(Fred Flemming).

Kingston waterfront in 1899.
(Marine Museum of the Great Lakes at Kingston).

trade remained strong. All these activities prevented a slump in canal traffic.

The Rideau also emerged as an alternate route to the St. Lawrence, rather than a competitor. Forwarding companies promoted the smaller canal system by advertising in newspapers, listing the services they offered. In 1857, the Ottawa River and Rideau Canal Company served notice to the public that its subscribers had purchased stock belonging to the firm of Macpherson and Crane, and subsequently to Robertson, Jones and Company. The newly formed company had the steamers *Bytown*, *Charlotte*, and *Juno*, and nine "First-Class Barges" all of which had been repaired, and the directors had hired Mr. James Walker, a well known forwarder on the route, to be their agent in Montreal. Rival firms ran similar advertisements for moving passengers and freight between Kingston and Perth, Oliver's Ferry (Rideau Ferry) and Bytown, or along the entire route. While the trade was never what Colonel John By envisaged, it was healthy enough to warrant keeping the canal open.

By the second and third decades of the waterway's life, technological improvements to steamboats helped keep it competitive with the burgeoning railways. Propellors replaced paddle wheels, which allowed more width for passengers and freight. Some of the barges, hitherto rigged or unpowered, were equipped with steam engines. One such was the *Breeze*, 91 feet long, 12 feet wide, 7 feet from her deck to her keel, weighing 42 tons, and built at Kemptville in 1845. Many others were similar, and the barges that travelled under their own power usually had names. All, whether named or not, were registered. One dual purpose steamboat whose dimensions are known, was a second *Bytown*, built at Montreal in 1842. She was 92 feet long and weighed 42 tons.

Gradually as boilers were improved and strengthened, high pressure engines could be installed with safety. These were usually the single cylinder type, and more powerful than the earlier low pressure models. After 1850, the steamboats that at first had been for all purposes were built for specific roles, for passengers and freight, and accommodation for the travelling public was more luxurious. One of the earliest tugs to ply the Rideau Canal was the *Mary Ann*, built at Sackets Harbor, New York in 1856, and owned by Henry Easton of Merrickville. She measured 50 feet long and 15 feet wide, and was still in service in 1877. The tugs *Forest* and *Francis* were built by the Chaffey brothers in their boatyard at Bedford Mills. The *Forest*, finished in 1861, weighed 33 tons, was 9 feet wide, and broke up in 1877. The *Francis*, built three years later, was 36 tons and 55 feet long, and towed lumber and barges into Lake Ontario as far as Oswego, New York.

Until the 1870s, all the steamboats along the Rideau burned wood, although the use of coal as a fuel was mooted in 1834. As long as timber was plentiful and therefore cheap, no change was contemplated by boat owners. In 1839, Benjamin Tett and his sons were supplying wood for Rideau steamers, and the records show that they sent Macpherson and Crane's ships *Meteor*, *Charlotte*, *Juno*, *Perth*, *Otter* and *Beaver* a mix of hard and soft woods. They charged 6 shillings a cord for tamarack, 5 shillings sixpence for hemlock and other soft woods, and 7 shillings and sixpence for hardwoods. Supplying wood provided cash income for many local farmers as well, and it was stacked on the wharves along the waterway.

When the canal first opened, a few vessels were registered under the Imperial Merchant Shipping Act, or under Lower Canada legislation. In 1844, the Canadian Parliament passed an act for registering all vessels over 15 tons that were not registered under the Imperial Shipping Act. The Collectors of Customs were responsible for these registries, and the name of a vessel could not be altered without reporting and having the registration amended. At the same time regulations were introduced, in part as a result of an explosion aboard the steamer *Dart*, when a 15 year old boy was scalded to death. The right hand rule was put in force, and any vessel riding at anchor at night had to show a light. In 1838, a guard-rail around machinery was made mandatory, and by 1851, the regulations of 1844 were stiffened. Lifebelts for everyone aboard, and one lifeboat for every 50 passengers were compulsory. Steamboats had to carry lifelines, fire buckets and axes, and were licenced for a specific number of passengers.

The canal building fever of the 1820s and 30s became railway fever by the 1850s. The St. Lawrence canals suffered from competition for passengers first. The Grand Trunk Railway received a charter to build a line between Montreal and Toronto, and it was opened by 1856. The Bytown and Prescott Railway Company received a charter in 1850 for a line between the two towns, to connect at Ogdensburg, New York, with a line to Boston, to carry lumber to United States markets. This line reached Bedell Station, near Kemptville by August, 1854, but the company went broke. On the final three miles to Bytown the rails were of hardwood, bound with iron, and the first train to follow the entire line reached New Edinburgh, Thomas Mackay's village, on Christmas Day.

A line was started to link Brockville with Bytown, and by 1859 it had reached Carleton Place. It was never completed, but it had the distinction of having the first railway tunnel in Canada at the Brockville terminus. The cornerstone was laid in 1854, by the then 74 year old Adiel Sherwood, the sheriff who lost the battle with canal workers

Kingston, 1875.
(National Map Collection, Public Archives of Cnaada).

at Clowes Lock some 25 years before. Another venture which received a charter, in 1884, was the Brockville, Westport and Sault Ste. Marie Railway, but only 45 miles, from Brockville to Westport, were built.

The Rideau Canal suffered less from railway competition because the lines did not provide a direct link between Kingston and Bytown. With the ever increasing demand for lumber in the United States, the Bytown-Prescott link to Ogdensburg was of vital importance, but no such motivation sparked a demand for a line following the canal route. Thus the little passenger-freight steamers continued on their way, and when coal was needed both for trains and steamboats and to heat homes, the Rideau Canal received a new lease on life.

5. Settlement Before Confederation

By the 1860s, most of the land along the waterway had been taken up and was being farmed wherever the soil depth and terrain were satisfactory. Where the soil was too thin over level limestone that had been logged over, it was grazed or allowed to regenerate as bush. Most farmers had left some portions of woodlot, and as the trees were thinned for fuel, cattle grazed among those that remained. The latter half of the nine-teenth century was the heyday of cheesemaking and milling, and the many villages at the powersites and crossroads continued to grow. Notable in these years were the erection of churches and better school buildings. The earliest settlers met at each other's homes for religious observances, and built small churches when they could afford them, or used the schoolhouses on Sundays. Few of the brick and stone churches that now grace these villages were built before 1840, and many date from 1870 or later.

The business directories of the villages show that they were prosperous, and the proprietors of the local businesses and industries were, if not wealthy, certainly a substantial middle class. In 1862, Merrickville had 39 commercial premises. These included millers, manufacturers, merchants, tanners, blacksmiths, a foundry, a printer and publisher, and two hotel keepers, shoemakers, carpenters, a nursery and seed shop. In addition the directory listed two bailiffs of the Number 5 Divisional Court, a Church of England clergyman, and two physicians, one in residence, the other at Eastons Corners, and a postmaster who was also a merchant. Kemptville boasted 65 such premises, while Burritts Rapids showed a similar mixture although it was smaller than Merrickville. Westport had 23 businesses, including a

Main Street, Westport, Ontario—1870.
(The Roberts Family, Westport).

(Rideau Valley Conservation Authority).

cabinet-maker, a joiner and a cooper.

Merrickville was a separated town, with a population of 908, although when the spill-over into Wolford Township was counted the urban population numbered 1,200. Kemptville, with 1,059, was also a municipality. The other villages near the canal in Leeds, Grenville and Frontenac were too small to be incorporated as towns. In Carleton County, Bytown had a population of about 7,800. Kars was still very small, as were Manotick and Billings Bridge. However, a driving force had discovered Manotick. The man who was to put that village on the map, Moss Kent Dickinson, born in Denmark, New York in 1822, was a Yankee by background. His father, Barnabas Dickinson, had moved from Massachusetts to New York about the time of the War of 1812. In 1828 Barnabas moved to Upper Canada to enter the forwarding trade.

In 1844, the 22 year old Moss Kent entered the same trade and moved to Bytown. He made his home there for many years, but Long Island captured his imagination, and he soon founded Manotick, on the left bank of the Rideau, moving the centre of the village off the island. Like others in the forwarding business, he saw the advantage in owning steamboats, and for years the ships of the Dickinson Line dominated the triangular trade from Kingston to Montreal and return by way of the Ottawa River and the canal. All told, 16 steamers and 84 barges and tugs were built for Moss Kent, among them the *Olive*, the *Kathleen*, the *Princess Louise*, the *Britannia*, and the *City of Ottawa*. Of these, the *Olive* was built at Smiths Falls.

In 1850, Dickinson was in partnership with Joseph Currier for the lumber trade. Currier was born in North Troy, Vermont, in 1820, and had removed to Canada by 1837 in search of opportunities. The two men leased for $50.00 per annum the rights to the waste water at a control dam that had been built in the 1850s to deepen the east channel of the Rideau at Long Island. In

152

1858, they purchased some 30 acres of North Gower Township, part of it on Long Island, where they planned to build mills. The following year they hired the firm of T. Langrell to erect a grist mill on their holding. The contractor employed Scots stonemasons who put up a building 64 feet long and 46 feet wide, and four storeys high. This mill was the last word for the day, and instead of the old fashioned waterwheel, it had turbines installed which lay flat on the rock of the river bed. Altogether, six sets of turbines operated, making use of the water power built up through the 27 miles of uninterrupted flow all the way from Burritts Rapids Lock. When this grist mill opened in February, 1860, it employed 20 men and was the largest of its kind in the eastern part of Canada West.

A year later tragedy struck, when Joseph Currier was showing his bride, Ann Crosby, through the mill. Her skirts got caught in part of the machinery and she was flung against a post with such force that she died. Broken hearted, Joseph Currier moved to New Edinburgh where he opened a lumber mill and sash factory. Later he built the fine mansion at 24 Sussex Drive that is now the official residence of Canada's Prime Minister.

Moss Kent Dickinson continued expanding his empire at Manotick, with a stone sawmill that employed 12 men, and beside the grist mill he opened a carding mill. Later he converted this mill for the manufacture of cloth, and he also had a planing mill and lumber yard. The sawmill was destroyed by fire, and afterward he opened a bung and spile factory on the site. For power he used a cable strung across the river that connected with one of the turbines at the grist mill. Some of those bungs and spiles were exported to distilleries in Scotland and other parts of Europe. In 1862, he had the townsite surveyed and registered, guaranteeing that more of Manotick would grow on the shore of the Rideau than on Long Island. A business directory of 1864-65 stated that Manotick had a post office, a flour mill that could grind 100 barrels a day, a sawmill that turned out two million feet of sawn lumber per year, a private school with 20 pupils, and a population of 100.

Unfortunately, Dickinson's mill ventures brought him into conflict with James Slater, the superintending engineer of the canal. Slater complained that Dickinson had two mills that restricted the free passage of water

downstream. It was Slater's duty to see that the water levels were lowered each year to avoid spring floods along Long Reach, the stretch of water between Long Island and Burritts Rapids. The King of the Rideau wanted the levels kept high, or he would not be able to operate his mills. The running battle raged on and on, and in 1863, Dickinson was demanding that Slater be fired for incompetence. "That idiot of a superintending engineer was damaging the mills." On his part Slater countered with a demand that the mills be torn down, and Dickinson was not the only mill-owner who was causing trouble along the canal. Slater wanted to have stoplocks opened in the various dams in preparation for spring runoff, but this precaution reduced the supply of water to the mills.

In 1870, Moss Kent moved his wife and four children to Manotick from Ottawa. For three years he had been building a three storey frame house and now it was ready for occupancy. All told he bought 200 acres in the neighbourhood and he also operated a farm on Long Island. The Dickinson house stood on what was known as Mill Square, but today it bears the family name. After Moss Kent settled in Manotick, he was a Member of Parliament for Russell County, before Gloucester Township became part of Carleton.

Dickinson's flour mill at Long Island was constructed on one of 19 pieces of property that were leased for millsites between 1847 and 1867. The Ordnance Department established a policy of leasing lots to encourage local industry along several canals in Canada where it thought the surplus water could be used to turn wheels and turbines. Others were granted on Green Island, at the mouth of the Rideau River, at Hog's Back, Burritts Rapids, Smiths Falls and Brewers Mills. All were classified as water lots, and the annual rent ranged from $1.00 to $360.00. The mills were built for a variety of purposes—sawn lumber, flour, carding, fulling, woollen cloth, shingles—and at least two of them are still standing and in good condition.

6. Queen Victoria Settles a 16 Year Argument

The issue of where the Province of Canada would have its capital had been the cause of heated debate ever since Upper and

Dickinson's residence in Manotick. Presently the Rideau Valley Conservation Authority offices.

Long Island or Watson's Mill, Manotick, Ontario, opened in 1860. (Public Archives of Canada—PA26958).

Interior of Watson's Mill, Manotick, Ontario.

(Rideau Valley Conservation Authority).

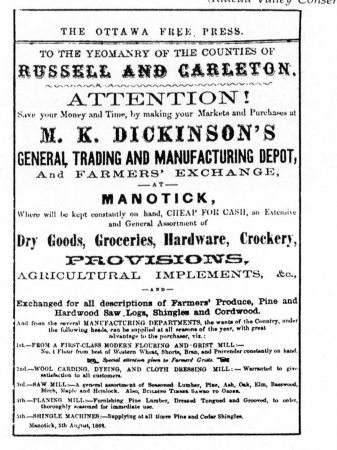

Lower Canada were first joined under one Parliament in 1841. Kingston, with a population of 5,000 at the time of union, had few suitable public buildings and a surfeit of gouging landladies. The members groaned over the length of time they endured there when the legislature was in session. Another who objected to that small town was the editor of the Bathurst Courier and Ottawa General Advertiser. In February, 1841, he claimed that Bytown was a more appropriate setting for the capital, overlooking certain embattled Orangemen and French Canadian lumbermen who detracted from what little dignity the rough frontier post could muster.

Ignoring the hint from the wilderness, the majority of the elected representatives voted to move the capital to Montreal. The first session of Parliament held in that city took place in November, 1844, in a market building adapted for the purpose on what is now the Place Youville. This satisfied the members from Canada East, but the debate did not subside. Matters reached a climax in April, 1849, with the passing of the Rebellion Losses Bill in a Parliament dominated by the Reform Party.

Briefly, the Reformers, led by Robert Baldwin of Canada West and Louis La Fontaine of Canada East, introduced a bill that would compensate all who had suffered losses as a consequence of the Rebellions of 1837, regardless of which side they had supported. The bill passed, and the Conservatives and their friends were outraged. Yet they were optimistic that Governor-General Lord Elgin would defer the legislation. Elgin, however, had been sent from Britain with instructions to be the sovereign's representative, nothing more. The members of Parliament had become, for the first time, the government in every respect. When, on April 25th, Lord Elgin gave the Rebellion Losses Bill Royal assent the fat was in the fire.

His Excellency's carriage was pelted with rotten eggs as it passed through the streets of Montreal, and that night a crowd gathered and marched on the Legislative Assembly. Inside, the members were in session, when the mob stormed the lobby, smashing furniture and setting fires. The members, led by the Speaker, marched out of the chamber in good order. Fire soon gutted the entire building. With that meeting place lost, the legislators met alternatively at Toronto and Quebec City, which satisfied no one. The verbal

swordplay raged over where a permanent capital could be housed, and the chief contenders were Montreal and Toronto, with Kingston still in the race. Quebec City, with the largest British garrison and the most elegant social life, remained the favourite of the governors-general. Another contestant was the brand new City of Ottawa. Upon incorporation in 1855, the name was changed and Bytown would soon become just a memory. The following year, the legislature more or less decided that Quebec City would be the permanent capital, and planned to erect Parliament buildings there. This move was foiled by the Legislative Council, which had not been consulted, and its members disallowed £50,000 from the Supply Bill that had been intended for these government buildings.

In 1857, the governor-general of the day, Sir Edmund Head, suggested sending a petition to Her Majesty, Queen Victoria, requesting that she make the final choice. In doing so, Head was turning to the last resort sanctioned under the Parliamentary system, a measure most politicians move heaven and earth to avoid. When all else failed the head of state could be called upon to break the deadlock. After some discussion, two petitions went off to London asking Her Majesty to exercise her Royal prerogative, "and select some place for the permanent seat of Government in Canada." With the petition Sir Edmund Head sent a private memorandum. He was careful not to take sides, but he did point out the divisiveness of the issue and recommended it be settled as quickly as possible. "Ottawa," His Excellency contended, "is the only place which will be accepted by the majority of Upper and Lower Canada as a fair compromise," and he continued:

> Ottawa is, in fact, neither in Upper or Lower Canada. Literally it is in the former; but a bridge alone divides it from the latter. Consequently its selection would fulfill the letter of any pledge given, to Upper Canada at the time of the Union. The population is at present partly French, English and Irish. The settlement of the valley of the Ottawa is rapidly increasing, and will be at once stimulated by making it the capital.

Next he emphasized the importance of Ottawa's strategic location:

> Canada is long and narrow; in fact all frontier. The rapid expansion of settlement up the Ottawa, and on each side of it, would give breadth and substance to the country.

156

In a military point of view (I speak of course with submission to higher authorities), Ottawa is advantageously situated. Its distance from the frontier is such as to protect it from any marauding party or even from a regular attack, unless Montreal and Kingston, which flank the approach to it, were previously occupied by the enemy. Stores and troops could be sent to Ottawa either from Quebec or Kingston, without exposure on the St. Lawrence to the American frontier.

A secondary consideration, but one of some importance as affecting the popularity of the choice, is the fact that the Rideau Canal, now handed over to the Provincial Government, would probably increase its traffic and become more productive by the transfer of the seat of Government to Ottawa. At present this great work is a dead loss so far as money is concerned."

Having expressed the hope that a more important Ottawa would help the Rideau Canal, Sir Edmund showed that he was not taking sides, from his comment on the city he was advocating:

The main objection to Ottawa is its wild position, and relative inferiority to the other cities named. But this wild position is a fault from which every day continues to diminish. The present population may be called 8,000 or 10,000, not of the best description.

Apparently His Excellency, if not acquainted with Bytown-Ottawa personally, had listened to countless tales of the unbridled conduct of certain elements in the lumbering community at the back of beyond. In Her Majesty's ultimate decision, the military aspect had the final say. Relations between Britain and the United States were again strained, this time by some injudicious attempts to recruit United States citizens for service in the Crimean War. This upset the American authorities and press. To a friend Sir Edmund Head wrote in March, 1856, from Toronto:

There is nothing as yet to hinder my being taken prisoner any day, for as things now stand the Yankees would have command of the

"Feu-de-joie"—Victoria Day gun salute, May 24, 1868, shortly after the completion of the Parliament Buildings. (Public Archives of Canada—C10978).

157

Lakes . . . If I am carried off to Boston or New York, I will apprize you of the change in my address.

In his official letter of December 31st, 1858, the Colonial Secretary Henry Labouchere informed Sir Edmund Head:

> I am commanded by the Queen to inform you that in the judgement of Her Majesty the City of Ottawa combines more advantages than any other place in Canada for the permanent seat of the future Government of the Province, and is selected by Her Majesty accordingly.

The die was cast. The voices of dissent were still heard in the land, and to placate Quebec City, until the move to the backwoods could be undertaken, the fortress overlooking the St. Lawrence would be the seat of government temporarily. Even then, Louis-Victor Sicotte and Hector Langevin, influential members of Parliament from Canada East, moved and seconded a want of confidence motion. The Toronto Globe protested the extravagance of moving first to Quebec City and then to Ottawa. At that, Richard William Scott, the sitting member for Ottawa and her former mayor, rallied the opposition and, joined by members from Carleton and other nearby constituencies, defeated the Sicotte-Langevin motion.

In May, 1860, a last motion to reconsider the seat of government was defeated, and after nearly two decades of infighting, Ottawa's future was ordained. When measured against this piece of historical scuffling, the flag debates of the 1960s were remarkable for their brevity.

Once the controversy over the location of the capital was more or less settled, the Department of Public Works advertised for architects to submit designs for government buildings, and to stay within these estimates:

A Parliament Building	$300,000
Two departmental buildings	240,000
A residence for the Governor-General	100,000

The deadline for submissions was August 1st, 1859. The winner for the Parliament Building was the Toronto firm of Thomas Fuller and Chilion Jones; for the two departmental buildings the firm of Frederick Warburton Stent and Augustus Laver. Both winning designs were Gothic, perhaps because they reminded the Public Works officials of the new buildings at Westminster to house the Mother of Parliaments. The sod was turned on December 20th, 1859, no doubt with difficulty the ground of Ottawa being frozen solid that late in the year. The laying of the cornerstone was delayed until the visit of the Prince of Wales.

His Royal Highness, later King Edward VII, officiated at this ceremony on September 1st, 1860, but the tentative wording on the stone hinted that some in high places were dubious over the choice his mother had made. It stated that the building was "intended" for the Canadian Legislature. Nor were all the reporters on hand convinced. On September 20th, the editor of the London Times commented:

> With the account of this ceremony, our correspondent has combined a description of the city of Ottawa, which we confess has filled us with very serious misgivings as to the wisdom of the step Her Majesty has been advised to take in selecting it as the capital of Canada.

Farther on the editor admitted that he hoped the question could still be reconsidered.

The finances of the Parliament Building and departmental quarters echoed the galloping estimates of the Rideau Canal. The original estimates—shades of the earlier triumph—were based upon inadequate preliminary surveys of the ground. The site selected was part of Colonel John By's Military Reserve, overlooking the Ottawa River from the heights. Workers had to do more excavating than anticipated, and the quarrying and transport of stone overran the estimates. By May 3rd, 1861, the deputy commissioner of Public Works Samuel Keefer—Thomas Mackay's son-in-law—suggested that the buildings would cost $1,436,408, a sum $400,000 more than the amount the legislature had voted. By 1863, escalating costs sparked a Royal Commission, and ultimately the buildings cost more than three times what had been envisaged in the beginning. By 1865, the Parliament Building and the two departmental buildings were nearly complete.

Little did the critics of this vast expense suspect that magnificence was in order. When the new Parliament was ready, plans for a confederation of the British North American provinces were well advanced. The Fathers of Confederation had started negotiations at Charlottetown in 1864, and by 1867, the British North America Act had been voted into law by the Parliament at Westminster—to whom it still belongs. Ottawa had become the capital of the new Dominion. The Confederation consisted of Nova Scotia, New Brunswick, Quebec (Canada East), and Ontario (Canada West), but the door was open for other provinces to join. The new government buildings, the butt of many unkind remarks in newspapers over their cost, served the old Province of Canada for just one session. By the second session, 181 members arrived in Ottawa to sit in a chamber intended for 130—65 from each of Canada East and Canada West. The chamber had been enlarged during the summer of 1867, but it was crowded and remained so until the fire of 1916 destroyed the building.

While the first Dominion Parliament met, malcontents were calling Ottawa the Westminster of the Wilderness. American editors, conscious of the reasoning behind the choice, agreed that Ottawa was safe because their soldiers would never find it. The city was also a mess, the original beauty of the setting marred by a jumble of lumberyards, sawmills, industries. Houses ranged from log shanties to the castle of Thomas Mackay, who had died in 1855. Ottawa was a boom town with no time for many frills.

Parliament Buildings from Russell House, Ottawa, Ontario, ca. 1860's.
(Public Archives of Canada—PA121538).

The 1850s had been years of prosperity, and the city's new status added momentum. Civil servants occupying the government buildings created a housing bonanza.

The Department of Public Works now had to find a suitable dwelling for the governor-general, at that time Lord Monck. Having spent so much on the government buildings, some way had to be found to establish His Excellency's household in visible munificence as cheaply as possible. Thomas Mackay's widow wanted to dispose of Rideau Hall, and Public Works leased it for 12 years with an option to purchase—another hint that some expected the capital would eventually move elsewhere. Lord Monck himself was never resigned to being in Ottawa. Writing to the Right Honourable Edward Cardwell in London, Monck confided that Her Majesty's choice bordered on insanity:

> to have fixed the capital of this great country away from the civilization, intelligence and commercial enterprise of this Province, in a place that can never be a place of importance and where the political section of the community will live in a position of isolation and removed from the action of any public opinion. My confident belief is that, notwithstanding the vast expense which has been incurred here in public buildings, Ottawa will not be the capital four years hence.

His Excellency resented having to leave the pleasures of Quebec City for the crude little frontier town. The road from Rideau Hall to his office in the East Block was so bad that the governor-general had himself rowed in a ship's boat along the Ottawa River by bluejackets of the Royal Navy. Alighting at the foot of Parliament Hill, up the slope he marched, lip curled in disdain. For better or worse, Monck's prediction misfired. Roads could be paved, the city eventually provided sewers, water and street lighting.

One who did not share the governor-general's pessimism was the first Prime Minister, Sir John A. Macdonald, the Kingston lawyer who had been a moving force behind the British North America Act and rewarded with the knighthood. Under that constitution Ottawa was to remain the capital unless Her Majesty deemed otherwise—most unlikely after the need to appeal to her. Returning to Ottawa from London in May, 1867, Sir John assured the citizens that their city's future was secure.

July 1st was Confederation Day, the scene of celebrations in Ottawa at least, although some Conservative strongholds felt mourning was more appropriate. To Orangemen, the self governing Dominion was the first step towards the disintegration of the great British Empire. That same day a new cabinet was sworn in, followed shortly by a general election. Ottawa was launched. Three years later the government purchased Rideau Hall as a permanent viceregal abode. The presence of the governor-general, his aides, and visits by many dignitaries lent some vestige of culture and refinement to what had been a volatile mix of wealthy captains of industry and brawling peasants.

Lord Monck and family, Rideau Hall, Ottawa, ca. 1867.
(Public Archives of Canada—C21006).

Rideau Hall, Ottawa, residence of the Governor General.
(Public Archives of Canada—PA53034).

Dining Room at Rideau Hall.
(Public Archives of Canada—PA27911).

7. More Irish Troubles

The years leading towards Canadian Confederation were tense ones because the American Civil War was raging to the south. Canada was in a quandary. Most citizens favoured the abolition of slavery, and their sympathies lay with Abraham Lincoln's Union. The British government—and the governors-general—favoured the south, Jefferson Davis's Confederacy. The administration tolerated the presence of southerners who made their way into Canada with the avowed intention of using it as a base from which to annoy the northern states. The climax was the raid on St. Albans, Vermont, in October, 1864, by southerners based in Montreal. After robbing the banks in broad daylight—Jesse James did not invent the procedure—the raiders withdrew to Montreal carrying $200,000.

The commander of the military district that included St. Albans ordered troops to go after the raiders, which might have brought Britain into the war on the side of the Confederacy, but President Lincoln wisely countermanded the order. Canadian authorities arrested 14 of the raiders, and the American Secretary of State, William Seward, asked that they be extradicted. Lord Monck, the governor-general, refused, but ordered the culprits to stand trial. To Monck's extreme displeasure all were freed on a technicality. He ordered them re-arrested, but the men were nowhere to be found.

By that time there was no doubt as to the outcome of the war, and the fact that large numbers of Irishmen were in the Union Army was well known to the then Attorney-General of Canada West, John A. Macdonald. Furthermore, the Fenian movement was gaining momentum in the north. The American branch of the Fenian Brotherhood had been organized to supply money and arms to the parent body in Ireland, for the liberation of the old sod from England's tyranny—an ongoing problem. By the 1860s, the Fenians in the United States were sidetracked. Why not, they argued, take possession of a closer piece of British real estate? Canada would make a fine new homeland, and already many Irish people had settled there, men who would greet the Fenians as an army of liberation.

Nobody had bothered to warn them that many of the Irish in Canada were members in good standing of the Loyal Orange Lodge. Macdonald had spies operating in the northern cities, who kept him at least as well informed as the leaders who were thinking of perpetrating an outrage against Canada. Since the Union Army would soon be disbanded, releasing seasoned veterans for nefarious schemes, the Attorney-General thought it prudent to co-operate with President Lincoln in preventing further excursions by southern guests in the provinces.

Along the frontiers of Canada West and Canada East the militia was called out, and a shiver ran the length of the Rideau Canal. As in 1837, the blockhouses along the waterway were occupied by militiamen and a few regular troops. This occupation had been mooted earlier, for on January 1st, 1862, the lockmaster at Merrickville, John Johnson, wrote to the superintending engineer, James Slater, enquiring as to when he would have to vacate the blockhouse and take temporary lodgings in the village. Johnson, a retired sergeant from the Royal Sappers and Miners, had had to leave his home in 1837 to make room for a garrison, and he was anxious to know what allowance would be forthcoming to cover the extra expense.

Excitement mounted when the civil war ended in February, 1865, and the disbanded Fenians were free to pursue their objective of tweaking the British lion's tail. Fortunately, John A. Macdonald's spies, who fraternized with the loquacious Fenians in bars, kept the Attorney-General fully informed, and he knew more about their intentions than some of the ringleaders. The crisis came in the spring of 1866, when groups of Fenians did cross the border, from Vermont into Canada East, and from New York into Canada West near Fort Erie. All were repelled without much difficulty, but everywhere the militia was on the alert.

Of immediate concern in the Rideau country was the safety of Kingston, Brockville, Prescott, and the canals near Cornwall. Mustered at Kingston were the Kingston Field Battery, the 1st Frontenac Troop of Cavalry, and companies of infantry from Garden Island and Portsmouth. At Fort Henry and in the six Martello Towers some regulars were on guard, and the 14th Battalion Volunteer Militia Rifles, established in 1863 at Kingston, was sent on a special train to reinforce Cornwall. Meanwhile, local militia units and regulars were strengthening Fort

North side of Princess Street looking west from Wellington Street, Kingston, Ontario, 1862-65. (Public Archives of Canada—PA62177).

Wellington at Prescott, and one division of the Ottawa Field Battery and two companies of the Ottawa Rifles were stationed there or in the town.

The Perth Rifles, and some infantry, as well as the Carleton Place Rifles, were sent to Brockville following an erroneous report that the Fenians were planning a St. Patrick's Day celebration in the town. At Cornwall the situation seemed particularly grave. A party of Fenians was reported to be moving in that direction, and among other units, one division of the Ottawa Field Battery and two more companies of Ottawa Rifles had been dispatched there. In the capital itself, the garrison consisted of the Civil Service Rifles, an artillery company, a company of infantry from Bell's Corners, several other companies from the neighbourhood, and some Home Guard raised for the occasion. The United States government acted with more alacrity than in 1838-40, and the Fenians threatening Cornwall were forced to turn back.

At Ogdensburg, where a party of Fenians arrived by train, M.D. Chapin, the Collector of Customs, received orders on June 1st, to prevent any of them crossing the St. Lawrence River. He ordered Captain Car-well, the commander of the United States revenue cutter *Chase* to keep his steam up, ready for an emergency. Next, Chapin sent an armed steamboat to escort the ferries that operated between Ogdensburg and Prescott so that the Fenians could not seize them. On June 24th, General Meade arrived with 250 regular soldiers aboard the noon train, and on July 16th, the armed steamer *Watertown* came to join the blockade of the harbour. In the interval General Meade had sent a detachment of troops to DeKalb Junction, on the main railway line from Malone, New York, where they intercepted a shipment of arms intended for Ogdensburg.

The Fenian ringleaders were lodged under guard at the Seymour House Hotel, where General Meade had his headquarters. On one occasion an angry crowd gathered in the street below, eager to see the Fenians retaliate for the raid on St. Albans of two years before. Guarded by 40 of his regulars, General Meade addressed the crowd, unaware that his feeling of security was misplaced. Later 40 balls were picked up in the street. The soldiers had opened their cartridges and removed the lethal part before loading their rifles.

163

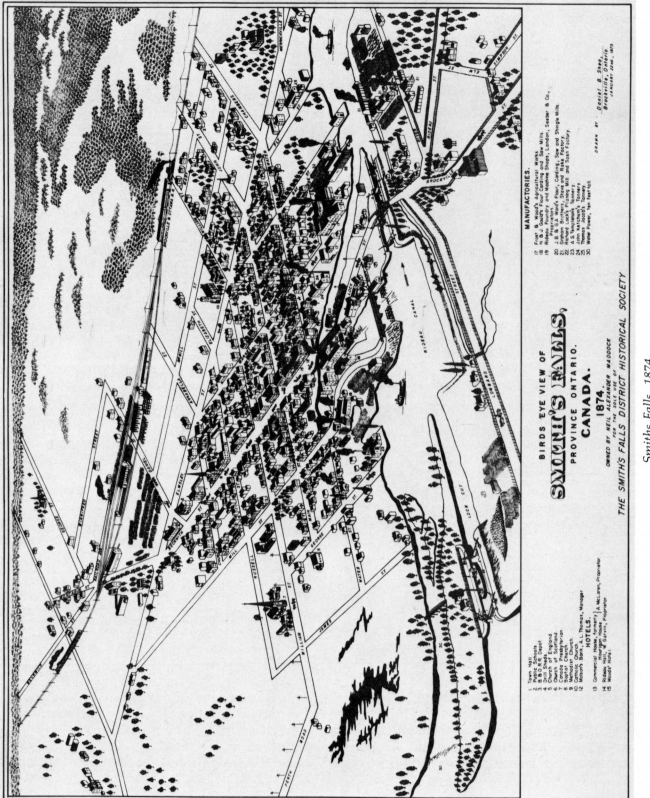

Smiths Falls, 1874.

(Reprinted by express permission of The Smiths Falls & District Historical Society).

164

The crisis blew over, and the American militiamen returned to their homes. The United States government dispatched other bodies of regular troops to patrol the border and prevent any further violations of Canadian sovereignty. Yet the trouble was not quite over. The Fenians kept a low profile for nearly four years, then in 1870, the leaders were ready to try again. This time the military situation in Canada had changed. Now that she was a self governing Dominion, the British regular troops had been withdrawn, and her defence rested on militia units that had been strengthened and better trained since the previous series of raids.

The militia battalions had been created from former independent companies and numbered, a process that had begun prior to 1866. For a second time the militia mustered and moved to guard the strategic border points, Kingston, Brockville, Prescott and Cornwall. The province of Ontario was divided into military districts. One, with its headquarters in Brockville, covered Leeds, Grenville and Lanark Counties. Raised to stand guard were the 41st Battalion of Rifles, from Leeds and Grenville, and the 42nd Battalion, from Lanark. Both regiments were organized in October, 1866, while the 14th Battalion Volunteer Militia Rifles, of Kingston, established in 1863, had been renamed the Princess of Wales' Own Rifles in 1868. In Carleton County, the 43rd Battalion was not formed until 1881, but the companies that were incorporated later were mustered. One division of the Ottawa Field Battery with two guns and one rifle company were sent to Prescott. The latter group was part of what was nicknamed the Carleton County Blazers, for no apparent reason, but they wore red coats, whereas the battalions of riflemen wore green.

All four battalions have their descendents in the present Canadian militia establishment. The 14th became The Princess of Wales' Own Regiment, home address Kingston; the 41st The Brockville Rifles; the 42nd The Lanark and Renfrew Scottish Regiment, with headquarters in Perth; and the 43rd The Cameron Highlanders of Ottawa. In 1870, men from all the battalions were on duty guarding border points between Kingston and Cornwall. The greatest threat came from Ogdensburg, where the Fenians were expected to congregate and attempt to cross the St. Lawrence. They were unsuccessful, but a party crossed from Vermont into southern Quebec, and the invaders were soundly trounced on May 25th, at Eccles Hill, by local militia. Canada's part time soldiers had demonstrated that they could fill in the gap between the departure of the British redcoats and the development of a professional army.

During the emergencies of 1866 and 1870, the Rideau Waterway was guarded, but it was not used to rush troops to the front. That role had passed to the railways, more suited to the rapid transport of soldiers. The mad incursions by misguided Irishmen marked the end of raids into Canadian territory from the United States, and vice versa. The 1870s ushered in an era of peace between the two neighbours, when the waterway would be used for commerce and pleasure boating to benefit Americans as well as Canadians.

Main Street, Newboro, Ontario.
(The Roberts Family, Westport).

Beckwith Street, Smiths Falls, Ontario, 1895-1900.
(Public Archives of Canada—C79399).

Street scene, Smiths Falls, Ontario.
(Public Archives of Canada—PA8811).

Mills on the Rideau River at Smiths Falls, Ontario.
(Public Archives of Canada—PA8803).

The William Merrick Mill ca. 1896, later the Percival Stove and Plow Works, Merrickville.
(Public Archives of Canada—C54506).

Merrickville, 1891.
(Ontario Archives).

View along the Rideau River, upstream from Merrickville, 1913.
(Public Archives of Canada—C54502).

Ottawa, 1876.
(National Map Collection, Public Archives of Canada).

Steamer "Olive" built in Smiths Falls, 1875, at the bridge in Manotick, Ontario, ca. 1880. (Public Archives of Canada—PA8808).

8. Commercial Navigation, 1870-1918

The most dramatic change following Confederation was the wider development of the tug and the luxury passenger steamer. However, at least six dual purpose steamers were built in that period. Freight remained an important source of revenue to the canal, and it was not suffering as much as the St. Lawrence canals from railway competition. The direct route to Ottawa from Lake Ontario remained the Rideau Waterway, and the triangular trade to Montreal of the early years did not die out. The railways helped increase the traffic along the Rideau, because of the demand for coal, used to fuel both the steamboats and the railway engines now that wood was growing more expensive. The coal was brought into the area on barges from American ports, and the black, sooty pyramids replaced the old woodpiles at depots along the waterway. Demand for coal was greatest at Smiths Falls, which became a junction on the Canadian Pacific Line. From 1875 onward, 4,000 tons were delivered there each year.

Known to have been in service along the Rideau Canal were a dozen dual purpose steamboats, so named because they carried both passengers and freight. One was the *Olive*, built at Smiths Falls in 1875, by William O'Mara; another, the *Quebec*, was built at Bedford Mills, on Devil Lake, in 1867 by William Gorrell. Until 1919, this vessel was registered at Kingston. The *Khartoum* was built at Ernesttown, on Lake Ontario, by Joseph Ward Pierce in 1885, and she broke up on the Rideau in 1892. Two others, the *Antelope*, and the *Victoria*, were built at Kingston in 1889 and 1900 respectively, and both were smaller than the first three. The sixth steamer was the diminutive, seven ton *Lee*, built at Brockville by James McGraw.

Plying the waterway, pulling barges, were several tugs. The little *Mary Ann* was owned by Henry Easton of Merrickville. The tugs *Forest* and *Francis* were from the Chaffey boatyard at Bedford Mills. These two were joined by the *Elswood*, from the same boatyard and named for one of the Chaffey brothers. On one occasion the *Elswood* towed the barge *Ontario* from Loughborough Lake to Montreal with a cargo of 263 tons of potash. Two others, the *Kitty Friel* and the *Edmond*, belonged to Benjamin Tett of Newboro, and were probably built at Bedford

171

Shipped In good order and condition, by _____ of Hull and consigned to Newton E. Graham _____ in and upon the Steamboat **OLIVE**, whereof **A. FOSTER** is Master for this present voyage. and now lying in the Port of _____ being marked and numbered as per margin; and are to be delivered in like good order and condition, at the aforesaid Port of Portland

(the act of God, the Queen's enemies, Fire, and all and every the Dangers and Accidents of the Seas, Rivers, and Navigation, of whatsoever nature and kind, excepted), he or they paying Freight for said Goods at the current rates.

In Witness whereof, the Master or Purser of said Vessel hath affirmed to _____ Bills of Lading, all of this tenor and date, one of which being accomplished, the rest to stand void.

Dated at Hull this 23 day of June 18 9

MARKS AND NUMBERS.	NO. PIECES.	DESCRIPTION.	RATE.	WEIGHT.	CHARGES.	TOTAL.
Newton E. Graham Portland		1 Paper Roll Jacky				1 50

Mills. The tugs provided rather cramped living space for two or three crew members. These small steamers gradually replaced the all purpose boats that had drawn the barges when the waterway first opened. Also, more of the barges, still built at Kingston and Bedford Mills in this later era, were powered by their own engines.

The newer single purpose passenger steamer, however, was the elite of all the carriers that plied the Rideau Waterway at the turn of the century. All told, five sailed the canal after 1885. The first was the *Rideau Belle*, built at Kingston by Robert Davis in 1885. Originally licenced to carry 40 passengers, in 1893, she was permitted 100 on inland waters. The Rideau system was classified as a minor waterway, and vessels were subject to less stringent safety regulations than the passenger boats that operated on the St. Lawrence and Lake Ontario. The *Rideau Belle* ran twice a week between Smiths Falls and Kingston, with a stop at Perth, and took 76 hours for the round trip. Her panelling of cherrywood, cushions of satin, and green velvet curtains in the lounge made her the last word in elegance.

She broke up on Sand Lake in 1895, at which time her owners were embroiled in litigation with the Department of Railways and Canals, which then operated the waterway. Some months earlier, the *Rideau Belle*

had hit the Beveridge Locks on the Tay Canal, inflicting $1,000 worth of damage to government property. For a time she had been impounded pending a settlement. After the fire her owners considered her a total loss, and the local lockmaster managed to salvage some of her panelling. With this cherrywood he built himself an outdoor convenience—or necessary house—of unusual splendour.

The *Ella Ross* was similar to the *Rideau Belle*, and she advertised 26 staterooms and a dining salon that could seat 50 people. The fare from Kingston to Montreal, or the reverse, was $14.00 in 1887. The *James Swift*, built at Kingston in 1893, was much larger and even more luxurious, and licenced to carry 100 passengers. Owned by Daniel Noonan of Kingston in 1899, her registration was changed later to the Rideau River Navigation Company, but Noonan remained one of her shareholders. Other owners were James Swift, for whom she was named, and Houghton Wilson, both of Kingston, George Kidd of Ottawa, and a Mr. Zimmerman of New York.

The *Rideau Queen* was built in 1901 for the Rideau Lakes Navigation Company. Advertisements informed prospective passengers that she had steam heat, electric lighting, electric fans, and cabins priced from $1.00 to $5.00, with meals at 50¢. Licenced for 300

Steamer "Olive" in Long Island Lock, 1891.
(Ontario Archives).

Steamer "D. C. West" in Brewers Mills Lock, ca. 1880.
(Public Archives of Canada—PA8831).

Steamer "Ella Ross" built in Montreal 1873 for the Deseronto Navigation Co., Northport, Ontario.
(Public Archives of Canada—C45429).

Parliament Hill from rear showing Rideau Canal Locks at Ottawa, ca. 1880.
(Public Archives of Canada—PA12384).

The steam-tug "Agnes P." built in 1913 at Buckingham, Que. and a barge in the Rideau Canal near Hogs Back. (Public Archives of Canada—PA45687).

The patrol vessel "Shanly" in the Canal Basin, Ottawa, ca. 1907. (Public Archives of Canada—C5277).

The old steam barge "Westport" hauled everything in the way of cargo, ca. 1900, builders: Geo. Chaffey & Bros., Bedford Mills, 1862. (Public Archives of Canada—C17364).

Steamer "Welshman" built in 1900 at Ottawa, in the Rideau Locks at Parliament Hill, 1907.
(Public Archives of Canada—C5275).

Government steam-tug "Loretta" built in 1907 at Toronto, Ontario to replace the "Shanly".
(Public Archives of Canada—C54497).

Tug "Loretta" in the Rideau Canal, Ottawa, 1920.
(Ontario Archives).

Steamer "James Swift" built in 1893 at Kingston, Ontario by Matthew R. Davis.

passengers on the Rideau Waterway, she was allowed 150 on the St. Lawrence. Her staterooms would not accommodate her full allotment, but many of her guests were day trippers. Her sister ship was the *Rideau King*, formerly the *James Swift*, which was gutted by fire in the turning basin at Ottawa in 1901. Acquired by the Rideau Lakes Navigation Company, rebuilt, refurbished and renamed, the *Rideau King* shared the Ottawa-Kingston run with the *Rideau Queen*, although the former was a slower vessel.

The last passenger steamboat to operate on the Rideau was the *Ottawan*. Built at Montreal by J. and R. Weir, she was similar to the *Rideau Queen*, and the only passenger vessel to sport a steel frame. After sailing the waterway alone for some years, the *Ottawan* was taken out of service when the automobile and road transport finally put her out of business.

The railways were not a threat to the passenger steamers on the Rideau, and the shipping lines and railway companies co-operated. The *Rideau Queen* and the *Rideau King* each made two round trips between Ottawa and Kingston every week. The *Queen* left Kingston on Mondays and Thursdays at 7:00 a.m., and reached Ottawa 23 hours later. The *King* left on Tuesdays and Fridays at 1:00 p.m. and made the same run in 27 hours. At Kingston the steamers connected with the Grand Trunk Railway's Montreal-Toronto trains, and with the Thousand Islands Steamboat Company and the Lake Ontario and Bay of Quinte Steamboat Company. At Ottawa the connections were with the Canadian Pacific Railway, the Ottawa-

Steamer "James Swift" subsequently rebuilt and renamed the "Rideau King".
(Queen's University Archives).

RIDEAU LAKES ROUTE

CLAYTON
SMITH'S FALLS
and
OTTAWA
to
KINGSTON
AND THE
CHARMING
RIDEAU
LAKES

MOST BEAUTIFUL SCENERY AND THE FINEST FISHING

BLACK BASS, SALMON TROUT AND MASKINONGE

GOOD HOTEL ACCOMMODATION & FIRST-CLASS STEAMER SERVICE

A Lake and Island Paradise

JULY 5 to SEPT. 5	CLAYTON, N.Y., KINGSTON, SMITH'S FALLS AND OTTAWA	JULY 5 to SEPT. 5
9.30 P.M. Lve.	CLAYTON, N.Y.	Arr. 8.30 P.M.
6.00 A.M.	KINGSTON	6.00 "
7.00 "	KINGSTON MILLS	5.45 "
10.00 "	BREWER'S MILLS	1.45 "
11.00 "	SEELEY'S BAY	12.45 "
11.30 "	JONES FALLS	12.00 Noon
1.00 P.M.	DAVIS	11.00 A.M.
1.30 "	CHAFFEYS	10.30 "
2.30 "	NEWBORO	9.30 "
3.30 "	WESTPORT	9.00 "
4.30 "	PORTLAND	8.00 "
5.00 "	GARRETT'S REST	7.45 "
6.30 " Arr.	RIDEAU FERRY	6.20 "
8.30 " Lve.	SMITHS FALLS	Lve. 5.00 "
9.00 " Lve.	SMITH'S FALLS (C.P.)	Arr. 8.30 P.M.
10.50 " Arr.	OTTAWA	Lve. 7.00 "

THE MAGNIFICENT PALACE STEAMERS

RIDEAU KING and RIDEAU QUEEN

Lighted by Electricity, Steam Heated, Ventilated by Steam Fans, and Equipped with all Modern Conveniences

CONNECTIONS

Passengers leaving New York Saturday evening, make connection with Rideau Steamers at Clayton on Sunday morning.

For further information apply to Agents of Thousand Island Steamboat Co., or New York Central Railway and Canadian Pacific Railway.

D. NOONAN, General Manager, Kingston, Ont.   H. W. WILSON, General Passenger Agent.

RIDEAU LAKES NAVIGATION CO. LIMITED

CLAYTON, KINGSTON AND OTTAWA

Rideau Lakes Navigation Co.
Limited

1910

Steamers will run during the season of Navigation as follows:

From May 2nd to June 28th, and from Sept. 4th to Nov. 1st.

Steamers leave Kingston Monday and Thursday at 6 a.m.; arrive at Ottawa Tuesday and Friday at 8 a.m. Leave Ottawa Tuesday and Friday at 2 p.m.; arrive at Kingston Wednesday and Saturday at 5 p.m.

From June 28th to September 4th.

Steamers leave Clayton, N.Y., Tuesday, Wednesday and Friday at 9.00 p.m., on Sunday at 3.00 p.m. Kingston, Monday, Wednesday, Thursday and Saturday at 6 a.m.; arrive at Ottawa, Tuesday, Thursday, Friday and Sunday at 8 a.m. Leave Ottawa, Monday, Tuesday, Thursday and Friday at 2 p.m.; arrive at Kingston, Tuesday, Wednesday, Friday and Saturday at 5 p.m. Clayton, N.Y., 8.30 p.m.

	O.W.	R.T.
Fare, Clayton to Kingston	$1.00	$1.75
" Clayton to Smith's Falls	3.00	5.25
" Clayton to Ottawa	4.80	8.35
" Kingston to Smith's Falls	2.00	3.50
" Kingston to Ottawa	3.80	6.60
" Smith's Falls to Ottawa	1.80	3.10

Meals and Berths extra.

Rideau King, Meals 75c., Berths $1.50, Rooms $3.00.

Rideau Queen, Meals 75c. to $1.00; Berths: lower berth $2.50, upper berth $1.50, Rooms $4.00.

Children occupying seats at the table will be charged for meals at tariff rates, as advertised. Stop-over allowed on application to purser.

N.B.—Clayton Service from June 28th to September 4th.

D. NOONAN,
V.P. & G.M.

Prescott Railway (which became part of the Canadian Pacific in 1885) and the Ottawa River Navigation Company's steamboats.

The larger Rideau steamers connected with the New York Central Railroad, by crossing the St. Lawrence to meet the evening train at Clayton and returning to Kingston to tie up for the night. At the more important points along the Rideau Waterway, the passenger steamers made regular stops, putting in at the smaller wharves only if people were waiting for them. The signal was a white flag, and when it was flying a captain knew he had customers. Some might travel to the end of his run, some only as far as the next wharf.

Also plying the waterway were several government boats and some private yachts. The *Ellen C* was a fishery patrol vessel built in 1906. The *Loretta* was a splendid craft built at the Polson Iron Works in Toronto in 1907, and owned by the Department of Railways and Canals. When she began her service that August, the *Loretta's* crew consisted of Captain Frank Nevens, Engineer Victor Riel, two deckhands and a cook. Aboard, a stateroom was maintained for the use of the superintending engineer, at that time Arthur T. Phillips, known to his employees as A.T.

Other government vessels were the *Agnes P* and two dredges, the *Rideau* and the *Tay*. The *Rideau*, which had no source of power, was built at Welland by Beattie and Company in 1889. Ten years later she was rebuilt in Ottawa by John Burns, when an engine was installed. Then in 1901, Selbey and Youlden of Kingston built a new boiler for her. The *Tay* was similar to the *Rideau*, and had five cabins. She was built at Buckingham, Quebec, in 1913, and was renamed the *Rideau* when the older boat was retired from service.

The earliest privately owned pleasure craft were steam yachts. One was the *Marquis of Lorne*, built in 1874 for a brewer of Portsmouth. After passing through several hands, by 1896, she belonged to John Carruthers of Ottawa. Others were the *Bella* and the *Willard*, 46 and 44 feet long respectively. The latter, built at Rideau Ferry in 1912, was owned by Mrs. Mabel Code of Smiths Falls. An early houseboat was the unpowered *Annandale*, 65 feet long and weighing 75.57 tons. She was built at Rockport, on the St. Lawrence, in 1903. Another that might be considered a pleasure yacht was the *Shanly*, owned by the government. She was actually a tug, but the superintending engineer, A.T.

"Rideau King", originally known as the "James Swift" was built at Kingston in 1893. Owned by Rideau Lakes Navigation Co. of Kingston. After being damaged by fire in late 1899 was completely refitted in 1900 and renamed the "Rideau King." Was commanded at times by Capt. Scott and Capt. Wm. Fleming (Brother of Capt. Ned Fleming). (Public Archives of Canada—C17366).

Phillips, used her for fishing trips on the lakes.

By 1910, some boats had internal combustion engines that ran on gasoline—noisier than the steam yachts but less expensive to buy and operate—the boat for the masses. One that may have plied the waterway was the *Little Queen*, built and owned by Grant Pike of Wolfe Island. By 1901, there were some 250 small power craft near Ottawa, and their owners had formed the Ottawa Motorboat Association. These plebian launches, buzzing past the aristocratic steam yachts, were a forewarning of things to come, the time when the waterway would be given over entirely to small pleasure craft, the day when the freighters and passenger carriers would vanish from the scene.

World War I marked the turning point. Until it ended the canal carried about the same volume of freight as it had done since 1875—between 50,000 and 150,000 tons per season. The total weight fluctuated widely from year to year. As war clouds gathered in the face of the strutting, arrogant German Kaiser, the men along the waterway were mobilized for duty at home and overseas.

The four regiments that had been formed between 1860 and 1880 all sent detachments to join the Canadian Expeditionary Force that was fighting in France and Belgium. Two members of the old 43rd Battalion, then known as the Ottawa Regiment (Duke of Cornwall's Own) that served with the 38th Battalion of the expeditionary force, were awarded the Victoria Cross. One was Captain Thane W. MacDowell, the other was Private C.J.P. Nunny.

With the coming of peace, faster cars and trucks and better roads, commercial traffic began a steady decline on the Rideau Canal. Apart from the small towns where some industries flourished, the waterway could aptly be described as a recreation corridor.

"Rideau King" in the Lock.
(The Roberts Family, Westport).

"Rideau King" at Newboro, ca. 1900.
(The Roberts Family, Westport).

"Rideau King" at the plating factory,
Westport, ca. 1910.
(The Roberts Family, Westport).

"Rideau King" leaving Jones Falls Locks.
(Mr. Joseph T. Kenney).

"Rideau Queen" built in 1900 at
Kingston, seen leaving the lowest
lock at Jones Falls.
(Public Archives of Canada—C17355).

The "Ottawan" built in 1904, at Ottawa
by J. and R. Weir, in the Rideau
Locks at Ottawa, ca. 1912.
(Public Archives of Canada—PA10370).

Steamer "Rideau Queen" of Kingston on the Rideau Canal, Ottawa.
(Public Archives of Canada—C6895).

Garrett's Rest, ca. 1912.
(Parks Canada)

Newboro Station, ca. 1912.
(Parks Canada)

Steamer "Rideau King"
in Newboro Lock.
(Parks Canada)

Rideau Canal locks at the Chateau Laurier Hotel, Ottawa. Painted by Richard Rummell in 1912. (Courtesy of Chateau Laurier Hotel Management)

Aerial view of the Royal Military College of Canada and Fort Frederick at Kingston, Ontario. (Courtesy of Health & Welfare Canada)

Chaffeys Lock and mill with the Opinicon Hotel.

The Long Island mill at Manotick, Ontario.

Aerial view of Jones Falls.
(Parks Canada)

In the locks at Jones Falls.
(Parks Canada)

Aaron Merrick house built ca. 1845, Merrickville, Ontario.

Log cabin on the River Road near Merrickville, Ontario.

Aerial view of Seeleys Bay.

Aerial view of Burritts Rapids.

The tug "Tay" at upper lock, Jones Falls.
(Parks Canada)

Pleasure boats in the Rideau locks.

Aerial view of Perth including the turning basin.

Aerial view of Smiths Falls and the locks.

Mouth of Rideau Canal and Parliament Hill, winter 1906.
(Ontario Archives).

Parliament Hill, Ottawa, 1906.
(Public Archives of Canada—C4962).

Captain Ned Fleming and staff in the dining salon aboard the Rideau Queen, June 1904.
(Fred Fleming).

Captain Ned Fleming and friends aboard the Rideau Queen, ca. 1900.
(Fred Fleming).

Captain Ned Fleming "looking for trouble" aboard the Rideau Queen at Newboro dock, ca. 1912.
(Fred Fleming).

Perth, Ontario on the Tay River.
(Public Archives of Canada—C18185).

9. Decline of Commercial Navigation, Local Industry and Agriculture

Passenger traffic on the Rideau Canal amounted to more than 5,000 bookings in 1890, and rose to 26,000 by 1910. Much of the increase rested on the popularity of the comfortable steamships that offered luxury staterooms and dining facilities, and deck space from which to view the scenery. The tugs and barges continued bringing in coal, carrying out lumber, cut and crushed stone, cheese and other foodstuffs produced within the region, as well as manufactured goods. By 1918, the situation for passenger boats had changed dramatically for the worse. The automobile had begun to supercede the more leisurely modes of travel, and the first to be struck down were the passenger steamers.

In 1916, after 23 years on the waterway, the *Rideau King's* engine needed an overhaul, and by 1920, she had been scrapped. The *Rideau Queen* had been sent to carry freight along Lake Ontario and the Bay of Quinte the year before, and she was sold to a Trenton contractor. In 1924, she was sold again, to the Valleyfield Beauharnois Navigation Company, and she operated on the lower St. Lawrence until her registry closed in 1937. By 1920, only the *Ottawan* was still plying the Rideau, offering sightseers and holiday makers the chance of sailing through the waterway. Roads and the Great Depression of the 1930s soon took their toll of this last vestige of a bygone era. The *Ottawan* made her farewell voyage on November 2nd, 1935,

departing from Ottawa. Afterward only privately owned boats carried visitors along the canal.

The death of passenger traffic was not unique to the Rideau Waterway. The same fate befell the steamers on the Trent-Severn Waterway, and the St. Lawrence. Everywhere people preferred to reach their summer cottages or the resorts by car. Freight remained a more viable commodity longer than passengers, but gradually, through the centralization of production in larger factories, local industry along the Rideau began to decline, and the story was much the same for agriculture. The farm operations were small scale, especially through the Canadian Shield country and on the limestone plain. As larger farms became the economic units, the poorest quality lands were abandoned, the scattered pockets of good soil gathered into bigger holdings. Only on the good farmlands of Carleton County along the lower Rideau were farmers able to hold their own against large operations in other parts of Ontario. With the decline in local industry and agriculture, the volume of freight the canal carried dropped off.

Cheese was a case in point. Before the 1930s, every town and village had a factory, and wooden boxes for its storage and transport were made at Westport. In 1892, to emphasize the region's cheesemaking capacities a group of Perth businessmen produced an eleven ton specimen measuring six feet high and nine feet in diameter, which was shipped to the Chicago World's Fair.

World's largest cheese, 22,000 lbs.,
loaded on C.P.R. flat cars in Perth, Ontario, 1892 enroute to Chicago World's Fair.
(Public Archives of Canada—PA91030).

If quality lived up to quantity the big cheese must have caused a sensation. Rapid road transport, and the notion that big was best, reduced the number of cheese factories. Fresh milk could be exported over longer distances, and most cheese making was centralized in a few large factories, the better to compete in the market place. The larger the plant the lower its prices. The last cheese boat, once a familiar sight, passed through the waterway in 1930.

Centralization adversely affected many other small industrial premises. Foundaries could not compete with Hamilton, the steel centre of Ontario, and woollen mills suffered from the competition of the Quebec textile industry, where labour was cheaper. The same fate befell the flour mills, which were not in a convenient location for grinding western grain. This industry became concentrated in a few large ports on the Great Lakes and lower St. Lawrence. Craftsmen were forced to close down their small shops, in the face of competition from factories that mass produced furniture, shoes and the like.

Technological change would in time mean economic stagnation for the smallest villages, but from 1900 until 1918, the canal carried a creditable volume of freight, because the economy was strong and goods moved by all forms of transport. Yet lumber dropped steadily as the trees were used up. In 1890, 38,600 tons passed through the

canal, and by 1915, this was down to 10,200 tons. In 1961, only 49 tons passed, although the pulp and paper industry flourished at Hull. The canal carried a surprising amount of ores and minerals until the crash of 1929—118,200 tons in 1914, and afterward an average of 70,000 tons a year. In 1956, only 26 tons, half a barge load, travelled on the waterway. Grain and other agricultural produce, which peaked in 1911 at 6,000 tons, was down to 608 tons by 1930, and by 1941, none moved on the canal because everything went by truck along the highways.

Coal, so important in the 1880s, fluctuated, but 17,770 tons were carried in 1901. By the 1920s, the amount was negligible. Merchandise, chiefly imported for local use, peaked in 1892 at 60,500 tons, and the best year for manufactured goods, some produced locally, was 1911, when 144,000 tons were carried. The figure by 1937 was 33 tons. The Rideau Canal had really lost out to the roads and the St. Lawrence canals by the 1930s. The latter canals were deepened in the 1880s from 9 to 14 feet, to allow the large iron freighters from the Great Lakes to reach Montreal. A comparison of the tonnages tells the story:

Year	St. Lawrence	Rideau Canal
1888	781,599	112,248
1914	4,391,493	151,739
1938	9,236,318	1,623

Steam-tug "Colonel By" built in 1882 at Ogdensburg, N.Y. Owner: David Eligh, Burritts Rapids, with the barge "Minnie" in the Rideau Canal Locks at Sparks Street, Ottawa, 1920.
(Public Archives of Canada—PA84504).

Therefore it was small wonder that by 1930 the members of Parliament were questioning the validity of maintaining the Rideau Canal. The Department of Transport (formerly the Department of Railways and Canals) had been operating the waterway since 1879, and wanted to dispose of the white elephant. In 1832, a proposal presented in Parliament recommended closing down the waterway and filling in the canals. Fortunately this was not feasible. Colonel John By and his engineers had drastically altered the natural environment, as had the lumbermen and farmers. To allow the lock walls and dams to deteriorate, and the water levels to drop in consequence, the spring runoff speeded up because of deforestation, would cause untold damage. The canal had to be maintained, the lockmasters and repairmen on duty.

The price of keeping the canal in operation, despite periodic questions in the House, was small for the indirect benefit it was to the region. Although visitors in pleasure boats would pay modest tolls for passage through the locks, they would spend money on food and accommodation while cruising the waterway. Here was a partial substitute for the many closed down industries and shops. The canal did have a viable future, and since it had been well maintained over the century when it was a commercial waterway, the upkeep would not be a heavy burden.

Since the first axemen had penetrated the forests, the landscape had been altered to the point where it resembled its original aspect only superficially. The countryside still looked well wooded, but the trees were second growth or later. Over large areas the hills of bare granite stood out, where, for lack of vegetation cover, rain runoff and melting snow quickly drained away. Over much of the limestone plain where the soil is shallow, farmers abandoned large tracts, and there, too, the runoff was rapid. Several streams that once supported mills were torrents for a short time each spring, dry gullies by late August.

Over the years the pattern was repeated at the many waterfalls. First came a sawmill to prepare lumber for markets outside the region. Ironically, many of these mills produced the railway ties that had a negative impact on water transportation. Second, a grist mill for the wheat that was invariably the first crop was built. Next, farmers turned to dairying and cheese making. Around the millsites a variety of small industries and shops or stores congregated. These activities increased until after the turn of the century, and then a slow downward spiral began.

Where local timber was exhausted the sawmills closed down, and with a decline in wheat growing the smaller flour mills lost out to larger competitors. Such were outside the corridor and were operated by hydroelectric power. Lacking a large source locally, nearly all the once-buoyant milling operations closed down, one by one.

On the better lands the dairy farms continued producing milk, fresh for the Ottawa

The locomotive "Georgia" crossing bridge over the Rideau River at Ottawa, 1882.
(Public Archives of Canada—PA12198).

market, or for cheese factories. Industries based on local resources gradually vanished as these resources dwindled, or were found in such small quantities that they could not compete with bigger firms elsewhere. The Rideau country became a quiet backwater, and many of the young people left for towns and cities in quest of employment. Farmers with enough good land remained on their properties, and their sons tended to inherit. Other offspring were inclined to depart, and the population began to stagnate. Population in rural areas declined, but the census figures show that some of the drift was to towns in the corridor.

The decline is best demonstrated through change shown on Figure I, which lists the numbers in cities, towns and larger villages. Figure II shows the numbers of people in the smaller communities that are still recognized as villages.

Locomotive and crew.
Brockville & Westport Railway, 1910.
(Rideau & District Historical Society).

"Ottawa," the second locomotive used on the Bytown & Prescott Railway, 1910.
(Public Archives of Canada—C5288).

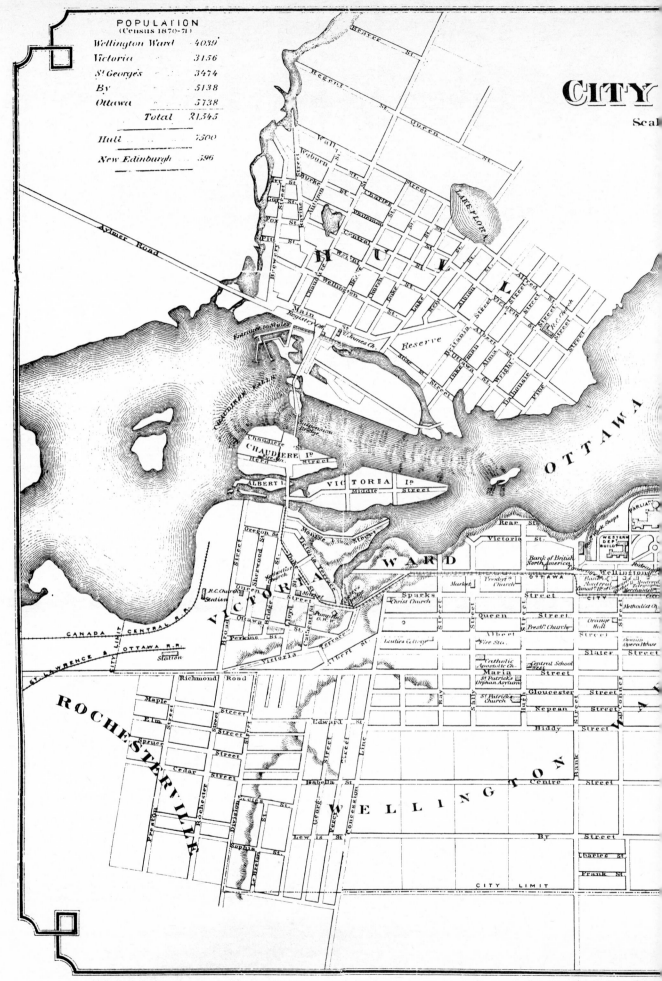

CITY

Scale

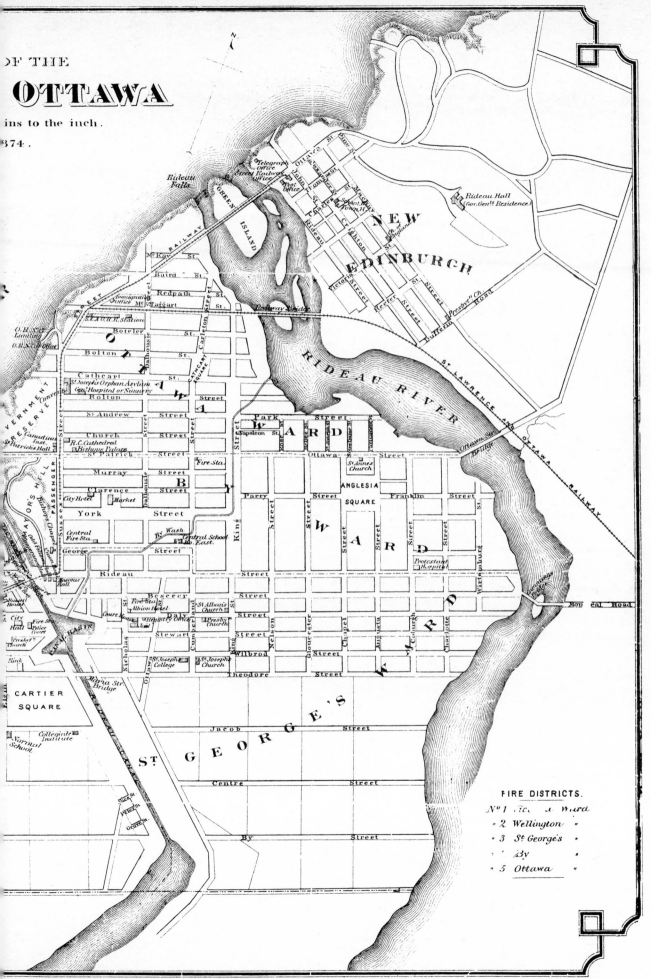

OF THE

OTTAWA

...ins to the inch.
...874.

N

Rideau Falls

Telegraph Office
Street Railway Office
Post Office

GREEN ISLAND
RAILWAY

Ottawa St
John St
James St

Sch. Ho.
Town Ho.

NEW

EDINBURGH

Rideau Hall
(Gov. Gen'l Residence)

McKay St.
Baird St.
Redpath St.
McTaggart St.

Immigration Office

Railway Bridge

S.A.U. R.R. Station

Boteler St.

St. Lawrence and Ottawa Railway

O.R.N. Co. Landing
O.R.N. Co. Office

Bolton St.

RIDEAU RIVER

Presby'n Ch.

Juffean

St. Lawrence and Ottawa Railway

Cathcart St.
St. Joseph's Orphan Asylum
Gen'l Hospital or Nunnery

CATHCART SQUARE

CARLETON STREET

DALHOUSIE

Convent

GOVERNMENT
RESERVE

St. Patrick's Hall

Canadian Inst.

R.C. Cathedral

Bishops Palace

Bolton St.

St. Andrew Street

Church Street

St. Patrick Street

Fire Sta.

OTTAWA

WARD

Park Street
Napoleon St.

Ottawa Street

St. Annes Church

WARD

Murray Street

BY

Clarence Street

City Hotel
Market

Bishops Chapel

SUSSEX

PASSENGER

York Street

Parry
King
Street

Street

ANGLESIA
SQUARE

Franklin Street

W A R D

Central Fire Sta.

By Wash
Central School No. East.

George Street

Rideau Street

MAYORS HILL

Masonic Hall

Protestant Hospital

Russell House

City Hall
Fire Sta.
Police Court
Protest. Church

Court House
Registry Office

Fire Sta.
Albion Hotel

Daly Street

St. Albans Church

Presby. Church

Beserer Street

NICHOLAS

CUMBERLAND

Stewart Street

KING

Wilbrod Street

Nelson
Gloucester
Chapel
Augusta
Charlotte
McCulloch
Wirtemburg

W

A

R

D

Montreal Road

Rink

St. Joseph College

St. Joseph Church

Theodore Street

ST. GEORGE'S

WARD

ELGIN

Maria Str. Bridge

Canal Basin

CARTIER
SQUARE

Normal School

Collegiate Institute

ST. *G E O R G E'S*

Jacob Street

Centre Street

St. St.
Peter St.
Grant St.

By Street

FIRE DISTRICTS.

No 1 ... ... Ward
" 2 Wellington   "
" 3 St George's "
" ... By   "
" 5 Ottawa   "

TABLES SHOWING THE POPULATION CHANGES IN THE AREA.

FIGURE I

Name	Population 1842	1891	1971
Kingston (city)	6,123	19,264	59,047
Ottawa (incl New Edinb.)	6,150	44,154	302,341
Frontenac			
Kingston (twp)	6,289	3,349*	17,390
Pittsburgh	2,132	3,000	9,445
Storrington	Not estab'd	2,285	2,515
Leeds			
Crosby North	863	2,097	635
Crosby South	1,003	1,849	1,395
Leeds & Lansdowne Rear	952	2,492	2,110
Bastard & Burgess South	3,058	3,319	2,285
Elmsley South	815	977	1,445
Newboro village	—	462	295
Westport village	—	—	600
Grenville			
Wolford	2,422	2,115	1,130
Oxford	2,960	3,307	2,615
Gower South	687	960	745
Merrickville	970	1,072	930
Kemptville	—	1,226	2,413
Lanark			
Drummond	3,451	2,202	1,640
Elmsley North	1,154	1,233	1,565
Burgess North	533	1,117	540
Montague	2,097	2,232	4,460
Perth	1,800	3,136	5,537
Smiths Falls	700	3,864	9,585
Carleton			
Marlborough	983	1,703	1,165
Osgoode	1,440	4,320	7,760
Gower North	855	2,383	3,725
Nepean	1,294	11,401	64,605
Gloucester	2,480	6,823	37,145
Richmond village	300	447	2,120
Osgoode village	—	—	823

* Kingston Township lost population through annexation by Kingston City.

FIGURE II—Small Villages and Ghost Towns

Name	1971 Population	Name	1971 Population
Kingston Mills	40	Portland	253
Barriefield	247	Rideau Ferry	107
Battersea	181	Port Elmsley	86
Seeleys Bay	406	Eastons Corners	119
Morton	91	Burritts Rapids	117
Chaffeys Lock	72	Oxford Mills	83
Elgin	322	Kars	183
Newboro	295	North Gower	363
		Manotick	476

Ghost Towns

Bedford Mills —mill restored as residence, church used
Opinicon —few traces, a landing
Allans Mills —mill being restored as residence
Andrewsville —six houses, some used as summer cottages

Kingston Mills Locks north.
(Ontario Archives).

At Foster's or Davis Lock ca. 1880.
(Public Archives of Canada—PA8817).

Chaffeys Lock, 1891.
(Ontario Archives).

203

As was to be expected, Ottawa absorbed New Edinburgh and her suburbs spread out over substantial portions of Nepean and Gloucester. A similar phenomenon on a smaller scale occurred at the other end of the waterway. The three townships close to Kingston have increased their populations. The drop of some 3,000 in Kingston Township between 1842 and 1891 was caused by an annexation to the city. Growth in Storrington was slight after 1891, but it was close enough to Kingston that it did not decline. Similarly Osgoode and North Gower Townships increased their populations after 1891 because they were affected by the proximity of Ottawa, as well as having good arable land.

In between, commencing at North Crosby in Leeds County, and extending to Marlborough Township in Carleton County, all the townships lost population by 1971, after peaking in 1891, with three notable exceptions. The population rose slightly in North and South Elmsley and substantially in Montague because of the presence of Smiths Falls, the urban area that had grown the most. In all three townships the percentage of good arable land is small, but the job opportunities were good. Many farmers could remain on their land and commute to work in Smiths Falls. Most of the smaller villages lost population, and this applied to Merrickville and Burritts Rapids. Perth grew slightly, and so did Kemptville, both of

which had a broader economic base.

Many of the small villages are shadows of their former selves, and four stand almost vacant. Dubbed ghost towns are Bedford Mills, Opinicon, Allans Mills and Andrewsville. At Bedford Mills, where so many boats were built, only the church was in use for some years. Now the mill building is being restored as a residence. The mill building at Allans Mills was used as a barn, and is now being restored as a residence, while down the Rideau at Andrewsville are six houses, some used as summer cottages. In other villages certain buildings might be renovated, but the merchants and craftsmen are gone, the factories and mills stand idle. Back from the waterway a village may now have only a gas station, convenience store, and a church or two. In the river ports are more convenience stores for local people and tourists, marinas and gas pumps, and resorts—hotels, cabins for rent, and campgrounds. The tourist trade has replaced the small industries as a source of sustenance along the corridor.

Then, too, as Ottawa grows larger, so does the need for recreation space, and even the most remote parts of the corridor are easily accessible. The closer to the city, the more picnic sites are to be found. The region is still noted for dairying, now mainly fresh milk for the urban market, but two cheese factories have survived. One is at Plum Hollow, the other at Forfar, their produce much in demand as it has more flavour than the

Andrewsville.
(Ontario Archives).

blocks of sanitary rubber of the large milk processing firms. Much has changed; much remains the same.

10. Emerging Playground

As the towns and cities grew, the middle and upper classes were able to take summer holidays. While the province was populated almost exclusively by farmers, a vacation was out of the question during the growing season, but increasing urbanization changed the pattern. Although few of the labouring class received wages high enough to save for a holiday, the situation was different for business and professional people. For them the passenger steamers offered an opportunity to visit faraway places, or to cruise and admire the scenery. For some the lure was hunting and fishing; the lakes abounded in game species, the forests with deer, and everyone who travelled needed a place to stay.

The first spot in the neighbourhood to attract tourists was the Thousand Islands section of the St. Lawrence River. The boom in tourism started before the 1870s, first with primitive shelters for fishermen, usually camps or small boarding houses. These were followed by summer mansions built by the wealthy; hotels; and cottages, owned or rented. Within a decade, proprietors along the Rideau Waterway, and the navigation companies, were advertising the charms of the smaller route, exhorting visitors to the Thousand Islands not to miss the opportunity to explore the inland streams and lakes

while they were close by. In 1875, John Fisher of Kingston operated a steam yacht with space for 100 passengers along the Rideau and Ottawa Rivers, but there does not seem to be any more information about it in the records.

Local people began building cottages close to their homes, and a few of the steam yacht owners built more sumptuous summer residences, especially along Big Rideau Lake. Men addicted to fishing and hunting sought solitude, if only to escape from wives and children for a time, by going into the more primitive parts of the waterway. Enterprising land owners provided campsites, some just tents, others wooden lodges. Soon a new profession developed, for city folk needed guides to show them where the fish were to be found; the shallows where large mouth bass basked; the grassy places favoured by pike; the deeper spots where pickerel floated; the depths of Big Rideau Lake where trout swam in the coldest waters.

The tourist industry, like everything else in the Rideau country, was on a small scale. Among the Thousand Islands religious groups sponsored large parks, where the social life revolved around a massive hotel; where cottages were owned or rented; and a pure moral climate best for young people prevailed. Along the Rideau, summer cottages were owned by local people, but a few larger resorts catered to tourists from farther afield who wanted creature comforts. Before the turn of the century the two most famous resorts—Hotel Kenney at Jones Falls and the Opinicon Hotel (later called the Opinicon) at Chaffeys Lock—were in operation.

Picnic party near Ottawa, ca. 1880.
(Public Archives of Canada—C11535).

Picnic party at Foster's Lock (Davis Lock) ca. 1880.
(Public Archives of Canada—PA8825).

Fishing for minnows at Foster's Lock, ca. 1880.
(Public Archives of Canada—PA8824).

Camping at Washburn Mills Locks (Lower Brewers) September 1913.
(Public Archives of Canada—PA16801).

Main Street, Portland on the Rideau, ca. 1910.
(Rideau & District Historical Society).

Original Hotel Kenney, Jones Falls, built 1877, photographed ca. 1880. One of the men in this picture has been identified as Thomas Bartlett Kenney.
(Hotel Kenney).

Hotel Kenney

In 1877, Thomas Bartlett Kenney and his wife Eleanor bought land on the north side of the waterway at Jones Falls. They erected the hotel known at first as the Hotel de Kenney. Immediately it was a hit with fishermen and pleasure boaters. The Kenneys added several wings to the original structure, where they played host to a stream of satisfied customers. One guest of note was William Howard Taft, the 27th President of the United States, who signed the register in 1909, during his first year in office.

In *Picturesque Rideau Route*, published in 1898, the hotel received high praise:

> We are glad to hear again, the torrent of Jones Falls and from the Vine-clad balconies of the Kenney House watch its snowy waters tumbling over huge boulders into the lake below. The house is so largely patronized by American sportsmen that the astute host flies the Stars and Stripes and the Union Jack side by side. It is a favourite resort for yacht owners and men of semi-nautical appearance lounge around and exchange fish stories.

In 1906, an annex with a store and post office was built across the road from the main building.

Hotel Kenney is now managed and own-ed by the fourth generation of the family by that name.

Thomas Bartlett and his wife Eleanor managed it from 1877 to 1922 followed by his son Joseph A. Kenney and his wife Suzanne from 1906 to 1943; then his grandson Thomas John Kenney and his wife Johanna from 1934 to the present day together with his son Thomas Joseph and his wife Linda who joined him in 1962. The greatest expansion of the facilities took place during the last 40 years.

Over the past few years the resort has become much more than a fishing lodge and vacationers from as far away as Arizona, British Columbia, France, Germany and the United Kingdom come to Hotel Kenney to enjoy boating, swimming, hiking as well as tennis, golf and riding nearby. The parade of private yachts entering and leaving the Jones Falls Locks creates a form of entertainment in itself.

The size of the Hotel provides for close attention by the management and staff and this may be one of the reasons why one couple from California recently celebrated their 50th consecutive year of Kenney hospitality.

May 24, 1915, celebrated by the local people with games and races at Jones Falls to commemorate the onset of summer.
(Hotel Kenney).

Fishing guides—Delbert Sly, Spence Baxter and Carl White at the Hotel, ca. 1950.
(Hotel Kenney).

Hotel Kenney ca. 1946.

Jones Falls Lock.
(Manotick Classic Boat Club—James Phelan).

Hotel Kenney and Lower Lock at Jones Falls.

Aerial view of Jones Falls Lock and Hotel Kenney.

210

Various modes of transportation in front of the Wardrobe Hotel, Westport, ca. 1909. (The Roberts Family, Westport).

In 1914, the Rideau Lakes Navigation Company published a brochure entitled "Rest and Sport Among the Rideau Lakes", enjoining visitors to come, stressing the steamboat links with the New York railway terminus at Clayton. Accommodation, the reader learned, was available at Kenney's, Fisherman's Rest at Westport, the Commercial House and Garrett's Rest in Portland, and a boarding house at Chaffeys Lock. Other resorts were Pringle's, Sea Breeze, Poppin's, Whitcomb's, Star Island and Rideau Ferry. Later the Tweedsmuir Hotel was built at Westport, Stirling Lodge at Newboro, Simmons Lodge at Chaffeys Lock, and a large resort close to Ottawa catered to honeymooners seeking privacy.

Other services expanded with need. Captain G.A. Davis of Smiths Falls, who had a forwarding business, undertook to supply cottages, and over the years his four boats were a familiar sight on the waterway. The *Vic II* was a gasoline launch, the *Lee*, the *Antelope* and the *Victoria* were steamboats all belonging to Davis. The Canadian Northern Railway built branch lines to Seeleys Bay, Crosby, Newboro and Westport, and a station less than a mile from the dock at Portland. There a shuttle carried passengers to and from the station. The steamboat fare was reasonable—$1.00 for the run from Smiths Falls to Portland, less for points in between. The *Victoria* remained in service until 1940, and was probably withdrawn because of extreme old age. World War II had started and gasoline for privately owned boats was rationed soon afterward.

By the mid 1930s, nearly all the traffic on the Rideau Canal was pleasure craft. Now the American invasion so dreaded in the past was welcomed. The local merchants were happy to have their patronage, although there arose what was called the flag controversy, which ruffled some plumage among the residents. Such were offended when American boatmen showed a lack of respect for naval etiquette, by not flying the host country's flag on their mastheads. They persisted in sailing along the waterway displaying only the Stars and Stripes. The matter became a non-issue when boats were smaller in later years. Few had mastheads of any size, and flying the Canadian flag was impracticable.

Most Americans were from New York State, but surprising numbers came from Pennsylvania and Ohio. On a first visit they were startled to find, through reading plaques put up by the federal government, that the canal had been built to keep them out of the country. In his book on the waterway, published in 1955, Robert Legget included a cartoon from the Columbus Ohio Sunday Dispatch for August 30th, 1936, showing two fishermen playing a whopper. The caption read "It's too bad the Duke of Wellington couldn't live to witness the battles of the Rideau."

As the numbers of small, privately owned boats increased, so did the need for aids to navigation. In areas where the land had been drowned by Colonal John By's engineers, many of the stumps were still there, submerged, and a hazard for the uninitiated yachtsman. At first many owners hired pilots to guide them through the complexities of the waterway. The channel was marked with buoys, but interesting byways beckoned to the explorer with a boat of shallow draft.

In the days when the Ordnance Department ran the canal, it was lighted by sperm oil lamps at the locks and wharves, which gave little light. By 1865, the superintending engineer, James Slater, and the Department of Public Works were considering installing coal oil lamps. The records do not show when the changeover occurred, but coal oil was cheaper than sperm oil and gave a better light. Undoubtedly it was used. In 1892, using power supplied by the Ottawa Electric Light Company, five arc lamps lighted the locks and canal basin in Ottawa. Gradually all the lights were electrified, and at many of the powersites small hydroelectric plants were built to serve local communities.

As another aid to navigation, the first map of the channel was published in 1905, for distribution to boat owners. The following year a speed limit of six miles per hour was imposed through the Ottawa portion, because the wake from fast boats endangered the safety of people in canoes and small rowboats at the foot of the high canal walls. In 1907, Dr. Elmer Lake of Kingston published a boater's guide at his own expense and sold it for $1.50 per copy. As another safety measure, steamboats and gasoline motor boats were never locked through together, lest a spark from the former set off an explosion if it came in contact with fumes from the latter's engines.

When commercial navigation was ending, a new type of resort was springing up in response to demand. Despite the Great Depression of the 1930s, people were restless and in their inexpensive Model Ts were on the move, wanting cheap places to stay. Tourist operators switched from opening more resort hotels to building small cabins along the shorelines. Equipped with a hot plate and ice box, a cabin catered to the families seeking a holiday on a limited budget, or just a night off the highway where they could cook, sleep and swim.

List of Hotels and Boarding Houses.

Name.	Proprietor.	Rates.
KINGSTON		
British American	W. Telfer	$2.50 and up
Randolph Hotel	J. S. Randolph	2.50
The New Windsor	McCue Bros.	2.00 per day
JONES' FALLS		
Hotel Kenney	Thomas Kenney	$2.00 to 3.00 per day
CHAFFEY'S LOCK		
Lake Opinicon Club House	M. H. Bartley	$2.00 and up
Boarding House	Mrs. Simmons	2.00 per day
PORTLAND		
Commercial House	W. H. Murphy	$2.00 and up
Garrett's Rest	Mrs. M. Garrett	1.00 to 1.50 per day
SMITH'S FALLS		
Hotel Rideau	C. O'Reilly	$2.00 and up
OTTAWA		
The New Russell	Mulligan Bros.	(European—) $1.00 to 3.50 per day
Grand Union	James Paisley	2.00 and up
NEWBORO		
The Rideau	Lev. Southworth	$2.00 to 3.00 per day

NOTICE TO PASSENGERS.

Passengers from New York by New York Central make connection with the Rideau Steamers at Clayton, N.Y., arriving in Kingston the evening of the same day, and can take a stateroom and have a night's rest preceding the journey through the Rideau Lakes.

The staterooms are always cool and airy, lying at the docks in Kingston, inhaling the delightful cool breeze coming off Lake Ontario.

Passengers leaving New York on Saturday evening make connections with Rideau Steamers at Clayton on Sunday morning.

STOP OVER CHECK

Good until close of season—will be issued on application to purser to passengers holding first-class, unlimited or summer tourists tickets. When passengers hold berth or stateroom tickets to a given port and then decide to give up their room at an intermediate port, no refund will be allowed for the remaining part of the journey for the reason that by their reserving room through, the Company is debarred from selling the space.

An entire room will be sold for use of one person, only on presentation of two full transportation tickets.

Husband and wife will not be sold a berth, but must purchase an entire room.

Through Tickets can be obtained from any Grand Trunk Railway, C. P. R., N. Y. C. & H. R. R. Agents; Thomas Cook & Sons, Raymond & Whitcomb, New York.

MISS BERTHA RUFFNER, Special Passenger Agent.
1122 Broadway, New York.

Reprinted from the brochure—"Rest and Sport among the Rideau Lakes," 1910. (Rideau Lakes Navigation Co.).

Hunting was an autumn pastime. Men from Kingston, Ottawa and points between, took to the woods after deer, or congregated near the marshes to shoot ducks gathered for the flight south. But fishing in the summer was the honoured attraction, and many of the best yarns concern the size of the one that got away. Some anglers were even able, however, to brag about the big ones they landed. One of the best, recounted by Legget, tells what might be termed a weighted tale about the fish scale at the Opinicon Hotel. A local farmer and his wife had a new son, and they brought the infant to the hotel to be weighed. Imagine the astonishment of his family when he tipped the scale at 22 pounds!

The Opinicon Resort

About the year 1868, John Chaffey, one of the famous brothers, built grist and woollen mills at Chaffeys Lock, and a residence which forms the oldest part of the Opinicon Hotel. For some years the house was let to mill workers. The entire mill property was purchased from the Chaffey estate by Thomas Houghes, who sold it to W. H. Fleming in 1899. After an appeal to the Department of the Interior, Fleming received the deed to the land, and he added several rooms to the house, which he opened as a tourist resort. In 1902, the property was bought by William Laishley, who named the resort Idylwilde and ran it for about two years.

Laishley sold Idylwilde to Mr. Robert Montgomery from whom it was inherited by Randall Montgomery. In 1906 he sold the property to the "Opinicon Club." (Opinacon, Opanacon) The name is Indian for "between two gaps of water." These men—Randall Montgomery, William Park and the Stambough brothers, E.L. Ford, John P. Hazlett, W.R. Beard, George J. Remer, J.H. Morris, F.M. Powers and J.F.W. Ritter formed a fishing club.

In 1921, Mr. and Mrs. W.E. Phillips from Pittsburgh, together with Mr. David F. Anderson of Youngstown purchased the property. After the death of Mr. Phillips the hotel was managed by his wife, together with her son Donald P. Jarrett and his wife, Hazel.

By 1929 the main building with two wings, the store and the annex buildings and one cottage, "The Pines" were in existence. Over the years additional facilities were added to improve on the resort facilities. In November, 1965, Janice Jarrett, the daughter of Donald and Hazel, took over the management of the resort together with her husband Albert Cross. A swimming pool, new docks, tennis courts and new cottages were built over the years.

Opinicon Club Hotel at Chaffeys Lock, 1925.
(Ordnance Land Photo).

213

Chaffeys Lock campsite, 1925.
(Ordnance Land Photo).

Chaffeys Lock view above the lock
showing boat houses and cottage, 1925.
(Ordnance Land Photo).

Opinicon Hotel at Chaffeys Lock.

Simmons Lodge

Until a sunny morning in the summer of 1886, what became Simmons Resort was a private farm house on the Chaffeys Lock Road overlooking the channel. Peter Hayden, a tourist from New York who had heard that fishing was excellent in those parts, knocked on the door and asked for board and lodging. The owner, Mrs. Thomas Simmons, agreed, and Hayden returned many times as a star boarder until his death in January, 1935. He was the first of many visitors who received wholesome food and warm beds in the Simmons household.

When Mrs. Simmons wanted to retire, her son James and daughter-in-law, Carolyn, assumed the proprietorship of the establishment. At first the Simmons named it "Cedar Grove Resort", but guests insisted on calling it after the owners. In time the name was changed to Simmons Lodge. The younger Simmons built several additions, one a dining room that ran the full length of the original building. They also built cottages and modernized the premises over the years. Today Simmons Lodge is still a favourite with visitors, set amidst delightful scenery,

The yacht "Dortha" at Chaffeys Lock in 1899. (Mr. George T. Fulford).

managed by Marwin and James W. Simmons, daughter and son of Mary Eunice and Ted Simmons.

Chaffeys Lock and the Opinicon Hotel.

During World War II, when gasoline was in short supply, cottage owners had to save coupons if they wanted to get back and forth. Americans had to save up longer, but many kept coming, as they had in the 1930s. As in 1914, the four regiments were mobilized. The Princess of Wales' Own Regiment, of Kingston, was on duty in Canada. Part of the Brockville Rifles went to Jamaica, but some served with the Dundas, Stormont and Glengarry Highlanders and took part in the Normandy landings. The Lanark and Renfrew Scots were redesignated the 1st Light Anti-Aircraft Regiment in 1941 in England, and landed in Sicily in 1943, participating in the campaign on the Italian mainland and in northwest Europe. The Cameron Highlanders of Ottawa were in the Normandy landings, and in the campaign across Europe, while the 3rd Battalion remained for a year following the war as part of the army of occupation.

With the growing popularity of the Rideau Waterway, more local men worked as fishing guides—men who became addicted to the disease in early boyhood. Such knew the best places to drop lines or troll from a small boat, rowed or powered by an outboard motor; this last an innovation of the late 1920s. Confusion arose over the Ameri-

Fishing near Nicholsons in the Rideau system. (Parks Canada).

cans' insistence that a pickerel was a walleye pike, thereby belittling a fine native species. Still, the more muddle and double talk the better the fish story, and the pleasure fisherman is a species himself. Who else would rise at dawn to sit for hours on end in a small, uncomfortable boat?

The steamer "Sport" a private yacht which was never used as an excursion boat. Built in 1881 and scrapped in 1942 at Cornwall, Ontario. (Parks Canada).

Sparks Street in the early 1900's, Ottawa, Ontario.

Bank Street in the early 1900's, Ottawa, Ontario.

American tourists in Ottawa, 1925.
(Public Archives of Canada—C30786).

Watering place—Billings Bridge, Ottawa.
(Public Archives of Canada—PA11357).

Tete de pont barracks at Fort Frontenac, Kingston, Ontario, 1915.
(Public Archives of Canada—PA61434).

Strauss bascule bridge at Kingston, 1917.
(Public Archives of Canada—PA12143).

Harbour front of Kingston and Tete de pont barracks.
(Public Archives of Canada—PA43932).

Princess Street, Kingston at night, ca. 1915. Note the streetcar tracks.
(Public Archives of Canada—PA56163).

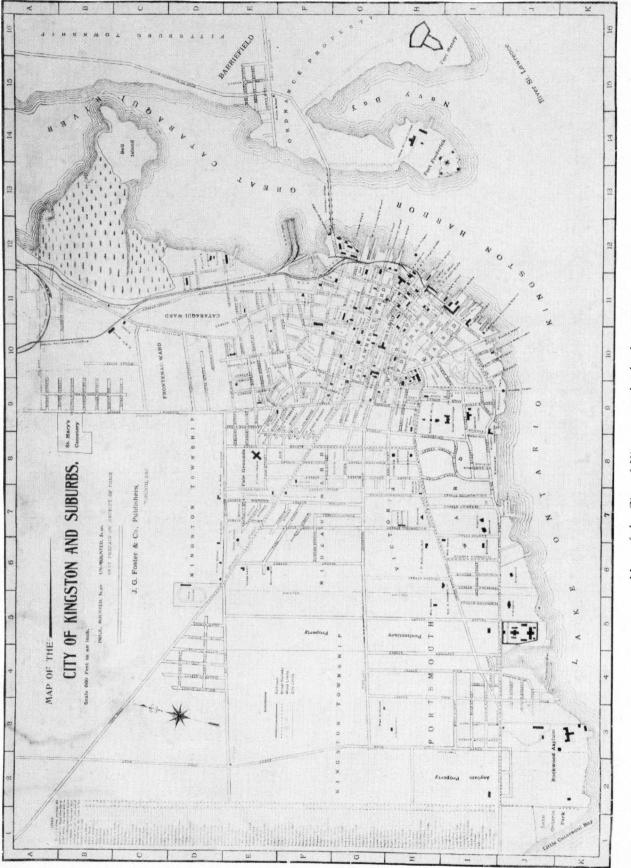

Map of the City of Kingston and suburbs, 1900.
(National Map Collection, Public Archives of Canada).

222

III

No Mean Museum

Until after World War II, the operation of the playground was a matter of private enterprise, with the federal government providing mainly the canal. Resort operators and storekeepers took care of the needs of tourists. Once gasoline was available, pleasure traffic increased rapidly, as newer and faster outboard motors became cheaper to buy. Gradually, however, the corridor was becoming institutionalized, as governments became more involved and the voters more preservation-minded. All of a sudden, planning by governments became the answer to all woes.

Master plans and restrictions had to have local support, and the Government of Ontario has generally pursued a policy of awaiting local initiatives before assisting municipalities in implementing Official Plans and zoning bylaws. Queen's University, from its ivory tower in Kingston, and the federal government, more removed from grass roots sentiments, took the earliest steps towards institutional supervision of the Rideau. The

"Ayuda" built in 1908 by the Truscott Boat Mfg., Co. in St. Joseph's, Michigan. Owned by Peter Elliott. (Manotick Classic Boat Club).

Antique boats at Jones Falls
1. 1928 Dowsett "Arawan"—J. Potter
2. 1923 Dodge Watercar—"Calypso"—S. Herwig
3. 1940 Andress "Riot"—J. Potter
4. 1950 Chris-Craft "Mista"—J. Lyng
5. Johnson/Port Carling—J. Lyng
(Manotick Classic Boat Club—Frank Phelan)

First Ottawa Antique Boat Show, 1975.
(Manotick Classic Boat Club).

Mahogany Harbour Rendezvous, 1978.
(Manotick Classic Boat Club—Frank
Phelan).

224

first opened a biological study centre; the second put a research vessel on the waterway to monitor the quality of the water and the ecology of the surrounding countryside. The 1960s and 70s were a time of increasing government involvement in the management of the Rideau corridor.

1. A Historic Site of Unusual Animation

In 1944, Queen's University opened a Biological Research Station on Opinicon Lake, and two years later purchased 65 acres as a permanent site, where students conduct field studies on land and in the water. They investigate the changes that are taking place in the flora and fauna and in the quality of the lakes and rivers throughout the system. Then in 1949, the National Research Council introduced to the canal the *Radell II*, 78.34 tons, to the waterway. She is a converted Fairmile, built at Midland in 1941 for the Royal Canadian Navy, and redundant when the war ended.

It is a sad fact that large congregations of the human species create problems of waste disposal. All too often, through expediency, wastes find their way into lakes and rivers. The Rideau Waterway is no exception. Nutrients seeping into the waters, or dumped directly, stimulate waterweed

Long Island Lock.
(Parks Canada).

Antique boats in Long Island Lock—"Ayuda" owned by Peter Elliott, "Shingebiss" owned by Murray Gould, 'Arawan" owned by James Potter.
(Manotick Classic Boat Club—Frank Phelan).

225

Lower Brewers Lock.
(J. C. Lamontagne).

Edmonds Lock.
(Parks Canada).

Chaffeys Lock.
(Parks Canada).

226

growth, and in the shallower lakes a deficiency of oxygen. This in turn influences the fish populations. One adversely affected is Opinicon Lake, classified as eutrophic, meaning that its water is rich in dissolved nutrients and choked with weeds. As a rule, the deeper the lake the less serious the problem.

Erosion is not serious throughout most of the waterway, because for much of its course it flows over solid rock. The lower Rideau River is the exception, for there the banks are of soft glacial material and old sea bed sediments. Once the original forest cover was removed these particles were easily washed downstream. By 1950, the Ontario Government had passed legislation permitting the establishment of Conservation Authorities to manage watersheds. The first authorities were set up for streams where massive spring flooding was a threat to property. With the exception of the Jock River, rapid spring runoff has not been too serious. Gradually, as more people became aware that improvements in their own neighbourhoods for other reasons were both practicable and desirable, more Conservation Authorities have been set up for watersheds in Southern Ontario.

By Order-in-Council dated December 17th, 1964, the Cataraqui River Conservation Authority was enacted. Now it operates the Little Cataraqui Creek Conservation Area, to the west of the entrance to the waterway. There the Little Cataraqui Marsh is extensive but it provides a habitat for only a few animals, because the shallows are dominated by cattails. Each fall, hundreds of wild fowl gather there before beginning the flight south, and the marsh is a stopping place for the migratory birds when they are returning north each spring.

The Rideau Valley Conservation Authority, established on March 31st, 1966, with the dividing line at Newboro, operates the Foley Mountain Conservation Area near Westport. A visitor may tramp a forest trail and stop at an interpretive centre, where staff on duty answer questions and give talks on the wild life and vegetation. On the dry slopes of the hills grow stands of eastern red cedar, and the area is the northern limit of the black rat snake—valuable for rodent control—that has almost vanished from the shores of the St. Lawrence.

There, some thirty years ago, a boater would come across one of these big snakes coiled upon a rock at the water's edge, sunning himself, soaking up the heat to raise his body temperature. Now they are a rare sight, because the Thousand Islands Parkway skirts the shore. After this highway opened——a make work project of the late 1930s—corpses of the long snakes lay on the pavement with each sunrise of summer. At night the creatures would crawl upon the road surface, still warm from the heat of the day, and fall prey to motorists. Now the snake is nearly extinct, and the few survivors have grown so wary that people almost never find them. The unpaved road into the Foley Conservation Area presents no such hazard.

Two other provincial conservation sites welcome visitors touring the waterway. The first, at Westport is a fish hatchery which opened in 1951, where all the large mouth bass released into Ontario waters are raised. The bass hatch in the early spring and are put into the lakes and streams in summer when the waters are at their warmest. Afterward trout that start life in cooler, spring-fed hatcheries elsewhere are brought to Westport for the winter, and are released into the deepest local lakes, by which time then have tripled in size. Trout stocking began in 1916, before the Westport hatchery was established. The Rideau system is also stocked with pickerel, but these are hatched at Glenora, in Prince Edward County, and brought in as fry.

The second is the G. Howard Ferguson Station. The name commemorates the Premier of Ontario during the 1920s, who was born and raised in Kemptville. The stone house where he lived was built following the 1837 Rebellion, out of funds collected by a branch of the Patriot Hunters. When that affair died down, the secretary-treasurer was certain that none of the members would dare admit the branch's existence, and he used the building as an inn. Later it was purchased by Dr. Charles Ferguson, G. Howard's father. Today it is again an inn where a visitor may have a meal. Ferguson was the epitomy of an Ontario Tory. From a fine old agrarian family, he was a staunch Protestant, member of the Loyal Orange Lodge, and keen imperialist. Franco-Ontarians remember him, none too kindly, as the back-bencher responsible for Regulation 17, which restricted the teaching of French in the province's schools. But he was flexible, or at least pragmatic.

Pleasure craft at the locks at Smiths Falls. (Parks Canada).

In 1925, seeing a need for Tory votes, the astute politician contrived to have the regulation relaxed, which won his party a measure of francophone support without losing Orange ballots. He ran a well-oiled machine, responsive to grass roots sentiments, and he knew when the time was ripe to end Prohibition that had begun as a World War I economy measure. In 1927, the Ontario Temperance Act was replaced by the Liquor Control Act, and the province, to the joy of some inhabitants, the sorrow of a few, became wet after a decade of drought.

The G. Howard Ferguson Station, a 1,500 acre forest nursery founded in 1945 by the province, raises pines, spruces and some species of hardwoods to reforest many places in southeastern Ontario. Here visitors are encouraged to walk or ride bicycles along forest paths, and in winter cross country ski among the trees. Some of the young saplings have been used on the south shore of the Rideau opposite Burritts Rapids where the land is limestone plain. The species established, with some success, are jack pine and white spruce. The work here is part of a larger scheme which in time may convert back to forest many areas that should never have been cleared.

Boats being locked through Nicholsons Lock.

Burritts Rapids village, summer 1980.

Burritts Rapids

In 1793 Stephen and Daniel Burritt, two brothers from Arlington, Vermont, settled in the vicinity of what is now Burritts Rapids. A bridge, sawmill and school were built at Burritts Rapids before 1826. In 1830 Henry Burritt, Daniel's nephew began to develop his property on the Oxford side of the river. In 1831 a store, tavern and several houses were built and on the Marlborough Township side, Christ Church was begun. A post office called 'Burritts Rapids' was opened in 1839 and later a town plot was surveyed and several additional mills built. With the opening of the Rideau Canal this milling centre flourished but the town was later bypassed by the railways and its importance gradually diminished.

Burritts Rapids village, winter 1981.

For vacationers wanting to pitch a tent or park a camper, there are many privately operated campgrounds, but the Ontario Government has set aside two areas as provincial parks. One is at Murphy's Point, where boats may tie up and camp, or just stop to cook a meal ashore or take a hike to see the abandoned mica mines in the north part of the park. Motorists may come along County Road 21 from Rideau Ferry. The spot is also a happy hunting ground for rock hounds. Big Rideau Lake is narrow here, and facing the park's shoreline are cliffs of conglomerate, formed of compressed granite boulders.

The other government-owned campsite is Rideau River Provincial Park, on the north shore of the river opposite Kemptville Creek. This one has been developed in the midst of a stand of red pine planted in one of the earliest reforestation projects in the region.

Federal government participation in the Rideau corridor now comes under the Department of the Environment. Often called by its bilingual name—Environment Canada—it assumed the role of the National Research Council in 1970 and gave the work to the Forest Services Branch, which assists the Conservation Authorities in improving the watersheds. This branch operates the *Radell II.* That same year, 1970, Indian and Northern Affairs took over the Rideau Canal from the Department of Transport and assigned one of its branches, Parks Canada, to operate the waterway. Since that time uniformed employees of this branch have staffed the locks and points of interest. In 1979, Parks Canada was transferred to the Department of the Environment, thus bringing both important functions under one jurisdiction.

The switch to Parks Canada is significant. The Rideau Canal is now an historic site. In keeping with its role as a museum, electrification of the locks was stopped; anachronism was out, authenticity in. Experts working for the National Historic Parks and Sites Branch, in turn a branch of Parks Canada, have undertaken studies and gathered vast quantities of information on the waterway's past. The staff members who work along the canal cater to boaters, and to the many visitors who come by car, travelling along side roads which lead to scenic parts of the route. At several points a tourist may obtain information on the history of the canal, both human and natural.

Lockmaster Anglin's residence at Kingston Mills, now an interpretive centre. (Doris J. Grant).

In addition to lockmasters and their assistants, who wind in the heavy chains of the crabs at each lock station, the canal is staffed with interpreters—historians, geographers, ecologists, and so forth—who inform visitors on points of interest. The headquarters of this fountain of information is the Parks Canada office in Smiths Falls.

Interpretive centres are located in the blockhouses at Kingston Mills and Merrickville, and the Bytown Museum that stands beside the entrance locks in Ottawa. At Kingston Mills and the museum a visitor may view slide presentations, while interpreters at Merrickville escort visitors on walking tours of the town. Other interpreters float, conducting walking tours of Burritts Rapids, giving demonstrations and illustrated lectures at various places. The office in Smiths Falls publishes a weekly bulletin during the summer season called "Of Steam and Stone", which contains historical sketches of important people and events of the past, news of current interest, and a diary of coming attractions.

For instance, one issue had a piece on some mysterious bones found in a gravel pit near Kingston Mills in the summer of 1963. These were sent to the Royal Ontario Museum in Toronto, where the analysts found that the bones were part of a horse, dated about 1135 A.D. From what is known of the past, this timing is too early, or else too late. Horses originated in North America, but were extinct when the Spaniards reintroduced them in the 16th century, 400 years after these bones were deposited in the gravel pit. The bones give rise to the speculation that Vikings, known to have had a settlement in Newfoundland about that time, paid a visit to the Rideau country.

Under the heading Rideau Canal Events, the bulletin reported on a forthcoming meeting at Hotel Kenney, where a canal interpreter would "unravel the mysteries of woollen mills by means of a slide show at 8:00 p.m." Another advertised bilingual walking tours through Merrickville, starting from the blockhouse at 2:00 p.m. each Sunday, while a third reported a programme on the development of British military strategy that would be held at Rideau Acres Campground near Kingston. A fourth informed visitors of a regular exhibit and activities for young people at the Bytown Museum. Like all publications of Parks Canada the bulletin is in both official languages.

In the summer of 1979, limited passenger traffic returned to part of the waterway. Parks Canada began operating a tour boat between Jones Falls and Chaffeys Lock, so that tourists coming by road could cruise on the most scenic part of the Rideau Lakes. Like the tour boats that now ply the waters among the Thousand Islands, this one is basic, lacking the glamour and luxurious appointments of the *Rideau Queen* or her sister ship the *Rideau King*, but at least it gives the landlubber tourists a chance to be water borne.

A tour boat firm is planning to build a 108' vessel equipped for three day cruises on the Rideau system.

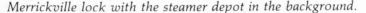

Merrickville lock with the steamer depot in the background.

The *"Canadian Empress,"* length 108', Canada's newest replica steamship, was under construction at the time of publishing this book for Rideau St. Lawrence Cruise Ships Inc. of Kingston, Ontario. The 72 bearth cruise ship will cost approximately $1.5 million. The luxury ship will be in the style of a turn-of-the-century decor and will be used to cruise the beautiful St. Lawrence River and the Historic Rideau Waterway between Kingston and Ottawa. For the evening dinner on the three day Rideau Cruises, guests will be taken ashore to antiquated Hotels and Inns along the system. It is intended that the ship will be in a port each night. The dates of the maiden voyages are in September 1981.

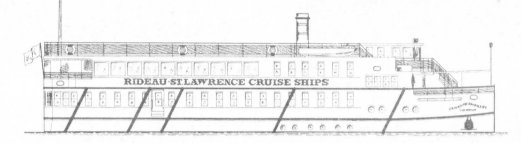

Pleasure craft in Nicholsons Lock.

At the Parks Canada Office and the interpretive centres and lock stations, a tourist will find brochures, maps, copies of the canal regulations, and a schedule of fees that lists the hours of opening and closing. Available for purchase are glossy soft covered books produced by the National Historic Parks and Sites Branch, and of interest are "A History of the Martello Towers in the Defence of British North America, 1796-1871", "The Canals of Canada", and "The Architectural Heritage of the Rideau Corridor". Then there is ecology. Back in the good old days this subject was the preserve of academics, who discoursed at length among themselves on misuses that would soon bring about the death of the planet. Now everything is spoilt. Laymen suspect that many resources are non-renewable, and advertising men tout ecology to sell humidifiers and air fresheners. A brochure called Ecotour, or Écotour, points out where a visitor may look at special natural features and some of the changes man's use of the region have caused.

*Rideau Locks with the Chateau Laurier Hotel.
(National Capital Commission).*

*Mackenzie King Bridge under construction over the Rideau Canal
and the Union Station railway tracks, Ottawa, 1951.
(Public Archives of Canada—PA111574).*

2. Exploring the Waterway

Today there are three ways of travelling through the Rideau corridor, and getting to know its scenery, accommodation and history, both human and natural. The best way is still by boat, be it a cabin cruiser with sleeping accommodation, a small outboard motorboat, even an old St. Lawrence River skiff loaded with camping gear or a canoe similarly encumbered. Because of the numerous side roads a tourist may see a lot of the route by automobile, following many of the delightful short walks at such sites as the Jones Falls dam. For the more ambitious a recent innovation is the Rideau Trail for hikers. Since 1971, it has been possible to walk along this trail from the foot of Montreal Street in downtown Kingston to the heart of Ottawa in the shadow of the Parliament Buildings.

Below Montreal Street begins the Little Cataraqui Marsh, and there the trail starts. Along its course, 70 species of plants find their northern limit. One of the first landmarks of note is a limestone quarry where Colonel John By's workers cut blocks for the canal works at Kingston Mills. The variety of plant and animal species in the marsh is not great, but it serves as a resting place for migratory birds each spring and autumn.

Boaters will have their crafts lifted up the first set of locks at Kingston Mills, named for the industry built by the government back in 1784, to prepare lumber for the first loyalist settlers, and later to grind their grain. The names of many of the lock stations are self explanatory, being the same as local place names, as is this one, but along the way are some that require clarification or defy the curious. On the lawn near the Kingston Mills blockhouse, now an interpretive centre overlooking the locks, is a delightful place for the motorist to pause for a picnic, the hiker to set down his backpack and rest, enjoying the view, the breeze causing the waters to lap gently against the stone walls. At every lock station the visitor finds beautifully landscaped government grounds, clipped lawns and flowerbeds which complement the neat stone and white clapboard buildings that once sheltered the lockmasters and their families.

Above the old millsite and the locks is a section of the Cataraqui River known locally as the River Styx, a stretch of drowned land where clumps of vegetation crowd close to the channel, which is well marked by sticks and buoys. Here swarms of insects provide food for black terns that swoop in from Lake Ontario. From rock knobs on the east side, granite is extracted, as it was during canal construction and later for the earliest homes following the log cabin pioneering phase.

The next lock station, Lower Brewers Mills, or the Washburn Lock, commemorates two local families. As the name Brewer suggests, the Brewer family founded mills at this site, as well as at the next set of locks upstream, making use of rapids and falls in the Cataraqui River. Washburn is another well known local name, of a pioneer family in the Township of Lansdowne, a few miles east of Pittsburgh.

Passing upstream to the Upper Brewers Mills Locks a visitor may inspect a small electric power generating station, and a second and larger one at Jones Falls. Between them these two stations supply about one quarter of the electricity used by the town of Gananoque. Jones Falls, locks and dam are named for the original land owner, Charles Jones of Brockville. Charles was the son of Ephriam Jones, a commissary to several below strength groups of loyalists that were eventually merged to form the Loyal Rangers during the American Revolution, who settled in Augusta Township afterward. Ephriam had four sons and four daughters, who, by intermarriage with other ambitious families along the St. Lawrence front and at Kingston, almost singlehandedly created the Family Compact. Charles was a merchant and miller, and he sat in the Legislative Assembly of Upper Canada, and was also a legislative councillor. He built a mill at Jones Falls that was destroyed during canal building. He also laid out a townsite, which he planned to call Charleston, but it never developed. Earlier he tried to have Brockville named in his honour, which led to quarreling with a faction seeking to name the community after a more deserving founder, William Buell. The name Brockville was a compromise, necessary because people outside the town had christened it Snarlingtown.

A short distance south of the village of Morton may be seen natural spires known as plutons. These are of hard rock and less susceptible to erosion than surrounding rock formations. Here, too, is a good habitat for pitch pine, rare in other parts of the Rideau

Upper Brewers Lock, 1980.

Chaffeys Lock, 1980.

Small runabout in Chaffeys Lock.

corridor. North of Morton, Highway 15 rings a section of drowned land that was once a swamp forest of elm, ash and maple. The trees were killed, not by the Royal Engineers' designs, but by later road construction and the feverish activities of beaver, which now abound in the neighbourhood. The dead trees are not without their value, since these make a fine habitat for the blue heron and several species of woodpecker.

Sand, Opinicon, Indian and Newboro Lakes were smaller before the canal was built. When damming raised the water levels these lakes spread out over low lying lands, forming new shallows, good conditions for the spawning of large mouth bass. Now these bays have been designated as sanctuaries, and fishing is prohibited. Davis Lock, between Sand and Opinicon Lakes, commemorates Walter Davis, a loyalist who removed from the St. Lawrence front in 1800, accompanied by his adopted son, Thomas Ripley. Chaffeys Lock, which separates Opinicon Lake from Indian Lake, is named for Samuel Chaffey, who built a woollen mill at this spot after he left Bedford Mills. The mill building was restored as a residence by the late Arthur Phelps, for many years a well known author and broadcaster.

Aerial view of Perth, Ontario, 1980.

Aerial view of the locks at Merrickville, Ontario.

236

Aerial view of Westport, Ontario, 1980.

The motorist travelling along Highway 15 can witness a phenomenon invisible to boaters. North of the turn to Elgin, road cutting has exposed an unusual rock formation, horizontal Ordovician limestone resting upon vertical Precambrian granite—what geologists call an unconformity. Meanwhile, the boater may make a side trip to see Bedford Mills, a ghost town, before passing through the Newboro Isthmus and the electrified Newboro Lock, where Colonel John By's men cut the channel linking the two drainage systems. Bank erosion caused by boat wake occurs, and this man-made channel across the isthmus must be dredged to keep it clear. Here, too, lie the bodies of many canal workers who perished from swamp fever. It seems a pity that this lock name does not remind a visitor of any of the poor souls who were sacrificed at this place.

After being lifted up Newboro Lock boats cross Upper Rideau Lake, the highest on the waterway, and owners may want to make a stop at Westport, to refuel and purchase supplies, before descending the three feet through Narrows Lock. Big Rideau Lake is the largest and coldest, possibly because it covers an elongated crack in the earth's crust known as a fault. Here the water is the deepest in the entire Rideau system, reaching nearly 1,000 feet. Fishermen may try for lake trout, which breed in this section, although 80 percent are stocked, brought from the fish hatchery at Westport.

Bacchus Bay, on Lower Rideau Lake, is a good place to look for osprey—or fish hawk—a large bird resembling in contour the bald eagle. These denizens of the air eat only fish, and drop on their prey feet first to seize it in their talons. Because of their exclusive diet, ospreys are susceptible to water pollution that builds up residue in the fish. While on this portion of the Rideau Lakes, many boaters will make a side trip up the Tay River to Perth, passing through the Beveridge Locks. How these came to be named is an open question. The Perth-born cabinetmaker, the Honourable John G. Haggart, was the Minister of Railways and Canals when the locks replaced earlier wooden ones. The name may immortalize one of Haggart's cabinet colleagues.

237

Aerial view of Poonamalie Lock.

Along the approach to Poonamalie Lock are stretches of eastern white cedar—swamp forest again—one of the most magnificent stands of this species in the province. The area lives up to its name, for the closely planted trees resemble stands of Tiger Bamboo that line the roads in parts of India. Perhaps the Royal Engineers, who knew both places, bestowed this Indian name because the spot reminded them of another British colony where they had worked before coming to the untamed wilds of the Rideau country.

Downstream towards Smiths Falls the banks are stockaded with cattails that conceal inner marshes, with water lilies, pickerelweed and sedges. The cattails are floating mats which waves from boats scatter. When the mats have become thickened with silt they create firm banks upon which elm and silver maple establish themselves. Passing through Smiths Falls, anyone in need of purchases may be surprised by the width of the main street, with its angle parking. It resembles an Irish market town, where the width allows room for trade as well as throughfare, once the parallel lines of donkey carts have

been drawn up to the curbing. Before quitting the town the boater reaches Old Slys Locks, named for the owner of a log cabin who received £50 compensation for the damage done to his property during canal construction.

Below Old Slys Locks is a woodlot that has not been interfered with for many years. Species found in the original forest cover have been seeding naturally and here a visitor may find black cherry, yellow birch, eastern hemlock, and blue beech, this last a very hard wood which lumbermen liked for making splitting wedges. Hop hornbeam, even harder and once popular for sleigh runners and tool handles, may also be distinguished. Other species are butternut, hickory, and prickly ash.

Edmunds Lock, the next downstream, was named for another early settler, James Edmunds, although for many years it was called Mills Lock. In the marshes near Kilmarnock, and also below Poonamalie, the warm, nutrient rich waters provide a feeding ground and a place where breed the black duck, blue winged teal, bittern and the too numerous red-winged blackbird. Each autumn

Aerial view of Clowes Lock.

ducks gather in these marshes, a favourite haunt of local hunters. About half way between Kilmarnock Lock—named by early Scottish settlers after the town in their homeland—and Merrickville, is a Migratory Bird Sanctuary. Here ducks and Canada Geese going to and from the Arctic may stop unmolested. This marsh is more exposed, thus easy for the birds to find, but not very suitable for breeding.

At Merrickville, where electricity has been generated since 1895 in a plant using the waterfall, stands the woollen mill built by William Merrick and enlarged in 1848. Later he sold it to Thomas Watchorn, whose family operated the mill until 1954. By that time it had ceased to be an economic venture. This mill had a unique feature, a bell that summoned workers and announced quitting time. Now Parks Canada maintains the structure as a restored ruin, although no plans are afoot to have it operate as a tourist attraction.

Clowes Lock was named, not, as might be expected, for Samuel, who made the early survey of the proposed canal, but for James. He owned a quarry in the vicinity and was

the contractor who supplied some stone for the canal works until Colonel By dismissed him. Clowes Lock is best remembered as the scene of the so-called Battle of Merrickville, between Sheriff Adiel Sherwood and his deputies and Irish canal workers. Nicholsons Locks keep alive the memory of another original settler, Robert Nicholson. By 1802, Robert had been granted some land in Montague Township, and he resided in Merrickville during the War of 1812. For his services in the militia he was granted a sum of money voted by the government for veterans of that conflict. As with Merrickville, the Burritts Rapids Lock is named for a place, yet it also commemorates a founding family.

Below Burritts Rapids, the countryside is more heavily settled, providing fewer opportunities for nature preserves, because so much of the land is valuable for agriculture. From this village to below Kemptville Creek, which has silted up, bank erosion is a serious problem. It is caused in part by the wake from fast boats, difficult to control although so many parts of the canal have speed limits posted because such boats pose a hazard to smaller craft. The other cause is overgrazing

Dalbeth Farm along the River Road, Merrickville, Ontario.

by cattle, and the trampling of vegetation that occurs when they come to the water to drink. Here reforestation is easy, as shown by the stands of red pine in Rideau River Provincial Park and the young trees at the G. Howard Ferguson Station. On the patches of limestone plain the task is more complex. Putting as much of the watershed as can be spared into forest would reduce some of the flooding that takes place inland from the Rideau, but, as Colonel John By's records indicate, spring runoff was formidable even before axemen began disturbing what was supposedly nature in balance.

North of Kars, visitors enjoying the setting by automobile may explore a drumlin field along both sides of Highway 16—elongated hills with a distinctive profile, steep at one extremity, tapering gently towards the ground at the other, resembling half an egg cut lengthwise. These formations were first defined in Ireland, which accounts for the Celtic name. They are also signs that the deposits of sand, gravel and clay in the area were formed beneath the continental ice sheet, rather than by meltwater flowing from its edge, or beneath the Champlain Sea. There are many theories about the origin of drumlins, none truly convincing, but they are thought to have developed when sand and gravel were deposited upwards, instead of down, as the temperature began to moderate. Ice erodes more readily than bedrock, and streams carrying fragments in suspension that flowed under the ice sheet dropped some of their load, which formed drumlins.

Wherever these hills are found, an observer may spot an esker—an inverted stream bed which cut upwards into the ice instead of downwards into the resistant bedrock. The traveller will not be disappointed here, for a gravel esker 17 kilometres long zig-zags along and is crossed by the side road between the highway and Kars. Drumlins contain finer material than eskers, and several are cultivated, because they are better drained than the surrounding flat lands.

On either side of the lower Rideau River, intermixed with and behind the rows of summer cottages, is some of the best farmland in eastern Ontario. The seepage of so much cattle urine stimulates the growth of algae and waterweed. One culprit is the Eurasian milfoil, an exotic plant that thrives on the nutrient rich river better than indigenous species. Similarly, when species of North

American waterweed were introduced into European waterways, they, too, became clogged. On both continents boats have found that their propellors become entangled and must be cleared frequently.

The name of the Long Island Locks, like many of the others, needs no explanation. At Manotick a tourist may stop and watch Moss Kent Dickinson's flourmill in action. The tall stone building has been restored at a cost of $100,000 by the Rideau Valley Conservation Authority, which purchases wheat and sells two pound bags of flour. June 2nd is the day to visit Manotick, the annual Dickinson Day, with craft displays, demonstrations of bread making, and a listening corner where older folk sit under a walnut tree talking about the days when the old mill was in its prime.

Downstream below Long Island, the Jock River joins the Rideau. The valley where the military settlers of Richmond congregated has changed greatly since logs floated down the Jock, today a shadow of its former self. Now the forest is gone, and the thin soil no longer retains water after the spring runoff. Early in the season Richmond village is sometimes flooded, but the Jock is likely to be entirely dry by the end of summer.

The name Black Rapids Lock is self explanatory, and below it spreads a flat sandy plain on which the Ottawa International Airport stands. In the heyday of commercial navigation, barges of sand moved into the capital for the manufacture of the cement required for streets and buildings. In the course of excavating the sand, bones of whales were unearthed, showing the extent of penetration by the post glacial Champlain Sea. At that period the huge mammals were able to swim this far inland. The sandy plain is deltaic, although it does not lie at the mouth of the Rideau. As the land floated upwards when the great weight of ice had melted, cliffs created at the mouth of the river left the delta marooned inland.

At this point the suburbs of Ottawa mushroom in all directions, with a corresponding increase in picnic sites. Here a new pollutant enters the picture. Many of the stately trees in the city are white pines that are sensitive to road salt and not in the best of health. Anyone who has ever negotiated one of the many snowstorms of a typical Ottawa winter can guess which will be the loser

Hogs Back Falls, 1981.

in the competition between motorists and trees. To return to the days when snow was packed down for the duration and the roads were ice-bottomed, slippery lakes each spring, implies bringing back the time when the capital was scarcely more than a bulging lumber town. It is hard to avoid concluding that the only way to check pollution is to get rid of people. In any case, should that happen the waterway would revert to something resembling the world Colonel John By beheld when he stood beside the Hog's Back Falls and decided that arch key work would do the trick.

The name Hogs Back defines a particularly steep hill, and that designation has been retained for both the dam and the locks. Hartwells, only a few yards downstream along the canal, poses a problem. The origin of this name has been obscured by time. No settler of that name pioneered in the neighbourhood, and although one of the contractors was a Hartwell, he proved so incompetent that he would hardly be remembered in this way for his efforts. No such difficulty is encountered in understanding the implication of the name bestowed on the last set of locks in Ottawa. Occasionally, however, they are

D. W. Cockburn residence—typical architecture along Rideau River Road, near Burritts Rapids.

Street scene, Burritts Rapids village.

Thatcher residence on River Road along the Rideau Canal at Merrickville.

242

referred to as the Entrance Locks, the name used during the construction era. Ottawa Locks is a more suitable choice, if only to avoid dissent. After all, the locks at Kingston Mills also provide entry, and have some claim to the other name.

3. Enduring Legacy

Great Britain's bequest to Canadian tourism is a civilized recreation area; a canal crossing a green and pleasant land, in spite of certain untidy looking abandoned farms and some crowded, stunted scrub woodland. At each lock station are trim, velvety lawns, and neat, freshly painted clapboard buildings. In addition to the blockhouses at Kingston Mills and Merrickville, those at Newboro and the Narrows have also been restored, and the log guardhouses at Jones Falls and Morton are needed to complete the defences as they once stood. Perhaps, one day the log guardhouses may be rebuilt, but it is unlikely that a visitor will ever behold block-houses at Hartwells and Burritts Rapids. Both have vanished with the spread of urban growth, and replacing them would be very expensive.

A restoration of note is the blacksmith's shop at Jones Falls. Many local blacksmiths built the iron fittings for the locks, but in 1843, the superintendent decided that a government-owned shop was justified at the highest set of locks on the waterway. This smithy, of stone quarried nearby, was built on the site of a log cabin that had housed canal workers and was torn down when it was no longer needed. The blacksmith's shop turned out lock gate hinges and kept the crabs in repair at Jones Falls and the other locks nearby. It closed down in 1933, but by 1979 it had been refurbished and opened for the benefit of the tourists. Now, five days a week, except Tuesdays and Wednesdays, visitors may watch the blacksmith, in his traditional leather apron, flexing the bellows at the forge, or standing over the anvil shaping the glowing iron with his hammer.

Blacksmith's shop 103 years old in Jones Falls, Ontario, August, 1930.
(Public Archives of Canada—PA89826).

Interior of restored blacksmith's shop at Jones Falls. Blacksmith Kevin Fox at work.
(Parks Canada—photo by Brian Tychie).

Deep blue lakes shimmering in the sunshine reflect the backdrop of wooded hills. Towards Ottawa the Rideau wends its way past the gently undulating farmlands of Carleton County. At either end of the waterway stand magnificent signs of refinement—the spires of Kingston's limestone churches and the massive Parliament Buildings. In between is the historic site built through Colonel John By's imagination and energy, the capabilities of his Royal Engineers, and the multitude of labourers on the project, some of whom went to early graves near the canal works.

Those who now operate the canal are a delightful blend of time honoured tradition and exuberent youth. Many of the jobs require little knowledge, strong arms, and enthusiasm. For one at least, the workers need special skills. Periodically lock gates must be replaced, and these can not be mass produced in the region or beyond. For years Fred Dawe and his partner Pat Murphy have re-

newed the gates. Fred started working on the waterway in 1945, with a party of lumbermen, and later he learned the art of gate building. Each gate must be custom made. The frost shifts the stone walls in the locks slightly as the years go by.

The space where a gate is to be fitted must be measured anew, for even the worn out one will not serve as a pattern. Dawe and Murphy have been passing their skills on to John Green and Dyne Carnaghan, who will carry on the tradition when the older men are ready to retire. They use modern tools, but the methods of squaring and cutting and mounting the fittings have not changed, except that the men apply wood preservative, so that a pair of gates lasts longer than when Colonel John By's men mounted the first ones at each lock.

Because the canal is open only during the tourist season, many of the staff are students. As the pleasure boats flock in, the lockmaster directs them into the locks and endeavours to take them through as fast as possible with the help of the students. On one occasion "Of Steam and Stone" reported, the "Lock Jocks" at Kingston Mills herded together fourteen powerboats at one time, something of a record, without mishaps or damage to any of them. The students are on hand for the opening of the canal in late May, but most have gone after the Labour Day weekend, and the interpretive centres which they help man, are shut down.

Yet cruising the waterway in autumn is a delight. The scarlet of the maples, deep reds of the oaks, and the dazzling yellows of the birches, interspersed with the deep greens of the conifers, dress the landscape in vivid finery. When Jack Frost rules the land, visit-ing has its rewards. The summer playground affords the cross country skier the opportunity to see the waterway in its winter garb. With the spring the trees drip, the azure waters peek through the ice, the land re-awakens, and the crowds return. Adventure and discovery await the newcomer, the promise of another rewarding summer the old hand.

Behind everything stands the stout figure of John By. Through the woods stalk wraiths in scarlet coats, tall shako hats and grey trousers. In the forest near Newboro lurk the pale, pinched faces of Irish labourers ill with lake fever. In London the Iron Duke spreads out the broad, linen-backed plan and insists that a canal is a necessity or Upper Canada will be lost.

Lower Brewers Mills Lock.
(Doris J. Grant).

Kingston Mills Lock.
(Doris J. Grant).

Trotting on the Rideau Canal—Courses sous harnais sur le Canal Rideau
Ottawa, Ontario
February 4, 1979 — le 4 février, 1979
Post time 2:15 p.m. — Départ 14h.15

Sponsored by the — Offert par la
Canadian Trotting Association
in co-operation with — en collaboration avec la
National Capital Commission
Commission de la Capitale Nationale

(Ontario Ministry of Industry & Tourism).

Canoe Festival 1980, near the National Arts Centre, Ottawa, Ontario.
(Photo by Edwald Richter, National Capital Commission).

Skating on the Rideau Canal in Ottawa with the Parliament Buildings in the background.
(Ontario Ministry of Industry & Tourism).

The Rideau Canal in Ottawa on a summer evening with the National Arts Centre, Parliament Buildings, the Convention Centre (former railway station) and the Chateau Laurier Hotel in the background. (Ontario Ministry of Industry & Tourism).

BIBLIOGRAPHY

Angus, M., *The Old Stones of Kingston*, Toronto, Ont.: University of Toronto Press, 1974.

Audet, Francis J., *Thomas McKay, Rideau Hall and Earnscliffe*, Ottawa, Ont.: Canadian Historical Association, Historical Papers, 1932.

Bell, M., *Painters in a New Land*, Toronto, Ont.: McClelland and Stewart Ltd., 1973.

Blue, Charles S., *John By: Founder of a Capital*, Toronto, Ont.: The Canadian Magazine, Vol. 38, No. 6, April 1912.

Bond, Courtney C.J., *City on the Ottawa*, Ottawa, Ont.: National Capital Commission, 1971.

Boyd, Mark F., *An Historical Sketch of the Prevalence of Malaria in North America*, Baltimore, Md.; American Journal of Tropical Medicine, Vol. 21 (1941), pp. 223-44.

Brault, Lucien, *Ottawa Old and New*, Ottawa, Ont.: Historical Information Institute, 1946.

Burleigh, H.C., *The Romance of Fort Frontenac*, Kingston, Ont.: Mastercraft Printing and Graphics, 1979.

Bush, Edward F., *The Builders of the Rideau Canal, 1826-32*, Ottawa, Ont.: Manuscript Report Number 185, National Historic Parks and Sites Branch, Parks Canada, Department of Indian and Northern Affairs, 1976.

Calvin, D.D., *Rafting on the St. Lawrence*, Canadian Geographical Journal, October 1931.

_____, *A Saga of the St. Lawrence; Timber and Shipping Through Three Generations*, Toronto, Ont.: Ryerson Press, 1945.

Canada, *The Regiments and Corps of the Canadian Army*, Ottawa, Ont.: 1964, Ministry of National Defence, Army Historical Section.

Canada, Parliament, House of Commons, Sessional Papers 1871, Vol. 14, No. 54, Ottawa, Ont.: Queen's Printer, 1871.

Camp, B.A., *Canada's Tribute to Lieut. Col. John By, Royal Engineers*, Chatham, Eng.: The Royal Engineers Journal, Vol. 85, (1971).

Carroll, Catherine L., *King of the Rideau*, Manotick, Ont.: Rideau Valley Conservation Authority, 1974.

Centennial Committee of Newboro, *The Isthmus, A Historical Sketch of Newboro*, Smiths Falls, Ont.: Centennial Committee of Newboro, 1967.

Chicester, H.M. and G. Burges-Short, *Record and Badges of the British Army*, 2nd Edition, London, England: Gale and Polden, 1900.

Connolly, T.W.J., *The History of the Corps of Royal Sappers and Miners*, London, England: 2nd ed., Longmans, Brown, Green and Longmans, 1857.

Creighton, D., *Canada: The Heroic Beginnings*, Toronto, Ont,: The Macmillan Company, 1974.

Cruikshank, E.A., *The Settlement of the United Empire Loyalists on the Upper St. Lawrence and Bay of Quinte in 1784*, Toronto, Ont.: Ontario Historical Society, 1934.

Davies, Blodwen, *The Charm of Ottawa*, Toronto, Ont.: McClelland and Stewart, 1932.

Durnford, H., *Heritage of Canada*, Montreal, P.Q.: Reader's Digest Association (Canada) Ltd., 1978.

Earle, Evelyn, P., *Linger in Leeds*, Prescott, Ont.: St. Lawrence Printing Co.

Eggleston, Wilfred, *The Queen's Choice: A Story of Canada's Capital*, Ottawa, Ont.: Queen's Printer, 1961.

Encyclopedia Canadiana, Toronto, Ont.: Grolier, 1970, 10 Vols.

Fryer, Mary Beacock, *Loyalist Spy*, Brockville, Ont.: Besancourt Publishers, 1974.

George, A.V., *The Rideau Corridor, 1832-98*. M.A. Thesis, Queens' University, 1970.

Greenhill, Ralph, *Early Photography in Canada*, Toronto, Ont.: Oxford University Press, 1965.

Guillet, E.C., *Early Life in Upper Canada*, Toronto, 1969.

_____, *The Pioneer Farmer and Backwoodsman*, Toronto, 1963.

Haas, R., *Ottawa—Our Nation's Capital*, Toronto, Ont.: Oxford University Press, 1980.

Hall, R. and Dodds, G., *A Picture History of Ontario*, Edmonton, Alta.: Hurtig Publishers, 1978.

Hannon, Leslie F., *Forts of Canada*, Toronto, Ont.: McClelland and Stewart Ltd., 1969.

_____, *The Discoverers*, Toronto, Ont.: McClelland and Stewart Ltd., 1971.

Harrington, Lyn, *Canadian Geographical Journal*, Vol. 35, No. 6, Dec. 1947.

Heisler, J.P., *The Canals of Canada*, Ottawa, Ont.: Canadian Historic Sites, No. 8, Dept. of Indian & Northern Affairs, 1973.

Hind, Edith J., *Troubles of Canal-Builder: Lieut.-Col. John By and the Burgess Accusations*, Toronto, Ont.: Ontario History, Vol. 58, 1965, pp. 141-7.

Humphreys, B.A., *The Architectural Heritage of the Rideau Corridor, Canadian Historic Sites, No. 10*. Ottawa, Ont.: Dept. of Indian & Northern Affairs, 1974.

Kennedy, C.C., *The Upper Ottawa Valley*, Pembroke, Ont.: Renfrew County Council, 1970.

Kingston Historical Society, *Transactions of the Kingston Historical Society*, Vol. 1-10, Belleville, Ont.: Mika Publishers, 1974.

Lake, Dr., *Chart of the Rideau Lakes Route*, Private Publication, 1911.

Lamb, W. Kaye, *Canada's Five Centuries*, Toronto, Ont.: McGraw Hill Book Co., 1971.

Latchford, Francis Robert, *Philomen Wright and the Settlement of Hull*, Ottawa, Ont.: Women's Historical Society of Ottawa, Transactions, Vol. 8, 1921, pp. 5-19.

Leavitt, T.W.H., *History of Leeds and Grenville, Ontario from 1749 to 1878*, Brockville, Ont.: Recorder Press, 1879.

Leggett, Robert F., *Rideau Waterway*, Toronto, Ont.: University of Toronto Press, 1972.

Lett, W.P., *Recollections of Old Bytown*, Ottawa, Ont.: Historical Society of Ottawa, 1979.

Lindsay, Coral, *Kars on the Rideau*, Kars, Ont.: Tweedsmuir History Committee, Kars Branch of the Women's Institute, 1972.

Martyn, M.P. and V., *The Story of the Lower Rideau Settlement: Merrickville, Burritt's Rapids and District*, Merrickville, Ont.: Merrickville and District Historical Society, 1976.

MacDermott, Hugh Ernest, *One Hundred Years of Medicine in Canada*, Toronto, Ont.: McClelland and Stewart, 1967.

MacLennan, H., *Rivers of Canada*, Toronto, Ont.: Macmillan of Canada, 1974.

MacKenzie, William Lyon, *Sketches of Canada and the United States*, London, Eng.: E. Wilson, 1833.

MacRae, M. and Adamson, A., *The Ancestral Roof*, Toronto, Ont.: Clarke, Irwin & Co., 1963.

McGill, Jean S., *A Pioneer History of the County of Lanark*, Toronto, Ont.: T.H. Best Printing Co., 1968.

McKenzie, Ruth, *Leeds and Grenville; Their First Two Hundred Years*, Toronto, Ont.: McClelland and Stewart, 1967.

Moon, R., *Colonel By's Friends Stood Up*, Ottawa, Ont.: Crocus House, 1979.

Morgan, H.R., *The Story of Colonel By, Founder of the City of Ottawa*, Toronto, Ont.: Saturday Night, 29 August 1925.

Moulton, James, *When Lumber was King*, Brockville, Ont.: Recorder and Times, February 2, 1933.

Ondaatje, Kim, and Lois MacKenzie, *Old Ontario Houses*, Gage Publishing, 1977.

Ontario Department of Energy & Resources Management, Conservation Authorities Branch. *History of The Rideau Waterway*, Toronto, Ont.: 1970.

Porter, Whitworth, *History of the Corps of Royal Engineers*, London, England: Longmans and Green, 1889.

Price, Karen, *Construction History of the Rideau Canal*, Ottawa, Ont.: Manuscript Report Number 193, National Historic Parks and Sites Branch, Parks Canada, Department of Indian and Northern Affairs, 1976.

Pritchard, James S., *Journey of My Lord Count Frontenac to Lake Ontario*, Kingston Ont.: Downtown Kingston Business Association, 1973.

Rideau Canal, *Historical Assets of the Rideau Canal*, Ottawa, Ont.: Dept. of Indian and Northern Affairs, 1967.

Rideau Canal, *Parliamentary Papers, 1830-31*, No. 395, London, Eng.: 1831.

Rideau Canal Preliminary Site Study Series, No. 1-13, Dept. of Indian and Northern Affairs.

Rideau Route, *The Picturesque Description of the Route of the Str. "James Swift"*, Toronto, Ont.: Lawson & Wilson, 1898.

Rideau Travelogue, Brockville, Ont.: Recorder Press, March 4-11, 18, (inclusive), 1830.

Ross, Alexander Herbert Douglas, *Ottawa Past and Present*, Toronto, Ont.: Musson, 1927.

Roy, James A., *Kingston, The King's Town*, Toronto, Ont.: 1952.

Saunders, Ivan J., *A History of Martello Towers in the Defence of British North America 1796-1871*, Canadian Historic Sites, No. 15, Ottawa, Ont.: Dept. of Indian and Northern Affairs, 1976.

Schuman, D.M. *Benjamin Tett of Newboro 1820-1843*, Kingston, Ont.: Historic Kingston No. 10, Jan. 1962, 3-14.

Seeley, J.H., *South Crosby, History of the Township*, Private publication, 1967.

Sherwood, Justus, *Account Book*, Metropolitan Toronto Central Library.

Shortt, Edward, *Perth Remembered*, Perth, Ont.: Mortimer Ltd., 1967.

Sneyd, Robert, B., *The Role of the Rideau Waterway 1826-1856*, M.A. Thesis, University of Toronto, 1965.

Stanley, G.F.G., and Preston, R.A., *A Short History of Kingston as a Military and Naval Centre*. Kingston, Ont.: Royal Military College, 1950.

Stewart, J. Douglas and Wilson, Ian E., *Heritage Kingston*, Kingston, Ont.: Queen's University, 1973.

Ten Cate, Adrian G. and Fryer, Mary Beacock, *A Pictorial History of the Thousand Islands of the St. Lawrence River*, Brockville, Ont.: Besancourt Publishers, 1977.

Ten Cate, Adrian G. and McNaughton, H.C.L., *Brockville, A Pictorial History*, Brockville, Ont.: Besancourt Publishers, 1972.

Tett, Edmund J., *Buttermilk Falls—A Lumbering, Milking and Shipping Centre of the Old Days*, Brockville, Ont.: Recorder and Times, February 4, 1933.

Tett Papers, Queen's University Archives, Kingston, Ontario.

Tulchinsky, G., (Editor), *To Preserve and Defend, Essays on Kingston in the 19th Century*, Kingston, Ont.: McGill-Queen's University Press, 1976.

Tulloch, J., *The Rideau Canal, 1832-1914*, Manuscript Report 177, Ottawa, Ont.: Dept. of Indian and Northern Affairs, 1975.

Tyrwhitt, Janice, *Bartlett's Canada*, Toronto, Ont.: McClelland and Stewart Ltd., 1968.

Van Cortlandt, Gertrude, *Records of the Rise and Progress of the City of Ottawa from the Foundation of the Rideau Canal to the Present Time . . .* , Ottawa, Ont.: Ottawa Citizen, 1858.

Walker, Harry James William, and Olive Walker, *Carleton Saga*, Ottawa, Ont.: Carleton County Council, 1968.

Walling, H.F., *Map of the United Counties of Leeds and Grenville*, Kingston, C.W.: Putnam, 1862.

Welch, Edwin, *Yankies and Loyalists*, Ottawa, Ont.: Historical Society of Ottawa, 1979.

Wells, Kenneth McNeill, *Cruising the Rideau Waterway*, Toronto, Ont.: McLelland and Stewart Ltd., 1965.

Wilson, Andrew, *A History of Old Bytown and Vicinity, Now the City of Ottawa*, Daily News, 1876.

Winter, Fritz, G.M., *Old Forts in Upper Canada*, Toronto, Ont.: School of Architecture Bulletin 146, University of Toronto, 1939.

about the editor . . .

Adrian G. Ten Cate, the editor and publisher of this Book, was born in the Netherlands. He came to Canada in 1951, and worked in various occupations throughout Canada.

He graduated in Medicine from Queen's University, in Kingston, Ontario. He then specialized in Ophthalmology and in 1967 settled in Brockville, Ontario.

Dr. Ten Cate became fascinated by the history of the area and in 1972 he published his first book, "Brockville, A Pictorial History". By 1977, he edited and produced "A Pictorial History of The Thousand Islands of the St. Lawrence River", Besancourt Publishers.

The success of these two volumes encouraged him to expand his interest to include the Rideau Waterway.

about the author . . .

Mary Beacock Fryer, who wrote the narrative, is a geographer with an absorbing interest in Canadian history. Born in Brockville, Ontario, she attended local schools, Toronto and Edinburgh Universities. She became fascinated by Loyalists of the American Revolution while researching her own ancestors. To date she has published *Caleb Seaman, A Loyalist*, 1970, Ginn; *Loyalist Spy*, 1974, Besancourt Publishers; *Escape, adventures of a Loyalist family*, 1976, J.M. Dent; and *King's Men: the Soldier Founders of Ontario*, 1980, Dundurn Press. She lives in Toronto with her husband and three children.

THE RIDEAU WATERWAY
by aerial photography 1976-77
Energy Mines and Resources Canada

KINGSTON

Chaffeys Locks

Opinicon L.

Davis Lock

Colonel By L.

San

Kingston Mills

River Styx

Cataraqui River

Cranberry L.

White fish L.

Jon

Washburn Brewers Mills

Seeleys Bay

PERTH

Tay River

Beveridge Locks

Lower Rideau L.

Poonamalie Locks

Rideau Ferry

SMITHS FALLS

Bass L.

Old Slys

Edmunds Lock

Burritts Rapids

Clowes Lock

Nicholsons

Kilmarnock

MERRICKVILLE